Yehuda's Revenge
By
William Shelley Gwynn

A Novel

In the format of a Diary
Written and created from "Heroes without Medals"
The memoir of Yehuda Adelman,
A Holocaust survivor and guerilla fighter
At the request of his son Alex

mustreadpageturners.com

Book cover by Robert Burke

Book cover photo credit; Meczenstwo Walka, Zaglada Zydow Polsce 1939-1945. Poland. No. 506, A Partisan group in Naliboki Forest

For comments contact wsgwynn@gmail.com

This book is dedicated to the following people:

Yehuda Adelman who lived to tell the tale
Alex Adelman asked me to write his father's story.
Peggy Barlow helped me get started
Betty Guttmann did an early edit
Quincie Hamby edited and encouraged me to finish
Martha Weinstein helped to make a better book
Bonnie Gadless edited and shared her insights of Belarus
Jeanne Lassia encouraged me to write a better book
Helena Hotmarova edited with Polish insight
Yvonne Richardson edited for content
Alicia Osborn helped with pictures and back cover
Robert Burke design the cover
Huldah Simpson did the final edit

Yehuda in 1935

Introducing Yehuda, the Narrator of his Story

My name is Yehuda Julian Adelman or Julie for short. For three hundred years my family lived in the village of Gorodok that lay between the cities of Minsk, Belarus and Vilnius, Lithuania. Most of the population was white Russian. From 1919 to 1939 we were Polish. Life was harsh, but the Polish Government made it more difficult. Anti-Semitic feelings were fueled from the propaganda coming out of Germany. Enrollment at the Universities was restricted, and Jews were forbidden to buy land. Encouraged by local Zionists, fifty young people waited to get certified by the British to go to Palestine. Few got certified. Everyone wanted to leave, but few countries wanted us.

We had about twenty-five shopkeepers and about fifty families of peddlers who traveled six days a week with a horse and wagon selling their wares to farms and nearby villages. They sold soap, cloth, raw herring, kerosene, flour, wheat, and chickens for the Sabbath. They were lucky if they had their own Sabbath chicken. Each week the peddlers would travel by train to shop in Vilnius with its many factories, wholesale markets and eighty-thousands Jews.

We became victims of Goebbels' propaganda and easy prey to a culture that envied our success in art, commerce, and medicine. They could forget that ninety-six percent of European Jews were impoverished third-class citizens with few rights and no land. We were shopkeepers, smiths, tailors, carpenters, and peddlers, because other opportunities were not open to us.

For a thousand years, the Catholic Church spread ill feelings against the Jews. The victorious Nazis, who actually despised Christianity, used it as a tool to get willing collaborators and the work was easy. They did not have to teach people new anti-Jewish ideas; the old ones were good enough. German brutality gave thousands of collaborators a chance to bluster and intimidate.

By luck and countless miracles, I survived the Holocaust in Eastern Poland and the battles of the Russian Front. It wasn't just luck that helped me live when others died. I grew up on a farm that gave me good food and hard work to make me strong and fit and the skills to feed myself. Then the Army taught me how to use a rifle and self-defense. My parents and college taught me to use my brain. Anger and hunger for revenge kept me alert and looking for an opportunity to escape the Nazi net and fight back.

My diary begins in 1942, when I am twenty-nine years old. I am of average height and have black hair and brown eyes. I got my looks and passion from my mother, who gave me a love for languages and math that I went on to study in college. After college in Vilnius, I did two years in the Polish Army and then got a teaching job in a grammar school where I became principal. That is the job I had when the Nazis came and made me a carpenter building barracks to house the occupation troops and the killing squads. We built houses for our murderers and sometimes dug our own graves.

I invite you to step into the heat of the Holocaust as I out run death while everything I love is dying around me. My culture, my family and friends were all murdered. I also want you to experience the satisfaction of revenge.

Chapter 1

Gorodok, Poland (Belarus)

June 1942

The Germans are occupying all of Europe except Russia and Britain and arc fighting in North Africa and Russia with mixed results. Nazis are busy shipping Jews to killing centers in Germany and Poland. The British are beginning to bomb the German cities. The United States has been in the war for six months and is shipping troops and supplies to Britain. The US is winning the naval battles of the Pacific and losing the battle for the Philippines.

It is daybreak on June 1, 1942 in the village of Gorodok Poland; near Minsk and the Russian border. I am one of ten Jews lying face down on the street with Gestapo troops standing over us.

Black boots move in six inches from my nose. I take a deep breath and try to exhale the budding panic. I search for a calm spot to focus as a tear releases and falls on to the grey cobblestone holding up my chin. Face down with hands on top of my

4

head; I feel the warm wetness of urine from the body to the left of me. Closing my eyes, I still see new knee high Gestapo boots. The stink of fresh dog dung layered on the smell of new leather stings through my nostrils and seeps down to join the fear in my throat. The squeak of polished boot leather cracks in my ears as I wait for bullets to enter my paralyzed body.

A frightened flow of mucous is choking me. If I spit, I risk hitting the boots. If I swallow, it might come back up with vomit, so it sits in my throat and waits with the rest of me to be expelled.

I retreat to a quiet, tranquil space deep in my memory. I see myself as a five year old slowly bouncing and catching a black ball on these same cobblestones. I try to predict which way the ball will bounce from the irregular surface. Each time I throw, it appears again in my hand like it never left. Whatever I do, it comes back to me. I am frantic to lose it, but it stays stuck to my palm like a black wart.

"God! You stink!" snarls the blond bully. "You're pissing in your pants, like babies"

I close my eyes into tight wrinkled slits and try to blot out the bully. I make white knuckled fists to still my trembling hands as I dart between the chaos of panic and the calm numbness of exhaustion. Clarity is interspersed with chills of fright. Wherever my mind runs, a childish bully is playing hopscotch with my life. By will alone, I am shrinking myself out of his sight. I feel myself becoming invisible as I compress into a single goose bump.

Beads of sweat burn my eyes as I boil with the humiliation of being intimidated by a simple idiot - a bully from the streets trying to win his first medal. Perhaps he is one of the soldiers drafted from the prisons. We are about the same age. I am sure this bully was putting a fist in some kid's face while

I was playing in this courtyard. This was the boy that punctured the thin rubber ball with the point of a knife and sent the other kids home crying. For the first time this new officer has more than self-appointed bully power. He throws out his chest and puffs himself up into a gangster's impression of an officer and inspects his victims with a swagger of arrogance and the intimidation of instant death.

Death wraps her cold wet bony fingers around my neck and kisses me in the mouth. As I gasp for breath I feel her close and stinking like vomit. The fact that life can be blown away in less than a second shows the absurdity of creation and the struggle to survive. Death is at the whim and the pull of a maniac's trigger. Will the bullet enter the head or the back? Will death be slow or quick? Now or in ten minutes? I am speechless and dumb with fright. I can say nothing, even if I were asked something - like my name. I feel a jolt of adrenaline and consider springing from the pavement, tackling the big blond bully, and trying to grab the gun off his hip, shooting the other two before they shoot me and the others on the pavement. It's all impossible and absurd. The officer is bigger, and I'm weak from hunger; but still I think about it. Even if I died trying, it would be better than being shot in the back and dumped in a hole like garbage.

"On your feet, so I can see you." the officer orders. "I need to select the best example of your race. Who is the most Jewish among the Jews?"

He plays with his blond mustache as his small green blinking eyes study his victims with alternating disdain and amusement as we struggle to our feet and try to stretch the cramps out of our muscles. He pauses and inspects each one with more scrutiny than a drill sergeant.

I am finally able to swallow and clear my throat. My breath is short and my heart beats quickly as the bully steps back and makes his choice with the point of a finger.

"You. You are the one. Step forward."

My heart stops like it's been stabbed. I am stunned dumb and unable to move or acknowledge that I have been chosen. I fear I'm about to be grabbed and pulled out of the ranks, when I see Moche, the victim on my right, step out of the rag tag line. It's Moche that's been chosen. I let go of my tension and relax. I look at the sky and thank God it's not me, but then I know my time is coming. I have been chosen for torture, and if I live through it, they will shoot me.

"Load the rest of them in the wagon," the bully orders.

I look at the wooden peasant cart with its empty harness, and wonder what is going to pull it, and how are we all going to fit in it. Where are we going? While we are packed into the wagon, I see Moche standing alone and regret being powerless to save him. What could be done? I feel helpless, guilty, and then relieved that I wasn't chosen. So many emotions chill and boil and grip me. Emotionally exhausted, I fall into a lifeless depression, and then I'm jolted by the fear of a bullet ending my life. Would I even feel it? Would it be relief? I try to clear my heart of the pain and confusion, and it becomes one big hurt in my ulcerating stomach, and then everything is replaced by intimidation and fear. If they don't kill me, I'll go nuts.

"I got my horse, or maybe it's my ass," the bully grins as he raises his hand and pops a buggy whip. "My Jewish ass. What is your name, ass?"

"Rabbi Moche," he says with a wide smile and shining eyes. He is a good example with his full black and grey beard, long black robe and ear locks. He looks very Jewish, but he is not as

7

intimidated as the rest of us - maybe that's why he's chosen for extra treatment.

"What kind of work do you do?"

"I am a shopkeeper," the rabbi responds pleasantly, like the officer might want to buy something.

The officer raises his voice and scolds, "You Jews refuse manual labor. You're parasites living off the backs of honest, hardworking people. Why aren't you a farmer, working in the fields, and doing a good day's work, instead of cheating honest people in your store?"

Still calm and not in a hurry to answer, the Rabbi responds logically, "Jews are forbidden to buy land, so farming is not an option for me. I have never cheated anyone in my store or anywhere else. In all my dealings, I do unto others as I would have them do unto me."

"Liar, we know better," shouts the bully as he slaps the rabbi's face with the back of his hand and looks to his two subordinates for approval. "See, even rabbis are liars and cheats. Everyone knows Jews refuse honest labor. We have scientific data that shows what parasites you are. Jews are hording all the gold in Europe. Jews have sucked up the wealth of the continent, and have always profited from war. You are no better than blood sucking leeches. Yes, you are parasites, enemies of the human race, and warmongers!"

The rabbi smiles and responds quietly, "Yes, I had some gold, but now Hitler has it. I am not a soldier or a rich man. I have never dunned a debtor or used money to manipulate people or events. I only want the best for all men and for you and your people as I seek peace and tranquility for myself and my family."

Irritated with the Rabbi's refusal to be intimidated, the bully shouts, "We are liberating the honest working man from the yoke of Jewish money and Jewish Pigs. Repeat: I am a Jewish Pig."

Moche hesitates at this juvenile stupidity and mutters in resignation, "I am a Jewish Pig."

"Louder!" shouts the bully with meanness and anger.

"I am a Jewish Pig, "he says in a slightly louder but in a reluctant voice.

The officer, red faced from anger, kicks the rabbi in the crotch, and Moche bends over in an agonizing grunt. He then jerks him by the beard and leads him to the cart and orders "Hook this pig to the wagon and let him pull the other pigs through the village."

Moche is yoked like a horse in the harness and the officer orders "Pull you bastard. Pull you lazy son of a bitch. Pull or I'll shoot you in the ass. Pull!"

The Rabbi is pulling as hard as he can. His neck is thrust forward protruding through the leather yoke with the veins popping out on his head, but the cart does not budge.

One of the soldiers cracks a whip across his back, drawing blood as it rips his shirt. Then the officer fires a shot at his feet; but still the cart doesn't move.

"Hook up three more pigs," orders the officer.

Daniel, Steven, and I are harnessed in with Moche. I am glad for the chance to help the Rabbi with his burden. The whip cracks - Steven groans as it hits his shoulder, and the wagon moves.

As we roll through the narrow cobblestone streets of Gorodok, people are coming to see. Many are laughing and throwing garbage.

"Now shout, 'We are warmongers'," instructs the bully trying to put on a good show.

We are walking in cadence to keep from stepping on each other's pitiful feet. We are using the words of our litany to stay in step and every sixth step we begin again, "We are warmongers...We are warmongers."

The whip cracks, the Rabbi groans, and the officer shouts, "Louder, we are warmongers, louder."

My shoulders, arms and leg muscles are taut and hurting from the strain as I lean forward and put weight into the pulling. My hands grip and pull at the poles of the harness and my feet slip in my loose second-hand shoes as I push with all my might against the cobblestones of my childhood. I remember how my mother salvaged these shoes from my father's tortured body as the Nazis watched. She dared them to shoot her and they did nothing, because at that moment being shot is what she wanted. Maybe they were afraid of her black piercing eyes.

A gang of adolescent boys bolt out of the growing crowd and marches beside the cart in a mocking swagger. With spiteful glee, the oldest beats each of us in the rump with his stick. The smallest jumps up in to cart and joins in with a mocking chorus of, "We are warmongers".

All this happens between laughs of encouragement from a bent gray-haired peasant who says, "Why use a horse or an ox when there's a Jew to pull a cart? Why, it's a talking horse."

"You mean a talking ass," says the bully.

"I'll give you a mark for a Jew."

"A mark is too much," laughs the bully. "I'll give you two Jews for a mark - you can make soap out of them."

"No soap," says another peasant. "There is no fat on them. You need fat to make soap - there's not two bars of soap in the whole bunch. You need to find something to do with bones - maybe bone meal - they got plenty of bones."

Others are chanting, "Go home you bastards. Go home."
I am muttering, "My family has lived here for three hundred
years, and it is not yet home? So, where is home? Maybe they
want to send me to Palestine or to my relatives in Texas, - well,
I'm ready to go. Where's the ticket?"

A second group of smaller boys pelt us with mud as two of
their mothers splash Moche and Steven with chamber pots.
Moche is in front and Steven is behind, so we all get at least
a splattering of fermented peasant piss. I vomit at the stink,
but only bitter bile reaches my mouth as I have no food in my
stomach.

Our tormentors leave us standing in the street still in the
harness and break for lunch. They eat in the mess hall built
with slave labor, eating food that Jews would be eating, if Nazis
weren't here. A soldier that we haven't seen before comes out
with a basin of wet, plain bulgur and feeds us as he might feed
horses by pushing a handful in our mouths. He then dips a cup
of water for each of us from a horse bucket. The grain and the
water are hardly enough to blot an appetite, but we are glad to
get it. We are not sure if we are being mocked or helped. Is our
benefactor a joker or sympathetic? For the first time since the
ordeal began, my stomach is soothed.

I'm startled by a scream. I turn and see Steven tearing off
his stinking piss soaked clothes and speaking to a few curious,
unsympathetic peasants.

"We are not animals," he shouts as he spits out the wet
grain. We are human. You are killing people - not rats." By
this time he is standing naked in the harness, covered only by
tears of fright, humiliation and anger. His voice breaks as he
speaks, "Don't believe the lies. We are innocent, honest people
who are being murdered. Resist or you'll be..."

"Bam!" Sounds a gunshot.

GORODOK, POLAND (BELARUS)

The light fades from Steven's eyes and blood gushes from his mouth as he crumples up at my feet. I turn and see the blond bully standing in the mess hall door pointing the smoking Luger at my face. I stare at the gun barrel and wonder if this is the end. I close my eyes, pray to God and wait for the gun to go off. After a minute, I open my eyes. The bully is gone, and somehow I am saved again.

By mid-afternoon the tormentors are finding it more work than fun, so they cut us loose except for Moche. Exhausted, I find the strength to quickly walk away. I don't want to see what they are doing with Moche. How on earth can I help him? The question does not absolve my guilt. At the first village well, I drown my thirst and clean myself. With my mother's glaring eyes I dare the peasants to object, and they don't. These people are like most victims of war - sheets blowing in the wind of fear and intimidation.

I barely have the strength to walk to the synagogue, where I collapse on my mat on the floor. It is all I have left since they took the Jewish homes and moved the 150 families into a fenced compound around the Synagogue. I ponder how we did everything the Nazis asked us to do, and still we are killed and tortured. I suddenly start laughing at a condensed version of all the conversations that the Judenrat has had with the Nazi Commander.

"If you cut trees for us, build barracks, make two hundred wool suits, give us your homes and all your gold, and stay in the ghetto, and no harm will come to you, I promise. I promise on my word of honor," says Gauleiter Schmidt.

"We will do everything you say, only spare our lives," says the Judenrat chairman, Rezkin, as he pushes five more gold coins in to the Nazi's pocket.

"Good Herr Rezkin," said Schmidt. "I will try to help you."

12

I am thinking no harm will come to us as long as the Nazis can milk us like a cow and as long as the cow is content and has milk. But what else do we have to give? They have broken too many promises and they know it. There is no way we can believe them anymore. I'm thinking this cow is about to be butchered.

Exhausted, I close my eyes hoping for a sweet dream to carry me away from my torment, but I toss and turn in an apprehensive sea of dead faces, and I am too agitated to sleep. Finally exhaustion wins over the torment. I dream of joining the resistance and running through the forest with a rifle, blowing up bridges and shooting Nazis from behind trees.

I feel a nudge and see the smile and sparkling eyes of Mama's face in the candlelight.

"Julie, I have soup for you, sit up so you don't spill it."

I find the vegetable soup thin, but delicious and sweet with mother's love, and I savor every sip and keep it in my mouth just for the taste. "Where did you find food?" I ask.

"I have friends among the peasants," she smiles as she watches me enjoy. "Today you are a hero, because you are alive. You were clever enough not to give them a reason to shoot you."

"How is Moche?" I ask.

"Dead," she says as she holds her head in her hands and releases a sigh of pain.

"I am so sad, Mama. Why are they doing this? I don't understand it. I loved him; his shining eyes, his wit and generosity. I didn't want him to die."

"What you have of Moche is what you see when you close your eyes and think of him, and also what you learned from him. The same is true of me and your father. You will carry memories of us throughout your life. Much of us is in you and you will give something of that to your children. That is why it is so important for you to leave here alive. We will live through you and your children, my love."

"You're talking like you're dead."

"I'm fifty-five years old. I've had a good life."

"Mama, you are still a young woman. There is no woman of any age that can do the work you do." I put my arms around her and say, "I can't leave you, ever."

"You must. If you stay here, you will be shot before you see another Sabbath. You were lucky today, and smart, because you didn't give them the excuse they were looking for. Today they wanted a reason - tomorrow they will shoot you anyway. There's another reason you must leave. I must have something to live for, or maybe some reason for dying. I need the hope that I will join you in America, and that you will give me lots of grandchildren. If you stay here and get killed, I have no hope and no grandchildren, and to bury you would kill me. So if you want to save your mother, leave tonight or tomorrow - the next day will be too late."

"How will I leave? It was hard enough to leave before the Nazis came and put up the barbed wire. And where is there to go? No one in the world wants us - not in America or Palestine. Every Jew in this village wants to leave, and has been trying to, for years. Mama, if I leave, they will kill you."

"They will kill me anyway, so forget that. I am telling you that you will have a chance, and it will last only a second. You must take it without thinking of me, or anything but saving yourself. My precious boy, I refuse to be the ball and chain that keeps you here. You don't have a wife and child or anything the Germans haven't killed or taken, just an old worn out mother, so get out of here. Save yourself."

She falls across my chest as to protect me and we embrace. I blow out the candle, and again I am too upset to sleep.

14

POLAND 1933

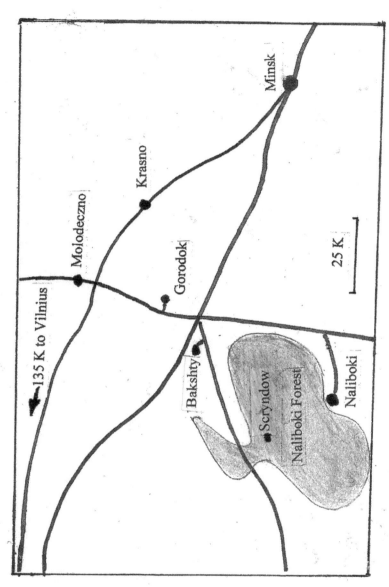

Chapter 2

The Selection

3 June 1942, 6:00 AM, Gorodok, Poland

I am waiting on the street in front of the synagogue with twenty other construction workers for the truck that will take us to the barracks that we are building for the occupation troops. No one is speaking, smoking or drinking tea as we might do in better times. Looking about, I notice my feet are lucky enough to have good shoes. Feet are spilling out of holes in the top, bottom, and sides of shoes and some have no shoes at all. The peasants have salvaged dead men's shoes among other things, but the Germans have left us nothing: no goods, labor or money to trade or buy shoes of any kind.

My dreams of a simple bread and cheese breakfast are interrupted by the roar and shake of heavy trucks that vibrate the cobblestones, and choke my chest with apprehension. They come into view, and it's a never ending line of monsters. I count twenty-eight before they finally stop with a screech of their air brakes. In addition to the drivers, a mix of sixty Gestapo troops and Ukrainian police climb out of the trucks.

Commander, Schmidt, steps out of his black Mercedes. I hear him give the order to assault the ghetto. Within minutes they are driving fourteen hundred Jews out of their quarters, some half-dressed, herding them toward the park between the two Synagogues. As they enter the park near the new community well, they separate them; young healthy men to the right, and all others to the left. I don't see my mother before I am loaded into the third truck in the caravan. In our truck, I count forty-four men and boys, all standing, shoved up against each other and packed like sardines pushing against the sides of the truck. I am able to make my way to the back left side of the truck. My left shoulder is pushed against the canvas top, so I am positioned to see the park through the large opening in the rear. I hope to see Mama. People are being sorted and loaded as quickly as they reach the park. I see one of my brothers, Ezer, his wife and two of his three boys. Finally there is no one left except some small children standing by the road, still I don't see Mama - maybe she is in hiding or loaded without me seeing her. I can hear the children crying for their mamas. After a few minutes two soldiers come over and try to find a place for the children in a truck, but the trucks are crammed full. Commander Schmidt, seeing the problem, gives one of them a whisper in the ear. I see them take the dozen children back into the park and throw them screaming down the well. I am horrified and sick. My poor stomach is suffering from no food and much trauma.

Schmidt steps onto an ammunition box and addresses the trucks. "There will be no more killing," he shouts. "You are all going to Krasno Ghetto to work, so be good, and we will be good to you. I wish you a safe trip and the best of luck in your new home."

The trucks crank up and move out toward Krasno. I am in shock and numb from watching the babies die, not knowing where my mother is, and leaving home for God knows what. First they took my possessions - then my labor. What is left but my life? Through the rear opening in the canvas, I look back at the rapidly shrinking view of my village - the picturesque castle, the two red brick synagogues, the three-hundred-year-old cemetery, and wonder if I will see them again. We cross the River Borezinka where as a happy child I bathed and splashed and rested my bare bottom on the smooth rocks. On the other side was the forest where we spent summer days, and where young couples walked hand in hand. With tears in my eyes I say good-by to all that I know and love.

The Springer brothers; Sabitai, Michael, and young Jeremy are standing beside me and are sharing all of what is happening. The elder Michael is thinking clearly with an accurate assessment of events.

"Some trucks are turning in to the forest," Michael says quietly, "the ones with our parents and the women and children. I'm sure they are going to kill them. I'm not going to wait like a lamb for life to end. Let's jump and make a run for it. We are close to the forest, and our chances are good, at least we'll die resisting."

"What about the soldiers?" asks the tall, commanding Grishka?

"So what can they do?" counters Michael. "There are three in the front seat of each truck. By the time the truck stops and they get out and are able to fire, we can be in the cover of the trees. There is safety in numbers - the more that jump, the better our chances. Whoever is in the front will be covered by people running in the back, so you had better be in the front and running for your life. Are you coming or staying?"

"I'm jumping," I say without reservation.

"Not so loud," Grishka whispers. "The guards are in the front seat - just on the other side of the canvas.

"Spread the word," commands Michael. We're jumping."

The truck is alive with whispers and excitement. My ten year old cousin Daniel has worked his way through the crowd and is pulling at me.

"I want to fight with you and join the resistance." he says. "Please let me jump with you."

"Yes, you will be a good soldier," I say. "We will jump out the back into the path of the next truck and be careful to stay in the middle away from the tires. The truck will pass over and we will get up and run for the trees."

"Are you crazy?" asks Itzke, my neighbor. "You could break a leg or be run over. If you stay, you won't be shot. They said no more killing."

"Do you believe them?" I ask as I look into Izke's eyes and see he has no hope. He is too intimidated and frightened to move.

"Quit lying to yourself," I say in quiet persuasion. "If you stay in this truck you are going to be shot and dropped into a hole. You could be dead within the hour."

"Then I'll be with God in peace," he says looking at the floor in resignation."

"I am not ready to meet the Lord in the lime pit," says Daniel. "I'm jumping with you."

Michael raises both hands as a signal the jump is about to happen. Daniel is on my right holding my hand. Michael lowers his arms, and we all jump together. Daniel lands first, then me. We fall flat on the ground to avoid getting hit by the truck behind us as it rolls over us. We scramble out of the path of the next truck and are on our feet running for the trees.

I can't tell how many have jumped, but it must be the entire truck, because the woods are alive with screams and crashes. People are fleeing like rabbits. I can feel the adrenaline flowing. I have never run faster in my life. We're a few feet from the trees when I hear the crack of rifles and zing of bullets coming by me. I hear Daniel scream in agony, but don't look back. I know Daniel was hit, but I can't save him. Six more strides and I am in the trees without Daniel. An empty sadness and shame is seeping into my mortified fear. Already I am rationalizing leaving him as I run for my life. If Daniel is alive - I have no way to treat gunshot wounds or the strength to speed him away from the Gestapo. What did my mother say? I can hear her voice like she's running at my side shouting, "Think only of saving yourself. Run! Faster! Run and don't look back. Live and give me hope. Save yourself. Run!"

I am no longer sprinting, but pacing myself at a speed I can sustain. My mouth is cotton. My heart is pounding. My lungs ache and scream for air, but I keep throwing one foot in front of the other with no lack of energy as I leap through the underbrush in a forest of tall trees. I have lost track of time. Finally I stop and walk to catch my breath.

I've never been this deep in these woods and don't know how far I've come or recognize where I am. There is no sound but the whisper of the breeze in the trees. Cold tears are running down my cheeks, cutting into my skin and slicing into the bone. No part of me escapes pain. There is no thought or place in my mind to retreat - to get away from what has happened. Mama is dead. This I know by the emptiness I am feeling. Everything I know is dead. I fall down lifeless, exhausted and emotionally finished.

Chapter 3

The Hunter and the Hunted

3 June 1942, In the forest between Krasno and Gorodok

I feel the sun, warm on my face and open my eyes to see from its position that it is well past noon. I find myself curled like a dog buried in leaves and pine needles. I roll over on my back and look up through the thickness of tree limbs into blue sky and feel my sudden freedom and autonomy and then anger filling my emptiness. Maybe I've dozed and rested for an hour. For several minutes, I stay still and listen, but hear no noise, no guns or anything human. I get up and stretch some of the soreness from my legs. I determine my direction from the sun and then walk west toward Gorodok. I welcome the first warmth of summer as the sun sparkles through the pines.

I am still walking toward the sun as it falls beneath the tree tops. It's near dark when I smell smoke, see a stone wall and know I'm near a farm. A farm could mean food, a hiding place and maybe contact with the resistance. I realize that I have the Star of David on the front and back of my shirt and should try to take them off before somebody sees them.

As if walking into a bad dream, I find myself on the edge of a plowed field near the smoldering ruin of a barn. Nausea and apprehension are creeping into my throat. Peasants are poking around in the dying fire. There is a burnt plow, an old cook stove, and other metal object protruding from the gray ashes. A stinking smoke is blowing my way, as I walk up to the ruin unnoticed and concealed in smoke. I can see that several men are pulling skulls up out of the ashes, some are clean but charred, and others have burnt flesh. They are using a bent rod to poke into the mouth or eye socket to pick up heads and toss them out of the fire. Nearby, two men are working on anvils with hammers and chisels to knock out teeth and smash them up in a search for gold.

Hundreds of burnt bodies are lying about in the ashes and scavengers are picking through them like thieves. Smoke blows up into my face and I begin to choke and cough. I am too stunned to move out of the smoke and find fresh air. Slowly I'm realizing this is the remains of my family and friends. The hurt of it is sinking into my gut. These were the people in the trucks. We were all loaded together. They were alive this morning and now - just burnt bones.

"It's the Star of David, a peasant screams in fear. "He has lived through the fire."

"Or come back from the dead," says another.

"It's a ghost!" screams a third as he drops his poker and runs off through the field.

Two more scavengers scream and run off in different directions leaving me alone with a hammer man at the anvil. He is staring in disbelief, but not moving from the small cache of gold that he's extracted from the teeth of the dead.

I start coughing - then crying uncontrollably. I turn away from the fire and walk a few feet back toward the trees and collapse into the dirt. Trying to find comfort, I curl up with my knees pressing against my elbows with my wet sobbing face in my hands. The deep eruptions of grief are streaming down my face. Exhausted, all the energy and hope of escape are gone. My lungs continue to cough up smoke, and soft cries spring deep from my guts.

Dirty boots step into my tear blurred vision. I look up and find the peasant from the anvil with his hammer. He is short, stocky and looks unusually strong and determined. He is bald with side patches of pepper-grey hair. He has a low bushy brow, a wide hairy nose, and a gaping mouth sparsely populated with yellow teeth. Squinting eyes, darting from side to side, are desperate and indecisive. His short stout arm pulls the hammer up behind his head in preparation to strike. I grab at his legs, and I'm a brown leaf falling through bare branches of oak trees into a wet black hole.

The world is a blur. I can't see through the fog in my brain or move my arms or legs. I blink to bring my eyes into focus and find myself in a lamp lit cottage, strapped to a straight back chair, staring across a well-worn table at the stout, stubby peasant. His mouth and chin are dripping wet with homemade grog. His wife, a larger version of him, stoops and stirs a hanging pot in the fireplace. Together they are a matched pair and the inspiration for gargoyles.

"Have some cheese," he says. Like he's feeding his dog- he reaches across the table and pushes a large chunk into my face.

I have more cheese in my mouth than I've seen in six months.

"You Jews eat chicken soup, don't you?" He waits for me to speak but sees my mouth is too gummed up and continues, "Olga has a rooster in the pot. My name is Ivan. What's yours?"

24

"Ivan? Did you say Ivan?" grins Olga from the cook fire. She straightens up, wipes her hands on her apron and walks over to the table, and laughs "No one ever called him Ivan except his mother. Stumpy is his name. The chicken soup is my idea. He wanted to take you right away to Krasno tonight and collect the bounty. You're worth fifty marks to Stumpy - more than a cow. They don't pay so much for cows, or they just take them. So Stumpy sells Jews rather than livestock. How many Jews you sold now - ten? Will that build the barn back? Never in your life."

"They said they would build us a barn," Stumpy mumbles.

"Even if you are their favorite bounty hunter, do you really think they will waste any lumber or labor on you? They've lied to everybody - even to the Pope, so why shouldn't they lie to you? And what are you going to do with all those bodies out there? I don't want to go outside. I throw up at the idea of it, and you're going to sit here and eat chicken soup with a Jew you're taking in to be shot when everyone he knows is lying dead in the yard."

"How are we going to eat, if I don't sell Jews?"

"Who can eat? I'm too sick to eat. I'm going to bed. The soup's ready - serve yourself and your guest, and while you're eating tell him how you're getting the gold out of his family's teeth."

"So far there is not much gold," says Stumpy.

"You idiot," she scolds. "Then why are you out there? Why did you let this happen to our property? The ghost of the dead will haunt us forever." Olga gives him a hard disgusted look and disappears into the bedroom.

Beaten down by his wife, Stumpy sulks over the problems of the day. "The fire was so hot it melted the gold. Some of it stayed in the mouths, but a lot of it burned through the flesh and fell into the fire. We'll have to rake the ashes and try to find it."

"It was terrible," Stumpy says turning to me with remorse. "Commander Schmidt had them undress and walk into the barn naked. The Nazis took everything they wanted and threw in the rest to fuel the fire. My two hundred year barn was framed with heavy timbers painted with pitch and full of hay. They soaked it with diesel, torched it with a flame-thrower, and made a fire hotter than hell. The ones that tried to escape were shot down by machine guns as they fled the flames - their bodies weren't badly burned. There were about fifty of them, and we did find more gold in their teeth."

"I would have chosen death by bullets rather than being burned alive," I say faintly without thinking. I am still dazed from the blow to the head and the shock of seeing and smelling the burnt bodies. The stench lives in my nostrils and forever in my memory. My skull is throbbing with pain and too sore to touch, and I am sick with fever and nausea. I am hollow and empty inside and tears are flowing down my cheeks. Every part of me hurts. There is no place or thought I can focus on that feels good or even neutral - there is no escape from the penetrating, throbbing pain.

I speak softly and more to myself than to Stumpy as faces flash through my brain, "There were children in that fire, beautiful women, mothers, grandmothers, grandfathers, my cousins, and maybe my mother and my brothers. A community, a tradition, three-hundred years of history, and a way of life is gone - vanished into smoke and stone cold dead. How can you pick through the bodies?"

Stumpy begins with a grunt of dismissal and says, "I have my own pain. Everybody has trouble. You cry for your people, but what about my pain? Do you think of my problems? My farm is dead. They have taken most of my livestock and grain. I have no way of making a living. The war is no good for me either and has made my life desperate. Now they burn my barn, turn my place into a graveyard, and make me a scavenger and a bounty hunter. They have me pulling teeth like a dentist, and living from dead bodies like a maggot."

"I would like the life of a maggot," I say. "To chew on Nazi flesh, and grow wings and fly away from here."

"I don't know if you can grow wings, but Jews are certainly maggots. Hitler is right in exterminating you."

"Why? It makes no sense even if you hate us. Every day, Hitler is killing potential soldiers, skilled craftsmen, nurses, doctors, and others that could help in his war effort. He is using precious resources to enslave, torture, and kill useful people. He's stirring up a nest of ants that's even now biting his ass."

"So you're a maggot and an ant - just a God damn insect. They'll step on your ass soon enough."

"Not before I bite them a few times."

"I don't see that you'll have a chance to do anything, my Jew," he says as he gets up, walks around the table and pinches me hard on the cheek with his dirty nails drawing blood.

I scream from the pain - like I'm pinched by pliers.

"Maybe you would like to lie down for the night," Stumpy says as his filthy army boot jams between my thighs, comes to rest on the chair seat, and pushes the chair with me in it straight back.

The chair crashes first then the back of my head slams into the floor. I am lying on my back, dazed, still strapped in the chair with the ropes cutting into my arms. Seized by anger, I shake my eyes into focus and scream, "You bastard!"

"Here's some grog to help you sleep," he says in a quiet voice as he slowly empties a full cup into my still, stone face.

I won't give him the satisfaction of another reaction. Stumpy gives me a kick into my empty stomach and still I don't react. He clears his throat and spits a wad of phlegm that hits my chin, drools around my neck and on to the floor. At that the peasant chuckles with amusement, and without another word he walks over to the cook fire, serves himself a bowl of chicken soup and sits down with his elbows on the table, soup bowl in hands, and slurps up his supper without taking the bowl from his mouth. After a couple of minutes, he puts down the bowl and chokes down some grog. He pushes himself up from the table on his thick arms and wipes his face with his sleeve. Without even a kick or a spit in my direction, he takes the oil lamp to the bedroom and leaves me captive in the dark.

The embers of the cook fire throw light around the room - casting flickering shadows like ghosts. It makes me think of the new spirits haunting this property. Maybe one of them could help in my struggle with the ropes. Softly I solicit my mother by closing my eyes, reaching out into the universe and thinking of her as I whisper, "Please mother, wherever you are, come to me. Come to me now. Please, I need your help. I'm not ready to die." I laugh at myself and say, "Who is ready to die?" I then look up at the ceiling and beg, "God, help me."

I struggle with the rope, then rest, try again with more determination but get nowhere. I think of how the ropes are moving about me. Maybe that will give me a clue as to how to get loose. My hands are tied with four rolls of rope, and then the rope travels under the seat and then makes turns around me and the chair. The knot holding all this together is on my back and at the top of the chair. Everything is tight and cutting into me - nothing wants to loosen up.

No amount of pulling and pushing or begging God and the dead gets me free. Although it seems impossible, it occurs to me that I might somehow be able to move this chair and myself to the fire. By shifting my weight, I am able to rock the chair until I turn myself on my side, and then I roll over onto my front. With my knees and using my head as a foot, I make my way inchworm fashion across the hard packed dirt floor. Beside the hearth I discover the black iron pot of chicken soup. I am completely consumed by the aroma of food. I make my way to mouth of the pot and plunge my face into it. It is still warm and feels good on my face - like the caress of my mother's hand. I slurp up the soup as quietly as I can, but in the stillness the sound is deafening as the noise is magnified by the cavity of the half empty pot. I am too hungry to care about the noise waking Stumpy or having to eat without hands. I dive for a piece of chicken and blow the soup out of my nose. My tongue finds a potato and then a carrot and I slurp them up.

With a full stomach I push away from the pot and think again about getting loose. I turn around and back the legs of the chair into the dying embers with the hope of burning the ropes. My legs are tied to the front legs of the chair with a space of rope in between. I am trying to straddle the fire, so as to burn the rope spread between my legs and not myself. I situate myself and wait, apprehensive that I might soon be burning or destroying my precious shoes.

As I lie with my knees and face on the floor and the chair strapped to my back, I can hear a door-rattling snore and higher pitched wheezing coming from Stumpy and Olga's room. There is a loft and open door to another smaller bedroom, where children probably slept. What happened to the children? Maybe they are casualties of the war. Olga and Stumpy are empty, without compassion. They are half-hearted survivors caring little for the future, and holding on to the day to day survival. I saw more hope in the ghetto than in this farmhouse. Like the Judenrat, they think as long as they throw the beast meat they won't be eaten themselves. At this moment, I am the meat.

I smell smoke and think the rope must be burning. Then I feel the heat on my ankles and realize that it's from my pants. "My God! I'm on fire!" I scream as the flames lick at my legs. "Help! Help! Please help! Wake up! Wake up! I'm burning!"

Suddenly I'm wet and cold from the waist down and my fire is out. I look up and see a match strike and the oil lamp comes to life on the table. The light reveals Stumpy bare-footed in a white night shirt with a puzzled look, and an empty wooden bucket at his feet.

"I've seen Jews burn, but it's the first time I've seen one jump in the fire by himself. You stupid ass, are you trying to join your family?"

I don't answer - I'm too depressed.

"Maybe you want to cheat me out of my money by killing yourself. You got to be crazy," Stumpy says as he grabs my chair and pulls me out of the dead fire. He then drags me toward the door, and pushes me and the chair into the vertical position.

"I wish they gave me the same money for dead Jews. I would be rich with eight hundred bodies in the yard, and it would be easier taking you in. I could cut your throat, hang you up by your feet to drain like a pig and go back to bed, but they want the pleasure of killing you themselves. You're going to Krasno tonight. You got me up, so I might as well do something."

Chapter 4

On the Way to Market

4 June 1942, before sunrise on the forest road between Gorodok and Krasno

A ground fog hangs a few feet above the country road, leaving the sky sparkling and clear. There is no moon or light to spoil the star studded blackness. I hear the horse give an occasional snort as it moves at a comfortable trot pulling the rickety wagon from bump to bump. In spite of the clip-clop of hooves and clatter of wheels, Stumpy is drifting in and out of consciousness. I am bouncing around in the back on the wagon's worn wooden boards still tied to the stout chair and looking up at the stars. For the moment the world is mine alone. My absorption in the vastness of the universe returns to the frantic reality of being tied to one earthly spot. Suddenly the back right wheel drops into a pothole. The jolt sends my chair teetering and yanking at the rope that is tied to the wagon seat. Quickly I shift my weight, and I'm able to remain upright. Stumpy doesn't look back to see what's happening with his load. His lack of concern makes me feel like a sack of onions or more like a fettered goat on the way to slaughter.

The knot at Stumpy's end of the rope has become loose with the bounces and my pulling. Slowly my tether is becoming longer. Gradually I am walking the chair to the rear of the wagon, so that it is soon teetering on the wagon's back edge. I am thinking that with the aid of the next pothole I might be able to bounce out without the notice of Stumpy, who has fallen into a grog induced stupor. So what if the rope doesn't break and I am dragged down the road. I must take the chance.

A sudden jolt throws me off balance and out of the wagon. The back legs of the chair break out of their sockets as they hit the gravel road. I find myself in the middle of chair parts and a loose tangle of rope. I am able to step out of the rope, and the only thing left tied is my hands. I get up and hobble toward the forest, pulling the rope and chair parts behind me. Stumpy, still slumped in his seat, is undisturbed by my absence and is moving on down the road.

I enter the forest and look back and see the wagon stopped seventy-five meters away and is now turning around. As I try to move into the woods I realize the rope is pulling at my hands, and I can't go any further. Somehow the rope has gotten tangled in a bush, and I am again tied to one spot.

Stumpy is standing in the wagon holding a lantern out front and over his head as he searches the road. In a panic, I pull at the rope, but find myself still caught and unable to move. Desperately I pull at the knot holding my hands with my teeth, but it holds fast. Stumpy is getting closer, so I drop to the ground and crawl on my belly back toward the road, pulling my way along the rope trying to find the tangle that's holding me.

Something in the road catches Stumpy's attention, so he pulls up the reins, ties them off and climbs down. His right hand pulls a knife from his coat pocket as he steps off in my direction shouting, "A cut Jew is as good as a dead one. They won't bother fixing you. So you will bleed, and die slowly. Don't worry. I won't kill you. I want to collect my reward. The bounty is for live ones only. Come out you bastard. You're not going to cheat me out of my money."

Stumpy is stopped by the sight of the rope. He holds his light over his head and searches the brush. His hat brim being lower than the light throws a mask across his eyes making him look like the bandit he is. With my heart pounding, I am lying in the bushes two meters behind him, holding a chair leg in my tied hands and waiting for my chance. Stumpy bends over again, grabs the rope, and pulls on it like he's got a fish on the other end. I feel the tug of the rope as I stand up in my bush, take two steps and bring my club crashing down on Stumpy's bald spot.

There is a groan of pain and surprise as the drooling troll crashes to the ground. I hit him two more times in the head before Stumpy is still.

With the help of the lantern I find the knife on the ground, I turn the blade on my ropes and cut myself free. I then trade my shirt for Stumpy's - leaving Stumpy the shirt with a Star of David on the front and back.

I take the lantern and the knife back to the wagon, climb up on the seat, take the reins and turn toward Gorodok where I hope to find a more sympathetic peasant. I am free and alive. My heart is leaping out of my chest. I have a horse, a wagon and revenge on a collaborating peasant. It is more elation than I can stand. Then I think of the burnt bodies in the ashes of Stumpy's barn, and I am again depressed.

Why did I let Stumpy live? He's as much a Nazi as any of them, but I never killed anyone. I still have respect for life. I grin as I think about Stumpy coming home to his burly, sarcastic wife without money, the Jew, or the horse and wagon. He will be coming home a complete failure with her already in a foul mood about the burnt barn. He will lose what little respect she has for him. She will be his punishment. I crack the whip and push the horse into a fast trot.

At daylight I find myself in the forest just outside Gorodok. I drive the wagon into the woods about a mile from the river, unhitch and camouflage it with underbrush that I cut with Stumpy's knife. I shorten the reins on the horse and ride bareback through the woods to the river. While my horse and I drink, I contemplate the next move. What peasant would be most likely to receive me? Anyone I pick will be risking his life. Do I have such a friend who will embrace the consequences of helping a Jew? How will I find the partisans, and will they take me? I have heard of people being refused. Certainly they would want a veteran of the Polish Army, even if I don't have a weapon.

Fording the river in a shallow spot, I enjoy the sound of splashing water and crunching gravel beneath the horse's hooves. The cool breeze flutters the newly waxed leaves and the warm sun is bright in a clear blue sky. When I reach the other side, I tie the horse to a tree and let her graze on the green slope. I take a deep breath, stretch and let go of the tension. I am relaxed and exhausted. I take off Stumpy's smoky shirt and my scorched pants and wash them in the river and spread them on a rock to dry. I then plunge in the cool water and proceed to pick off lice and scrub off the grime with sand.

I pull myself up on the rock where my clothes are spread out, shake out my hair and lay down in the sun to dry. I feel myself falling asleep. When I wake, I see the sun is climbing toward noon. My clothes are almost dry and my skin is parched and about to burn. I put on the damp ill-fitting shirt and see the horse is still content munching grass on the slope. I am wondering how safe she is in this spot, or whether I should go back to the forest to hide until darkness before I look for a meal and a place to bed down. My stomach is telling me to find food.

As I listen to the splashing of the water spilling over the rocks, I am startled by the faint sound of voices. They seem to be coming from the Gorodok side of the river, from where the horse is tied. Apprehensive, I scramble into my pants and quietly pick my way through the brush along the river toward the voices. They are very close now. Crouched behind a bush, I steal a view.

"My God," I mutter. "It's Stumpy. How did he find me? I left him ten kilometers from here with his head bashed in."

Besides Stumpy there is a tall, thin man in peasant clothes and a huge policeman with a rifle looking small in his hands. The policeman points the rifle in my direction and says, "He has got to be down here on this side of the river. Maybe a stone's throw away."

"You can shoot him in the leg, but don't kill him," Stumpy says." Alive, he's still worth fifty marks."

"Hush," the policeman scolds. "You're too loud - he might hear you. Look for some sign of him - footprints, a broken bush, anything. You, Kris, go up hill - from there you'll have a good view of the river. Stumpy, you search the bank, and I'll stay between you with the rifle. He must be close by. He wouldn't leave the horse behind."

They become quiet as they spread out and start walking downstream toward me. I run back along the horse trail toward my bathing spot. I cram on my shoes, and tie them tight. I jump up into a run and follow the path along the river. I look for a place to cross. I am thinking how stupid I was to keep the horse. Why didn't I kill Stumpy? If only I could run faster. I must get around the bend in the river before I can cross to the forest undetected. Looking back I have a clear view of the tall man on the hill pointing at me and then leaping down the hill as he runs towards me. Now I know the misery of hunted rabbits. My heart jumps to my throat as a gun goes off. The tall man must be holding a pistol, but he is too far off to be accurate. If I can only get across the river and into the woods before they shoot me.

I turn at a bend in the river and find a crossing place where the river spreads out and is less than knee deep. Thinking I am out of sight of my pursuers, I splash through the shallow water. Two shots ring out as I enter the woods and dive behind a tree. Scrambling back to my feet, I am off running again. Fifty meters inside the tree line, I turn right and run a zigzag path parallel to the river. I soon reach a familiar thicket where I once played hide and seek. I crawl in and lie down on a bed of leaves, exhausted.

Chapter 5

Trapped

4 June 1942, near Gorodok, Poland

It is well after dark before I find the courage to move from my hiding place in the thicket. I make my way back to the river and take a long drink. The cool water fills my empty stomach, but does nothing for hunger pains. I must find a farm house and beg at someone's door. But should I risk it? What peasant would feed me? I remember the day I pulled the wagon down the street and try to remember a sympathetic face.

I find the same shallow point in the river and wade across. As I am climbing the bank on the other side, a hand reaches out of the darkness grabs an ankle and pulls me off my feet. Stunned and held by a foot, I am on the ground, face down, being drug back downhill toward the river.

"I've got you now," I hear a voice chuckle before everything goes black.

I wake to find myself again in the wagon and bouncing down the road. I am lying on my stomach with my hands and feet tied behind me. I am hurting all over like from a beating. Each bump in the road aggravates a bruise. I try to roll over on

37

my side, but the ropes won't allow it. I am tied, so I can't turn my head to see the driver. Who else could it be, but Stumpy? Finally the wagon stops and I feel the weight of the driver get out. Two uniformed guards untie my feet and drag me out of the wagon by the arms. I see the entrance of a barbed wire compound. I am disoriented, stiff and sore. With a guard on each arm, I hobble toward the gate.

"Catching you was like trapping a pig," Stumpy says as he steps into view. "I knew hunger would bring you back out of the woods, and you would come out the way you went in and cross the river in the same place. You crazy Jew, please die, so I don't have to catch you again."

His big belly quivers with laughter as he brags, "I beat you, you bastard. It feels good to win, and even better when I collect the money. How does it feel that I am laughing in your stupid face?" he asks with a chuckle that ends with a wad of spit that hits my forehead and spatters my eyes.

I am silent in my suffering as I wipe my face on my sleeve. I know better than to speak. My anger would only bring a slap to one of my bruises, so I ignore Stumpy and keep my eyes on the ground, so no one can see into my pitiful soul.

The compound looks much like the Gorodok Ghetto and has been created by sectioning off the part of the village surrounding the synagogue. With a Lithuanian guard pushing me in the back, I am escorted to a cottage near the main gate and deposited in a small room with a stack of five beds against one wall. The bottom bunk is on the floor, and the top one is too close the ceiling.

Besides the stack of bunk beds, there is only a dirty bucket in the empty room. I lie down on the thin mattress of the second bunk and feel each of the hard wooden slats and the void between them. I keep shifting about, trying to find a spot in the bunk where my bruises don't hurt. I fall asleep thinking if this is the Krasno Ghetto, some of my family could be here.

In what seems like a few minutes, I am awakened by a poke from a rifle and taken to the showers where I give up everything but my belt and my shoes. After a short cold shower, I am given a tin bowl and clothes, a size too big. Thank God I have a belt to hold up my pants.

I am left in a small cluttered room where a bright eyed middle-aged man in a prison uniform is seated on a small cot in front of an old ammunition box that serves him as a desk.

The man points to a smaller box in front of the desk, and says, "Be seated. I am the Kapo in charge of your section. I need to ask you some questions."

Then there is a pause and prolonged eye contact as we study each other. The Kapo breaks the silence with several questions with pauses for answers that don't come: "I must determine if you are a parasite or a productive worker... Do you have production skills? Tell me, what work you do? If we can't find any use for you, you will be shot.... Silence is not golden but deadly.... Speak up or you will be deported today...."

"I'm a carpenter," I say, finding my voice." I can build most anything. I've been a math teacher and grammar school principal. I speak German, Polish, Russian and English."

"And of course Hebrew," adds the Kapo.

I nod yes.

And the Kapo continues, "We are building quarters for the occupying troops. Would you like to be a carpenter on this project?

"Yes," I say.

"It will mean working hard every day, but work is your meal ticket. If you don't work - you don't eat."

"I understand," I say.

39

"If you work and do a good job, you'll have nothing to worry about. Understand?"

I nod my head.

"Good," says the Kapo. "Where you slept last night is a place for people arriving and leaving. Your quarters will be in the Synagogue. You must make your own space. Everyone is up at five and at work at six. You will work until six and have soup at seven. Lights out at eight. Any questions?"

"Is there anything to eat?" is my weak response.

"Come," he says getting up. "I will take you to the kitchen cottage, and then a visit to the doctor. Hurry, we haven't much time."

I am stiff and hurting from Stumpy's beating and sleeping two hours on boards, so I'm having a hard time keeping up with the quick cadence of the Kapo. I am afraid of losing my guide and consequently my meal in the crowded narrow street. The stink and closeness of unbathed bodies is more than I can stand. The stink has found its way to my stomach. If I had something to vomit, I would. A bony elbow bumps me hard in a broken rib, and it brings back a pain that shoots up into my armpit. I am becoming anxious about the doctor's inspection. I must try to look healthy - my life depends on it.

Damn Stumpy. He tried to cripple me, so I couldn't work - so I'd be expendable. I should have smashed his head in with the chair leg.

When we reach the mess hall, the Kapo goes to the front of the line and picks up two cups of steaming soup from a small window and pours one into to my tin bowl.

"We must eat on the run or you will miss your work detail. The next stop is the doctor."

I gulp down the last bit of hot watery soup as I enter the doctor's cottage, and I'm ordered to take off my clothes. Blotches

40

of discolored swollen tissue are as plentiful as spots on a leopard. The doctor is not available, so I'm examined by an assistant, a short stocky man of about thirty. He can be identified as a Polish political prisoner by a "P" in a red triangle on his shirt. With blue vacant eyes the examiner looks me over for less than a minute and dismisses me without commenting or offering any first aid for my wounds. I quickly dress and follow the Kapo to the front gate where I am left with a group of men waiting to go to work. My new Kapo is a large, gray haired man with a "P" on his shirt. He blows a whistle; the men form up in ranks and come to attention. The Kapo makes a quick count as two stragglers join us.

"Forward, March," orders the Kapo, and we are out of the gate and on our way to work. In a few minutes of marching we enter another barbed wire compound where barracks are under construction.

The Kapo comes up from behind me and puts a strong hand on my shoulder and says, "Come, I'll take you to your job. You'll be building door and window casings. The windows will be here in two weeks, and we've got to get ready for them. If we're not ready, it will be my ass and yours. See that tall, skinny Pole looking out the window," the Kapo says. "He'll be your partner. He's young, arrogant and illiterate, but an okay carpenter. Try to make the best of it."

"Pavlic," the Kapo says to the Pole with a wave of the hand. "I'll leave you two to work it out," is all he says as he walks out the door.

As the man approaches I hold out my hand out for a greeting. The Pole makes a weak begrudging handshake. At that instant I know the man doesn't want to work with me or any Jew.

"You are new here", the man grunts in bad Polish. "So, I'll show you the ropes. Just do as I say. We are building window casings. The measurements are the same for each opening. Your job will be to measure and cut the materials while I nail them up. Call me Pavlic."

"I'm Yehuda," I say looking at the ground with resignation.

"OK Yahoodee. Here's the measuring stick. It's worth more than you are. Break it, and they'll make the next one out of your leg bone."

As I put the saw horses in place, I am thinking that talking to this guy will not be fruitful. How can I be silent all day? I make a pattern for the window, so I only need to use the precious stick once. Pavlic is just looking out the window hole, wishing he were somewhere out there beyond the fence. I make the first cut and hold the board in the top of the window with my left hand.

"Nail it." I ask.

Pavlic slowly moves to my left side and places a nail near my holding hand. He takes a big swing at the nail and smashes my little finger. The board falls striking me in the top of the foot. The pain shoots up my arm and flashes through my brain in anger. My right hand feels strong as it makes a fist. I look into the Poles eyes and see a mocking grin. Anger overpowers hurt as I step toward Pavlic on my sore foot. I stop myself in mid-swing, slump over and put both hands on my knees. I look at the floor, and think I'll have to suffer this bastard.

"Watch it," says the Pole, backing up. "Are you going to hit me? It was an accident, honest to God."

"Don't do it again," I grunt, looking up.

"I won't. I never meant to do anything."

"You had better start doing something," I say standing up. "You're not going to blame me for the lack of production."

"Who's blaming you? I'm not feeling good today."

"The Nazis don't care what you're feeling. We've got to get something done. Take that board and hold it yourself, and nail it while I cut another one."

I go back to measuring boards and sawing. The Pole is still slowing me down. I help with the nailing until we catch up. It goes like that most of the morning with me doing two-thirds of the work. Then all of a sudden the Pole is nailing like a machine gun. He is suddenly caught up and waiting for me to finish sawing. I finish, turn and see the Kapo has been watching.

"Jew-boy, you got to work quicker," says the Kapo in scolding voice. Your partner is waiting on you. You pull your weight around here, or you won't be here tomorrow. Okay, lunch. It's in the yard at the bottom of the steps."

I turn and whisper to the Pole," I know you set me up. You do it again, and there will be consequences."

"Sure," says the Pole, "I'm shaking in my shoes."

I mutter my way to the lunch line. I hold out my bowl for the thin soup, get it, and sit down on a fresh oak stump left from clearing the building site. I take a deep breath and try to let go of my aggravation. As I sip, I look around for someone I know, but there is no one.

The afternoon passes without incident. Sunlight is fading, as the whistle signals to stop and clean up. I make my last cut and place the board in the top of the door and wait with sudden apprehension for the Pole to nail it. I see the hammer coming toward my left hand, and I am unable to move in time. The left hand is hit again. Before the board hits the floor, my right fist is on its way to the Poles face. The Pole takes the hit, stumbles back, regains his balance and makes a swing at my head with his hammer. I duck and push up with my legs driving the top of my head into the Poles chin. The Pole falls back into the

43

wall with blood spilling out of his mouth. The hammer falls out of his hand, and I kick it across the room.

The noise of the scuffle attracts the other workers who hope to see a fight. A tight circle of spectators is made around us. They are telling Pavlic to get up and fight, but the last blow has made him drunk. He stumbles to his feet and leans against the wall to steady himself. His eyes are vacant in his bloody face. I grab up my hammer thinking the Polish workers are becoming angry enough to attack me. Someone kicks a hammer to Pavlic's feet, but he doesn't have the courage to pick it up.

Pavlic's girlfriend steps out of the crowd, hands Pavlic her hammer and shouts, "You will pay for this, Jew."

"The fight is over," shouts the foreman. "You, Jew, don't come back tomorrow. Everybody, outside in formation."

I have so much unspent energy, I can't restrain it. I double time down the steps and find my place in formation.

"Attention! Forward March! Hup, two, three, four," fills my head, as I fall into the cadence of the march. I sob in relief as the tension flows out of me. I sob for being captured after such a magnificent escape. Then I feel better and find my strength. The wetness of tears feels cool and refreshing on my face. I tell myself that I am going to escape again. I've got to get out of this camp, or one way or another I'll die here - maybe before the killing squad comes.

I leave the formation and follow some Krasno Jews who are walking toward the synagogue. I begin talking to a middle aged man named Simon.

"There's always room for one more," says Simon. "People are continually coming and going. Don't worry about bedding. There's plenty."

"Are there any people from Gorodok?"

"Yes, there are quite a few," Simon replies.

"Do you know of any Adelman's?"

"Yes, several of them. There's a man, Ezer Adelman, who escaped."

"Good," I say. "I hope he found the partisans."

"That would be fortunate," smiles Simon as he holds out his hand. "Are you Ezer's brother?"

"Yes," I smile."

"I admire his courage. Most of us would like to be partisans. If we could only find the way to take our families with us. We have talked about a mass escape."

"It's a good idea," I whisper. "Half of us would be killed, but some of us would be free. Better than all of us dying. It must be coordinated with the partisans. The best time would be early Sunday morning when the guards are dead drunk asleep. This project is near completion. We will be going somewhere to another job or to liquidation. Something must be done before the mobile killing units come, and you know they are coming."

"Yes, maybe sooner than you think, "nods Simon. "It's not a happy thought to take to bed."

I break away and walk quickly with the anticipation of seeing my family - maybe even Mama. But I never saw her get in a truck, and some trucks didn't come to Krasno. As I enter the synagogue, my nose expects the usual fresh scent of candles, but I'm hit with the musty smell of dirty clothes on dirty bodies. There are too many beds and makeshift walls to get a clear view of the whole place. My heart is racing, and I am breathing hard as my eyes dart into one small space and then another. I grow anxious. Where are they? Are they alive? They must be here - work is over for the night.

"Julie!" I hear.

Startled, I stop, see nothing and then feel a hand on my shoulder. I turn and I am face to face with my younger brother,

45

David. As we embrace my arms reach all the way around his bony body. Tears are flowing from our eyes as we push back and look at each other.

"I thought you were dead," we both say at once.

Still holding each other at the shoulders, we look at each other in delight and wonderment. Then David lets go, and his arms fall limp at his side.

"My Sarah, Ezer and Helen and her family are here. Ezer escaped the day we arrived. He swam the river and went back to Gorodok to look for Mother and his little Moshe. He found them dead in her bed. They were killed the day of selection and left to rot."

We embrace, hug and cry. After a few minutes, I wipe my eyes, and ask, "Why did Ezer come back?"

David wipes his eyes, clears his throat and continues, "Ezer was shot leaving Gorodok as he was crossing the river. He was in shock, crying and stupid with grief. He crossed the river too close to the bridge. Someone on the bridge shot him in the arm. He came back under the fence in the early morning. He is exhausted from the loss of blood and the ordeal. The bullet passed through without breaking a bone. It's a matter of controlling the infection and getting his strength back. We're hiding him under the floor until he is strong enough. If he's too weak to work, they would kill him. All he needs is food. We do what we can, but it's hardly enough."

"Poor Ezer," I lament. "Too bad he couldn't stay on the other side of the fence. It was the bounty that did me in. This stubborn peasant wanted the money, and he wouldn't give up on me. So I was caught, tied like a pig and taken to market. I'm a commodity, worth more than a cow. So here I am. The first day, I'm in trouble already."

"What kind of trouble?"

"I got into a fight with this Polish kid."

"Did you win?"

"How can you win?" I say exasperated. "I butted him in the chin with my head. That bloodied his mouth and knocked him down. Still in a daze, he got back on his feet but never got it together to lift his arms. The Kapo called the fight to save him. Something he wouldn't have done for me. I don't see him giving up. His pride was hurt, and his girlfriend was there. He'll take another hammer swing at me, when I'm not looking, but it won't be tomorrow. They gave me the day off."

"You won the fight and a day off," smiles David. "I'm proud of you, but you've become noticed as a trouble maker. Come, we will make a bed for you in our space on the other side of the room."

I follow my brother through a maze of temporary walls. Sister Helen is the first to hug me, then her five and six year old children, Shusona and Matthew. David's wife, the petite, sparkling eyed Sarah, kisses me on the lips and hugs and holds me with a warmth that helps sooth the reality of Mama's death. I am chilled and surprised as I pull her close, as no woman in the family has ever kissed me on the lips. I'm reminded of the first kiss of adolescence and of all the love I've lost. It's the most affection I have had since I kissed my mother goodbye. One kiss and I am in love with her and life again.

"Thank God you're alive," says Sarah as she pulls away but still holding me at the shoulders and smiling with love in her bright green eyes.

"Yes," I say. "Thanks to you I am coming back to life. I was worried that I would never see any of you again."

Overwhelmed and speechless in a cocoon of affection, I wipe the tears out of my eyes.

"You must be tired," says a sympathetic Helen. "I'll make you a bed. It will only take a minute. We will all lie down and talk until we fall asleep. But it must be in whispers."

She steals bedding from each of the others and makes a place for me between Sarah and five year old Matthew. I lie down, dizzy with exhaustion and fall asleep in a bed of love.

The next morning, we are up before sunrise pulling on our shoes.

"It will be your job to take care of Ezer today," Sarah whispers as she hugs me. She pulls back and gives further instructions. "Follow us to the soup line and take him your breakfast. The boards are loose in the closet behind me. Knock four times before you pull them up. Close the door and replace the boards after you drop into the crawl space. Have a good visit. He talks of you often. He loves you very much."

I get the watery soup in my tin bowl and return to the empty synagogue with my heart racing. I place the bowl on a low closet shelf, and pull the door shut so as to a leave a crack of light to see the boards that I must take up. I get on my knees and make four raps on the floor. I then proceed to pry up the boards with my fingertips. Once the boards are up, I quietly close the closet door, and drop into the crawl space and quickly work the boards back in place.

Before my eyes can adjust to the dim light spilling through the cracks in the floor, a hand reaches out and grabs my forearm.

"Ezer is it you?" I ask with my heart in my throat.

"Yes, my dear Julie," returns a hoarse whisper. "Thank God you are okay. I thought you could be dead. But somehow I knew you were alive. You are too resourceful and stubborn to die."

48

"How are you doing?" I whisper as he grabs me with his good hand. "Your grip feels like you have some strength in you."

"I'm getting stronger. I'm thinking of coming up."

"Why do you want to come up? Let's escape together. We can go out the way you came in. Here, have your soup."

"That's the problem," groans Ezer. "It's not my soup. It's your soup. You will die without it."

"It's okay. We are all taking turns. Tonight it will be somebody else's soup. So drink it or I will pour it out."

"Thank-you my dear Julie. I do appreciate your sacrifice, and I will drink it, but tomorrow I'm coming up and getting my own soup."

"Are you strong enough?"

"I'm as strong as I will ever get down here. I can't stand up or walk. My muscles are cramped. This is as much a prison as it is up top. The first couple of days will be hard, but I will get through it."

"I want you to escape with me," I plead.

"I have no reserve, no strength left. The awful sight of Mother and Moshe haunts me. It was either come back or die. At least I have my family here. Maybe in a couple of months, I will find the strength and courage to try again."

"Please, escape with me," I plead. "With the two of us, it will be easier."

"I'll slow you down, and we'll both be caught," Ezer says as a matter of fact. "I will tell you how to escape. Here is the plan. You will go to the saw mill in David's place. He will take your place in your job. Once you are at the mill you will see how to escape. David will tell you how. It's much easier at the mill, because you are out of town and in the forest."

"I would feel better if you would come with me."

"No, I can't leave the family. After you leave, I will take your place and start earning my keep. When I am stronger we will all try to leave."

My eyes have adjusted to the dim light. I can see the bones of my brother's face are covered with scraggly hair. "You must get someone to cut your hair and clean you up."

"Yes it's been arranged."

I sob, and grab my brother by the neck and kiss him on the lips. I blink to control my tears as I look into his eyes.

"I love you," he says.

"I love you too, brother. When I find the partisans, I will be back for you and the others. We will have a mass escape."

Chapter 6

Sonia and Rose

3 June 1942, 8:00 AM, In Gorodok, Poland on the day of the Selection.

The Gestapo has surrounded the ghetto and is efficiently doing its work. Everyone was quickly sorted and loaded into trucks. In the process several people were bludgeoned to death, and two older men were trampled and injured by the panic of inmates being herded into trucks. Several were yanked out of hiding. Only eight escape detection and are huddled in a small bunker dug out of the brown dirt under the synagogue floor. They hear the bangs and crashes of the Gestapo and the Ukrainian police shouting and stomping about as they turn over beds, tear through makeshift closets, and search attic space looking for hidden Jews.

"Look, there's a Jew in this piano. He's in the box," the police chief reports to the commander. "I was looking at it for myself. My wife plays the piano. Christ, who would think a man could be small enough to fit in this box full of strings? I push a key and it doesn't play, so I open the lid to see why. And here he is - this skinny, sickly creature. What should I do with him?"

"He's got dysentery," replies Commander Schmidt. "He's too weak to work. Put him in the last truck with the old and crippled. But wait. Before you move the piano, have your men tear open this wall. I want to see what's behind it. I heard something. I think it came from there."

Sonia is hearing this as she crouches in the hole beneath the floor, tightly holding her two year old Rose who is frightened by the noise. Rose kicks Sonia in the stomach and cries out, "Mama, Mama!

Sonia puts a handkerchief over her baby's mouth to muffle her crying and whispers, "Hush, quiet - Mama is here - no need to cry. Hush."

Still the child continues wailing and Sonia is not able to completely muffle the noise. Everyone in the hole is fidgeting and nervous that the noise will be the death of them. Dania, a large, hard faced woman, grabs the child with both hands. In desperation to quiet it, wraps her hands around Rose's neck and chokes her until she becomes pale and falls limp. When her big hands let go, the baby's neck is red and deformed. She then gently picks up Rose and lays the small, still body down in Sonia's lap.

Sonia is shocked, and tears begin spilling out of her eyes. In disbelief she looks to Dania for an explanation of her brutal behavior. Dania refuses eye contact, and without apology bows her head and retreats into a protective silence.

"Stop! Be quiet," they hear from above. "I heard something, like a baby crying. It's coming from the floor. There, in that spot. Chop a hole."

They hear an ax chipping at the floor, and soon splinters of wood are falling four meters from their tiny bunker. Sonia feels every blow of the ax like it's chopping into her chest. With silent prayers and trembling hands, she shakes her pale bloody child and blows into her mouth and shakes her again and again as she looks for some sign of life. Finally the baby starts breathing quick, deep breaths and Sonia pulls her to her breast and Rose begins to suck her thumb.

Sonia's racing heart freezes as she hears, "Juden raus! Come out." The voice is now coming to them unmuffled through a large fresh rip in the floor.

"Come out or you will be shot where you are. Come with us and you will live. We are only taking you to a new home."

No one moves or even dares breathe. The joy of finding life in her child is replaced by a knot of fear in Sonia's chest. Like a break in the clouds on a dark day, a shaft of light is spilling through the newly cut hole into the blackness of the crawlspace.

A head decorated with an officer's hat pokes through the hole. As it looks around, the hat slips off into the void beneath the floor. Like a turtle, the bare bald head retreats back into its body leaving the fugitives with the immediate urge to flee, but with nowhere to go but down. So they crouch lower in the bunker and try to become smaller with the hope that somehow they won't be seen.

"I lost my hat," they hear. "You go down and get it and take a look around with the flashlight."

A tall, lanky soldier makes an awkward drop through the hole. He is hatless, crouched with one knee on the ground and his head up between the floor joists. The light from the hole is on his face, so the nervous fugitives can see that he is blond with no beard, and looks to be a boy suffering from the clumsiness of a growth spurt. He picks up the hat and gives it to a black gloved hand waiting in the hole of light. He then turns on his flashlight, bends his head down below the floor joist, and makes a slow half circle of light around him until the light

53

stops on the faces of the eight Jews crouching in the dirt three meters away.

The focus of the light is on Sonia and Rose. Sonia's face is wet with tears. She is looking past the light into the soldier's eyes and making her message understood. Her head is shaking no and her finger is on her lips, and through the silence with her hands and her eyes she is saying, "Please go. Don't say we're here. Don't kill my precious baby. Just go back up and say you saw nothing."

The boy soldier is hypnotized by her radiant presence. He sees the love of mother for child, his own mother's love, her beautiful face and the wife he would like to have. He wants to hug and hold her, embrace her helplessness and tell her it's all right. He wants to lie down in her arms and have the most peaceful sleep of his life. He feels relaxed and warm just looking at her. Although she has a power over him, he feels his power too. He is judge, jury, and executioner. Never has he had such powers. Now he has them all at once and all to himself.

Lost in the moment, the soldier doesn't move until he hears, "Is there anyone there? What did you find? What's taking so long?"

There is silence as the soldier frets over his decision. What should he do?

"There is nothing here," the soldier finally says as he turns off the light and climbs back up through the hole. "I saw some rats. It must have been squealing rats."

The fugitives wait and wonder, but there is only silence. Finally they hear the trucks drive off taking some of their apprehension with them. But it's hours before they have the courage to leave the crawl space and push through the barbed wire of the compound. They find the town outside the ghetto has gone to bed and the streets are pitch black. They try to stay together as a group as they run toward the countryside with Sonia following behind carrying baby Rose. The anxiety of the escape gives them energy in spite of their hunger. They are moving quickly through the shadows except for Sonia, who can't keep up with the group and soon falls far behind.

Baby Rose is crying and spitting up blood. In her desperation Sonia thinks of her friend Piotr, the peasant. She knows him to be an honest, caring person. She had often purchased eggs and produce from him at the market. Even in the compound, he would bring milk for her baby. She is afraid to use the bridge to get to his farm, so she finds a shallow place in the river to cross. She steps into the cold water holding Rose over her head - not trusting her ability to navigate the river crossing in the dark. She carefully picks her way across the rocky river bottom, hoping not to step in a hole or twist an ankle. She is soaking wet from the waist down and cold before she reaches the other side.

Piotr is sleeping in his small bed next to the stove. He is a tall, bent man with a small potbelly. His gray hair is curling wildly out of the edges of a black wool cap that never leaves his head. A thin white mustache is drawn half way between his large fat nose and his thin lips. At seventy he still milks the cow, herds the sheep and tends the fields. He is widowed, and lives alone with his sheepdog. He has lost his soldier son to the war and has no love for the Germans. He responds to the knock on the door with a sleepy, apprehensive, "Who is it?"

"It's Sonia Essers," she shouts trying to reach through the door, and his deafness.

He lights the lamp, opens the door and greets Sonia and Rose with a hug and a peck on the cheek.

"I'm so glad to see that you are alive," he says. "I heard they came today and took everyone away and closed down the ghetto."

"Yes," she says showing her fatigue. "I was able to hide under the floor and escape detection. I've lost my husband and my baby is hurt. We are hungry and tired."

"Please come in," he says. "I'll find some food. See this belly. There is no shortage of food here."

The small cottage has two rooms and the cooking is done on a large wood stove which also provides heat. He opens the cupboard and pulls out a loaf of bread, makes several cuts and places it on the table where Sonia and Rose are seated.

"Eat up. I made this bread yesterday and I also milked the cow," he says, as he pours two cups of milk for Rose and Sonia.

"Listen, there is no way you can stay here and not be noticed. My neighbors live too close and are too much in my business. When they come out at daybreak to work the fields - they'll know you are here. There is a fifty mark bounty, and they are eager to collect it. I can hide you in the forest, and I can feed you as long as you like. Let me help you."

The next afternoon he brings milk, bread and the latest news to her in the forest. "Everyone in the ghetto was sorted - the old and sick were disposed of," he tells her. "All the young healthy men were sent to Krasno to work. Most everyone else was killed and burned. Today the Nazi's announced that there would be no more killing of Jews."

"I know nothing of my Pesach," she laments. "Please find out if my husband is alive."

"Such an excellent cobbler is sure to be alive. The Germans need boots to march across Russia. They need many Pesach's working night and day. You have heard the phrase, "For the lack of a nail the battle was lost. Well, Pesach is the one who drives the nail into the shoe. He is essential. They will keep him alive. I'm sure he's in Krasno working. When they find out how good he is, they will never let him go."

That night she lies down in a canvas shelter Piotr has made for her at the base of an old oak tree. Trembling with fear for her family, she hugs her sleeping child and tries to fall asleep but can't. Finally, she sits up and leans against the fat trunk. She covers the baby with a rag. Sonia listens to the rasp of Rose's breathing and imagines the hundreds of spiders, snakes and wolves that must be in the forest all around her. It's the first time she's sleeping under trees. Something could bite her baby. Just before daylight she collapses against the tree and falls into a harsh snoring sleep.

The sun is bright and high in the sky when Sonia wakes. Piotr is standing over her with bread and milk. Without a word she tears off a piece of bread and eats it. She wakes her sick child and gives her some bread and a cup of milk. Sonia is dull and tired from the lack of sleep and desperation.

Piotr sits and waits for her to finish tending to Rose. Finally he speaks, "Your Pesach is alive and in Krasno working as a carpenter. They are building barracks for the German troops. There are about twenty children there with their parents who escaped the massacre. They have stopped killing Jews, because they need workers. They are giving amnesty and welcome any Jew that wants to come to Krasno."

"Thank-you Piotr," she says looking up at him. "I have no choice. I must go to Krasno to be with my husband. It's only twenty kilometers. I can be there tonight."

Chapter 7

Homeless

June to November 1942

US bombing starts in Europe. First reports of gas being used to kill Jews reach the West. Germans develop first jet plane. The Selection of Jews in Warsaw Ghetto continues. Germans continue to advance toward Stalingrad until they totally surround the city on September 13. Hitler boasts that Stalingrad will be taken. Germans launch the first rocket into space (84.5 kilometers). The Red Army begins to encircle the Germans at Stalingrad in November.

7 June 1942, 6:00 AM on Sunday, at the entrance to Krasno Ghetto

I'm one of thirty hollow eyed men with chins on chest leaning back on one of two stone walls that face each other just inside the ghetto gate. Still in a dream state, we wait to march to work. Last night I was too nervous to sleep. I would like to drop down on the crack where the wall meets the ground and steal a few winks on the cobblestones. That would only bring a beating or a bullet.

My droopy eyes become focused as I break out of a stupor at the sight of my younger brother. David embraces me, and we become the only animated ones in the group. We grip hands, look into each other's eyes and embrace again. If any guard cared to look, he could see that something was unusual, but the four Lithuanians are stinking of Saturday night vodka. Their eyes can't see beyond their lids.

As agreed, we are trading work assignments with me going to the sawmill and David joining the carpentry crew. As the workers are called to fall into their respective platoons, I take a last look into David's watery eyes and kiss each of them shut.

"Give everyone my love," I whisper in a cracking voice - unable to suppress my tears, excitement and apprehension. "You must take care of the family. I will come back for you as soon as I find the partisans. I promise. It will only be a few weeks. Look for me at the mill at sunrise. I'll be there with a gun in my hand."

"My love and my hope go with you," says David as he lets go of my warm hand like he is seeing life walk away from him."

I march out of the Ghetto in a squad of twenty sawmill workers. At my side is the comfort of my childhood friend, Niomke. There is a spring in my step and I feel taller than yesterday. My spirit is soaring up into the tops of the tall trees. I don't mind the early morning march in the mud. Each step is a step closer to freedom.

The mill is at the edge of the forest about three kilometers from the village. When we reach the work site, I stay close to my friend and follow his lead. The twelve man squad breaks up into groups of two or three. Some workers are pulling the newly cut lumber out of the saw and are stacking it on to carts. Niomke and I push the full carts to a large fenced area and stack the lumber to dry. There are over a hundred stacks of siding and framing lumber each standing two meters high in a lumber yard that is half full. Two guards walk the perimeter. We wrap rags around our hands for protection against the splinters of the rough boards, but still the boards bite. At mid-morning the large circular saw is shut down to replace the blade which has become dull. This gives Niomke a chance to take the Star of David off the back and front of my shirt.

"I wish I were going with you," says Niomke. "But I must stay with my family. My wife and boy would be lost without me."

"I understand, I say grabbing his hand to say good-by. "I have no wife or child, so it is easier for me to leave."

"Take care my friend," says Niomke. "May God go with you."

Our eyes lock in a final good-by and I slip away. I squat, run on bent legs to stay low and try to keep the lumber piles between me and the guards as I make my way to the fence. Hiding behind piles of lumber, I watch and wait for the perimeter guards to pass and turn the corner. A panic chills my body as I slip under the fence and dash for the cover of the trees, all the while expecting bullets. There is nothing but the pounding in my chest.

The sun is in a blue sky and the forest is cool and sympathetic. Large fir and pine trees tower above me and rock with a gentle sway in the breeze. I run with my heart in my throat until I am exhausted and sit down on a log to rest. While resting, I hear the nearby whistle of a train and the screech and bang of box car metal against metal and hissing of steam.

"My God," I mutter. "Where am I? Have I come the wrong way?"

I walk in the direction of the sounds and I am soon peeking through a bush, looking at a railway station that I don't recognize. There are German troops and barbed wire everywhere. I dare not leave the safety of the forest and go any closer to identify the place. I look to the sun to orient myself and realize that I must be northwest of Krasno rather than southwest. In my haste to escape I took-off in the wrong direction. A panic seizes me. I take slow, deep breaths and try to remain calm and clear headed. I must go toward Gorodok where people are more likely to help me and the partisans are more likely to accept me. Some of the people who jumped off our Gorodok to Krasno truck must have become partisans by now.

"This must be Molodeczno," I mutter while drawing a map in my head. "Then I must go south to Gorodok."

All day I move parallel to the road on paths through the fields and forest until my feet ache. I am getting stomach pains from hunger as the sun becomes a faint red glow in a black cloud sky. I must find the cover of a barn or someplace out of the threatening rain.

I am especially tempted by the sight of thick brown smoke swirling out of a white stucco chimney and the warm glowing yellow lights of what looks like a friendly cottage. I hesitate trying to find the courage to enter the yard and knock on the door. I have used every ounce of energy covering what I think must be thirty kilometers. It must be another ten kilometers to Gorodok. I can't go a step further until I have food and rest. As I approach the cottage, I put my hand on the gate and hear a deep voiced dog make a guttural growl and bark a warning. Before he can attack, a tall blond fortyish peasant is at the door shouting in Polish. I must make him think I'm Polish - he might not accept a Jew.

"What is it, brother?"

"Long live Poland," I say in an energetic voice using my best Polish. "I'm seeking a bite to eat and refuge for the night."

"Come in," says the man as he leaves the front door for the yard. "I'll chain the dog. We have just eaten, but we have leftovers. I'll call my neighbor. Nicholas will want to meet you. He likes anybody who will drink with him. We don't get much company, so we have to share our guest. I make the best vodka in the village. You are welcome. My name is Moreno," he says as he covers my hand with both of his.

"I am Ivan," I say as I become comfortable with Moreno's generous smile that's pushing out wide wrinkles in his sun burnt, boney face.

Nicolas arrives soon after Moreno's deep voiced shout across the fence. Nicolas is stocky with short legs and a long torso. His hair and full mustache are black with streaks of grey. His eyes twinkle with curiosity, and his teeth are yellowed from smoking the pipe that passes from mouth to hand as he greats me. His hand shake like Moreno's is strong and calloused.

With the wife and children in the two bedrooms, the three of us share ham, eggs, cheese, bread and vodka at the kitchen table with me doing most of the eating and the peasants nibbling and drinking. I am basking in the pleasure of being welcome in a house again and leisurely eating solid fresh food while sitting at a table in flickering firelight. Pleasures once taken for granted are making me ecstatic with tears that I conceal with blots on my sleeve.

"Have you heard the latest from the Russian front," says Nicholas pointing his pipe at me.

"No," I say as I awake to the conversation.

"The Germans are attacking Leningrad and are pushing toward Stalingrad. They have also launched an attack on the Russian oil fields in Azerbaijan."

"Then the war will soon turn in our favor," I say as I hold my vodka up for a toast. "It's Napoleon all over again. Hitler has bitten off more than he can chew. He has too many objectives in Russia. With the Americans in the war and bombing his cities, Hitler will soon be busy on the western front. If nothing else the Russian winter will defeat the Germans. A salute to Stalin's troops and the brave Partisans."

"Salute," echo the peasants.

"Russian, Polish, and even some Jewish partisans are in the forest," says Moreno wiping the vodka off his chin. "It's believed that Moscow is dropping in supplies by air, and they are using Russian rifles. What do you think?"

"Yes," I say. "For the most part, the Partisans are commanded by Russian officers sent behind the lines with orders to organize a resistance."

"Last week, Partisans burned out one of our neighbors." says Moreno. "Other Nazi sympathizers are getting worried the same will happen to them."

"The Germans will have a harder time collecting their taxes and maintaining control as the Partisans grow stronger," I say. "And people will begin betting on the Russians and a German free Poland."

"I'll drink to that," says Nicholas. "Salute to getting the Nazi bastards out of here."

"And may Stalin's troops leave soon after," salutes Moreno.

Moreno shows me to the barn and gives me a blanket. I make a bed in the hay loft and lay down with my first full stomach in months. As I fall asleep my nose twitches with the stink of cows and horses, but it's better than the work camp's smell of dirty bodies and rotting clothes. In the morning I help Moreno with the milking and feeding - thank him and leave. I think it best to stay on the move. Stumpy has made me skittish and suspicious of peasants, even if they are generous.

From Moreno I get a blanket, soap, a razor and a knife. I take my treasures to the river, and shave, bathe, and feel energized and new again.

October 5, 1942

For four months I am on the run - never staying in the same place twice. All the while I keep an eye out for the Partisans. Somewhere I get some bad food and develop a terrible case of diarrhea. I have to stop eating and become too weak to move about. Now I am back at Moreno's and hiding in his barn. He is allowing me to stay here until I recuperate. I have promised to repay him with my labor.

November 6, 1942

I have been helping with the chores - mostly thrashing wheat and shucking corn by hand.

"Are you Jewish?" Asks Moreno as we shuck corn.

A chill runs through me. I look into Moreno's eyes and know it's OK. I find my voice and say, "Yes, my name is Yehuda. I told you Ivan, because I didn't know how you felt about Jews. I thought you would be more likely to take an Ivan in."

"You were smart to rename yourself," says Moreno. "Maybe I should have changed my name. Most of my neighbors are Russian and speak nothing but Russian. They go to the Russian Orthodox Church and I'm a Roman Catholic. I can never be one of them, because I am Polish and the wrong kind of Catholic. On that first night when you answered me in good Polish, I knew I had a friend. I had to sit down with you and have a drink and speak some Polish.

"We have the same thing - Jews that don't get along. There are Orthodox, Conservative, Reformed, Zionist, East and West European Jews, Middle Eastern Jews and Jews that don't want to be Jews. In our community there were two factions competing with each other for members - Zionist and Conservatives. In preparation to immigrate to a Kibbutz, Zionist started recruiting young people at an early age to live on a local collective farm. The Zionists are determined to have a Jewish state in Palestine, and the Conservatives think it would displace too many people and bring conflict with the Arabs. The arguments are heated and there is no compromise between the two groups.

Moreno adds, "When a Catholic can't get along with a Catholic, and a Jew can't get along with a Jew - how can you expect anyone to get along?"

"Somehow we will," I say as I offer my hand. "I hope we can reach across our differences and be friends."

"We are friends, Yehuda," he laughs and takes my hand. "Now that I know your name. How did you come to choose the name Ivan?"

"Five months ago - I was caught, beaten and sold for fifty marks by a bounty hunter named Ivan. His name will always be in my head. I underestimated him, because he had bad grammar, bad teeth, and seemed stupid. My university education didn't make me smart in the way that he was. He beat me at our game of cat and mouse. I thought I was smart, but I didn't do anything smart. At first it was like losing to an idiot at a game of checkers. Not only was there the humiliation of losing, but my freedom and my life were in jeopardy. My education is in math and languages. He is an expert in primitive survival, trapping, and hunting. He was better prepared for our game of survival. He was a persistent unrelenting bastard with a single focus - collecting the bounty offered for my head. It became more than the money. He had an obsession to win."

"Like Ivan, you will need to be persistent, stubborn and a mean bastard, if you are going to stay alive. The woman next door thinks you're a Jew. She's already thinking of how to spend the bounty money."

"Thanks for the warning, my friend. It's to be expected. I have been here almost a month. When there is a bounty on your head, it is not wise to be in a place very long. Thanks to you, I'm strong again; I'll leave before the sun breaks."

Night falls and I eat Moreno's soup and go to bed early. I wake in the middle of the night to the sound of voices and a light coming through the cracks in the barn. I'm sure the Nazi's are coming for me. I crawl underneath the hay and lie very still as I hear them enter and then I hear a curse in Yiddish and recognize the voice.

"My God I've found you," I say rising up out of the hay like a ghost and looking down into the barn." Is it you Abram?"

"Yes," says the husky, brown bearded Abram as he holds up the lantern to see into the loft. "And who are you?"

"Yehuda!" I exclaim in glee as I run down the ladder. "We jumped off the truck together. Remember?"

"Yes, I remember. And how are you my friend?"

"Free at last," I say laughing and happy to see someone from Gorodok. "I was recaptured and ended up in Krasno. Anyway, my life is absurd."

"And so will be your death," says a tall thin Russian as he steps into the light."

"Why are you here?" I ask, regaining some of my depression.

"We've come for horses and provisions," says Abrams.

"Please, not here, go next door to the farm south of here. The woman would like to be a collaborator - maybe you could change her mind. This man is my friend and has saved my life."

"Ok, we'll go and let you sleep."

"No. How can I sleep?" I plead. "I've found you at last. Take me with you. Please, you must."

"Impossible," says Abram sternly shaking his arm to free himself of my desperate grip. "We are pressed for time. You would only slow us down, and you have no weapon. Come," says Abram as he pulls me aside and whispers in Yiddish. "The Russians would shoot me if they knew I told you. Go to the village of Scryndow, twenty kilometers south of here. Maybe they will take you. Goodbye and good luck, my friend. We will try the neighbor next door."

"Thank-you," I say in disappointment.

8 November 1942

Before daylight, I leave to look for the Partisans. At least I now know where to go. And thank God it is not difficult to go in that direction, because no troops are stationed in that region. There is little farming and the area is undeveloped and uninhabited. The Germans don't value the place and have never been able to control it. It's low and swampy, has no railway and only the law of the gun. It's only dangerous, if I fall into the hands of robbers or anti-Semitic guerrillas.

As I wander the countryside searching for the Partisans, I pretend to be a peasant looking for my horse. In a way the Partisans are my horse - my vehicle for survival. I surely won't make it on my own. A peasant believes my horse story and takes me in for the night.

It's the middle of the night when I wake to the sound of horses and Russian voices.

"Is there a stranger here?" One of them asks the peasant. In a flash they are in the barn and have me by the collar with the cold steel muzzle of a rifle on my neck.

"Who are you?" asks the large burley black bearded commander.

"I just escaped from the work camp at Krasno. I'm a Jew and would like to join the Partisans."

"No!" he screams, knocking me to ground with a fist to my face. He then leans over and grabs me up by front of my bloody shirt and continues his rant. "You gave the Germans all your gold, and now you come to us. For what do we need you? Jews are cowards. You lie down and let the pigs walk on you - shit all over you. Then you do nothing, but give them all you got. Who in the hell needs you? Get out of here. Go find the guts to fight or die - you bastard," he says shoving me toward the door and kicking my ass.

I flee into the dark with my blanket, but not my shoes. I don't notice the sticks or mud as I fly over them. I hear a shot and dodge behind a tree and keep running. I don't know if the bullet was meant to scare or kill. I heard them laughing as I left - maybe I am just the brunt of a Russian joke. No matter - it all has the same effect. My heart is pounding out of my chest, and I am running and dodging like a rabbit. Finally I feel safe enough to stop and lay down under a tree exhausted. I rub my cold wet feet until they are warm again, wrap up in my blanket, but can't sleep. It is turning colder and the first snow is beginning to fall. I bundle up into a ball and pull the blanket tight about me, but I am still cold. I get up and decide to risk returning to the barn rather than freeze to death. The nights are getting dangerously cold. I find the barn has lost a couple of goats and the Russians have gone, and my shoes are where I left them.

9 November 1942

I resume my search for the partisans. I keep my blanket wrapped around me as I walk through the fresh fallen snow. I walk until midday and beg a cup of soup from a peasant family. I continue my journey into the late afternoon.

I feel intensely alive with an unexplained joy as I watch a red sun, dressed in a black hat of clouds, sink into the snowy evergreen forest. I am thinking how lucky I am to be alive and free, and it doesn't bother me that I haven't found a place to spend the night. I am startled by the approaching snort of a horse, and I turn to discover a sleigh coming up behind me. As they approach, I see a peasant is driving and three men are in the back. I am sure the peasant's passengers are Jewish and look to be in their twenties. I can see the one on the left is holding a shiny pistol. We make eye contact, and I recognize them from Krasno but don't know their names.

"Take me brothers," I shout in Yiddish as I run along beside the sleigh. "I'm trying to get to the Partisan town."

"No, Get out of the way," the one with the gun says.

The man in the middle looks sympathetic, but doesn't say anything.

"Please, I must get to the Partisans," I beg again.

"Get back," says the peasant driver as he cracks the whip and the sleigh pulls away."

I am left alone in the cold dark night. There is only the sound of wind and no light in sight, but there is hope in the tracks the sleigh has left in the snow. Now I have a road to follow and a direction to go in. I refuse to be depressed by the rejection of the three selfish men. An hour of following the sleigh tracks brings me in sight of village lights. I see it's a natural fortress with a moat of swamps and lakes and has a river running through the middle of town. The only road is blocked by a pile of trees and debris that runs for about twenty meters. It is dead center in the wild forest of Naliboki which has many tall and broad oaks, fir, birch and thick underbrush. No tanks, cars, or even motorcycles could pass through this area. Only a single file of soldiers or guerrillas could get in and out. I remember studying the geography of the Naliboki, and thinking, except for hunting, it's useless land. There is plenty of valuable timber, but very difficult to get to market. Now I see that it is perfect for guerrillas. They can live on small islands in the swamps and make night raids against the Nazis. When they are tired, they have a safe place to come back to.

It doesn't take long for me to find the Partisan headquarters in a large house in the center of town. After a short wait, I am ushered into a big room lit by a huge fireplace and a single oil lamp. My eyes are immediately drawn to a plump middle-aged Colonel in a Russian uniform. He is sitting in a comfortable chair by the fire. He is smoking and admiring his cigar and looking more like a professor than a soldier. I judge him to be Jewish in spite of the fact he is called Platonov. He is surrounded by six armed guerrillas sitting and standing around the room and scrutinizing the three Jews that refused me a ride. I would like to speak up and say how ungenerous they were, but I don't. One of the candidates is holding up a shiny new Browning for the Colonel to see. A guerilla grabs the pistol and hands it to the Colonel.

"How did you get this new Browning," the Colonel asks as he turns the gun over in his hands.

"Hanah, a friend of ours, took it from a German officer."

"Are you telling me the truth?" The Colonel asks as he looks into their eyes.

"Yes, sir," says the spokesman as he fidgets nervously and cracks his knuckles behind his back."

"Do you have bullets?" ask the Colonel with increased interest.

"Yes, sir," he says holding up a belt of bullets he has just unbuckled from his waist. "There are fifty of them."

The Colonel is impressed as he takes the belt and fingers the bullets. "Where is Hanah?" He asked putting the belt on the table beside him. "She is the one we need."

"They were chasing us, and we lost her," one of them replied. "Maybe the S.S. caught her."

The Colonel whispers something to his secretary and they agree. "We will accept you. You will belong to the Kuznetzov detachment. You will each get a rifle, but you will leave the Browning and the bullet belt here."

"Thank you sir," the spokesman says gleefully like a boy who has just seen his birthday cake.

"We will do our best," another one says.

"If you don't, you won't be with us long," says the Colonel. "By giving you a rifle we are giving you the chance to be brave and cunning. We have more volunteers than rifles, so you must be a good soldier, or your weapon will be given to someone else. We are only giving each of you an opportunity to prove yourself."

"Thank you, sir."

"And when you find Hanah, bring her to me."

I think I know the Hanah they are talking of. I saw her at Krasno, so it could be her. She was a medical student forced out of school by the Nazis. I remember her as beautiful and happy-go-lucky from the nearby town of Smorgon. Hanah would come to visit her relatives in Gorodok and drive men mad with her beauty. She would push them away and leave them pitiful and pining. I had once watched her look at herself in a full length mirror for half an hour. She fretted with her hopelessly tangled hair. She sucked in her checks and squinted in an attempt to be sexy in the way young girls flirt. She was completely enjoying her changing image. As she walked away she said, "I want a job looking in the mirror."

I wanted to be her mirror and tell her how beautiful she was. I envied these three men, because they had some kind of relationship with her. But why didn't she come with them?

"You sir," says the secretary in a raised voice. "You are next. Come forward and tell us who you are."

"Yehuda Adelman," I respond as I break away from my dream of Hanah and step into the hot spot with a military bearing.

"Tell us something of yourself," commands the Colonel. "What kind of work do you do?"

"I served in the Polish Army, and have training in the infantry where I operated a machine gun. In civilian life, I was the principal of the elementary school in Bakshty. I am fluent in five languages."

"Where is your weapon?" The Colonel asks.

'I have no weapon, but I have three hundred bullets. I buried them near Gorodok. I will try to recover them."

The Colonel thought for a minute, looked to his assistant for some silent confirmation of his thoughts, and said, "First, bring the bullets, and then we will see."

Rejected, I turn and step away, with my focus falling to the floor. As I reach the exit door I feel a hand on my shoulder, and I turn to face the assistant whose eyes are large, intense and magnified in gold wire rimmed glasses. I can smell the breath of the secretary's last meal and know it was finished off with coffee. Where did he get coffee? I am reminded of the empty spot in my stomach.

"You gave everything to the Germans and now you are coming to us empty handed?"

I refuse to listen to the rest of the speech that I've heard before. I wait for the hand to lift from my shoulder. I nod good-by and walk out in to the cold.

Chapter 8

Grishka's Ten Rifles

June 3, 1942, on the outskirts of Gorodok, the day Grishka jumped from the truck with us.

Lying in the shadows of sunset, Grishka watches from the pines in back of Dimitri's cottage and waits for the safety of darkness. He must see Dimitri without being discovered by a neighbor. A publicized visit could be deadly. He hasn't eaten or even talked to anyone since this morning's escape. Demetri could give him food, a place to hide and maybe a weapon. Again he wipes his brow with the back of his hand and pushes the dirty mangle of black hair out of his broad dark face. He's become thin to the point of showing bones. He moves only on the energy of anger and the passion for revenge. His body wants to fall asleep here on the ground. He feels vulnerable and is terrified by his fatigue, since he no longer has the strength to fight or get away. He blinks and shakes his head to stay awake. If only he could eat, he might find the energy to save himself.

His fingers find the gun-shot gash of dried blood on his scalp and push hard on either side of the wound to force the fluid out. The pain splinters across his skull as the discharge

74

drips down on the back of his ear. Satisfied the wound has drained; he lets his head fall into the softness of the rotting leaves and again finds himself this morning's madness.

His eyes close and fill with tears as he sees his two small boys being thrown down the synagogue well, and his mother being bludgeoned by the butt of a rifle. All the tragedy, loss, trauma, and hardship of his sparse twenty-eight years as a peddler and a peddler's son cannot add up to the trauma that he suffered in today's selection. The pain of a life time was concentrated into a few minutes.

He has hope that his wife is alive, since he saw her go into the truck with the young women, and that truck did not turn off into the woods. "She is too beautiful to die," he mourns, muttering, "Damn, if she weren't so pretty, it would be easier. Surely some Nazi bully or fat Ukrainian guard is going to demand sex. What should she do? Resist or try to save her life by giving into sexual favors? The bastards! I hate them. I won't think about it."

He watches the cottage for an hour and sees no one come or go. Finally it's dark enough, so he moves through the shadows avoiding the light of the half-moon as he approaches the window on the backside of the cottage. He wipes the dust off the glass and looks in. Looking distorted through the old window glass, he sees white bearded, wrinkled Dimitri, alone, eating a plate of stew and drinking his Vodka.

"God, I'm hungry," Grishka mumbles as he visualizes the food in his mouth and remembers his hunger and the last time he ate at this table. With two steps he moves to the back door and gives three raps. Already he tastes the stew on the table. The noise arouses the German shepherds sleeping in the front yard, and they are soon at the back snarling and showing their teeth.

"Hush, hush, Toby, Tanya," commands Grishka. The dogs stop barking and let down their ears. They sniff him, wag their tails, and push their heads in position for a pet. Grishka hugs both of them with his hands pulling them into his thighs as the back door creaks open a crack and a squinting Dimitri says, "Who is it?"

The tall figure moves toward the door and whispers, "It's Grishka, my dear Dimitri."

Dimitri nervously opens the door and says, "Come, quickly. No one must see you."

Grishka slips through the door and sits down at the table. Spreading two long fingers he steals a potato out of the stew pot and throws it into his mouth. He grabs the bottle of home-made vodka, chokes down a mouth full and pours some on his wound above his ear. The Vodka stings his scalp, eases the tension in his neck, and sends the room spinning around him.

The spider web of wrinkles in the old man's face blends into a frown, as he lights a short fat candle over the fire place and turns out the oil lamp on the table leaving Grishka in the dark.

"Finish up the stew," Dimitri offers as he hands him a clean fork and sits down and watches him eat in silence. Grishka gobbles up the left-overs in three bites, pushes back from the table still hungry, and looks to Dimitri for something else.

Dimitri ignores his silent dog-eyed request and looks into the empty fireplace as he speaks, "Always I look for the safe way. I go around mountains. I don't try to climb over them. I don't take chances. I like to sleep at night. Do you understand me? At my age I don't need your kind of aggravation. I'm an old tree that bends with the wind and by so doing have survived." He pauses, clears his throat, spits in the fireplace and turns to Grishka and continues, "Your mother and the boys are dead. I hear your wife is still alive in Krasno, but she will die. You too will die. All Jews will be killed. Your fate is sealed. May God help you. I can do nothing for you. I can't keep you in my house. You put my life at risk by coming here. Yesterday, my neighbor was shot for keeping a Jew. Do you have any regard for me? I don't think so, or you would not come here. Go off and die you son-of-a-bitch, by yourself, or join your wife, but don't take me with you. Accept it. You are a dead man."

The anger in Grishka's eyes is quenched by tears of rejection. Desperate and pleading he says, "Dimitri, my friend, my family has loved you for years. We have often exchanged gifts and sat down together and shared the best we had. Look, I have a ring, the gold ring of my father's. It's worth at least 200 Marks. I will trade it to you for your hand gun. And I will give it back to you as soon as I find another... I know you have a gun... Please give it to me. My life depends on it."

Dimitri looks at him with a contempt that builds into rage as he leans into his Grishka's face and spits on the floor, "And my life depends on you leaving here now. If they found my gun on you they would shoot me with it. Go. Get out of my house! I don't want to see you again, ever. Do you understand? If you come back here, I will shoot you and feed you to my dogs."

Without a word, Grishka with tears in his eyes gets up and doesn't look back. In three quick steps he is out the back door and gone. He is angry, still hungry, and the vodka has given him courage to disregard his fear of the neighbors who might turn him in for bounty money. As he passes through the back-yard he impulsively grabs a roosting chicken out of Demetri's coup and carries it squawking by the legs as he leaves the yard. He has now left absolutely everything of the old life behind and the humiliation of being a chicken thief is sinking in. He is feeling rejection, the loss of his family, and realizing he's a fugitive with no friends.

As he walks he thinks of where to spend the night and cook the chicken. A few meters down the road he remembers and finds the small hut in a flax field next to a stream. The peasants have piped water in from the stream and use the hut for a bath house. As he enters the hut he lets the chicken loose, and she flies up into the rafters to roost. He then undresses and turns on the valve and takes a cold bath. Chilled and refreshed he shakes himself off and gets back into his clothes. Tomorrow he promises to wash his clothes. His hunger has subsided and exhaustion has overtaken him. He decides to go to sleep and let the chicken live until dawn. For safety and to get out of the way of the next bather, he climbs into the attic and sits down with a sigh of loneliness and despair. As his unfocused eyes stare into the darkness, he's startled by the outline of three figures squatting across from him that are close enough to touch.

With his heart racing and braced for attack, he demands, "Who is it?"

A chorus of laughter fills the attic. Confused, Grishka doesn't know if it's friend or foe. In a panic he drops down into the hut below, knocking the chicken off its roost and sending it squawking and fluttering through the air.

"Wait! Grishka." A voice stops him at the door. "It's me, Matus. Ele and Hirsh are here too. We didn't know it was you until we heard your voice."

He climbs back up in the attic and greets his friends by hugging each of them.

"We jumped from the truck just behind you," says Hirsh. "You run too fast. We couldn't keep up and didn't know where you went. Where did you go?"

"I don't know," laughs Grishka. I was just running and when I stopped, I didn't know where I was."

"Look, says the stocky, bright-eyed Matus, holding up his weapon with a strong arm. "I got this ax from a peasant, Feel the edge - you can shave with it."

"That's good," says Grishka feeling the edge with his thumb, but we need guns. With this ax, we will get a gun."

"And it will kill our first chicken," says Hirsh, the tall, husky blacksmith. "What do you say we cook your chicken? None of us has eaten today."

They build a fire, roast the bird, and talk over their next move as they eat.

"Our village is not the only one that's been purged of its Jewish population," says Ele as he pushes his thick blond hair out of his blue eyes. "We know of Smorgon, Rokov, Ivanictz, and Molodeczno. If we don't find guns and start fighting, we too will die. The Nazis won't stop until every Jew is dead. The Chinese guerillas drove the Japanese out of their country. Russian guerillas did their part in defeating Napoleon. And we can become guerillas and do our part in defeating the Germans. At least we will die fighting and not like sheep in the slaughter house."

"What do you say to the fact that they are still holding our wives and children in Krasno?" asks Hirsh. "If they find out who we are, they will take it out on our families."

"We'll have to take that chance," answers Matus. "Given enough time they will kill us all. They have my wife and Grishka's wife. All of us have someone in Krasno. We can only hope to be strong enough to save them before the killing squads come."

"I know where a gun is," says Grishka. "Three kilometers from here, the bastard Nikita has one. His son has become a policeman doing the Nazi's work. Nikita does what he can to help his son. He caught my ten year old cousin, Benjamin, tied him up and took him to the police. He was awarded three pounds of salt for his good deed. Tomorrow night we will find Nikita."

They have trouble falling asleep. The events of the past few days disturb them so much that only exhaustion overcomes their fears and heartbreak. They dream about their parents and their once intact families, and how they lived before the war and how that quiet, meager existence, shattered and gone, now seems a perfect life. At least it was much more perfect than now.

Grishka is having a fitful dream about his children and how he sometimes carried his small boys in his peddler's wagon. He sees them playing among the soap, herring, and hardware that he trades for produce, flower, and rags. In his nightmare they are screaming and dying among blood soaked rags in his wagon. He sees them rising up out of the rags bloody, broken and pleading to be brought back to life.

Tired and hungry, the four friends wake to the reality of a bad situation. They need food, shelter and guns. Enemies and spies are everywhere.

"To get food we must deal with the peasants who are also feeding the Germans and themselves," says Grishka. "Like Demetri they won't risk giving us anything, nor do they have much to spare. They will say, 'Get out Jew or we will send the dogs after you."

"We must intimidate the peasants and force them into our camp," says Ele "They must come to fear us more than they fear Germans. We will teach the peasants a lesson, so they will not betray our hiding places no matter what bounty the Nazi's place on our heads."

That night while the others are sleeping, Grishka shakes Matus and says, "Get up. Come with me and bring your ax.

Let's find the murderer Nikita - now in the middle of the night. We'll do it alone - just the two of us."

Their shoes sink in the soft, wet plowed earth as they walk through long rows of lush green fields about to explode with its fruits. Everything looks vibrant and greener in the dark. Matus grips the ax handle with strong hands, and is ready to use it. Most houses are dark, and dogs are barking, and a sinking moon is showing half its face. Grishka knows exactly where Nikita lives, but they pass his unlit house and make a visit to Paul, Nikita's neighbor.

"Who is it?" asks Paul.

"It's me, Matus and Grishka." answers Matus. "We're hungry. Do you have food for us?"

"Sure, come in my friends," says Paul as he opens the door. "But talk softly; the wife and kids are sleeping. Good to see you. I miss the peddler's wagon and your conversation. There has been no one to replace you. I'm just doing without things that I need."

"So are we," says Matus. "We've missed eating today."

"I'll soon fix that," says Paul as he puts a pan on the stove and drops in some lard. "How about eggs? Do you eat eggs?"

"Of course," laughs Grishka. "If it can be eaten, we eat it. You know there isn't much food in the woods. If we were only wood beetles, we would be in paradise."

"There are truffles, mushrooms, berries and nuts in season and some roots, if you know then," says Paul. "There is deer and wild boar, but you'll work hard for them, and you need a gun and some bullets. Did you know you can eat stinging nettles? You don't believe me, but it's true. If you cook them, they no longer sting and you can eat them like spinach. Try them; they are all over the place now."

"Eggs sound much better," says a skeptical Grishka.

"You are right, you need me. That's why I'm here. What brings you out so late?"

"Your neighbor Nikita," says Grishka. "You know, he murdered my small cousin Benjamin."

"So you are seeking revenge," muses Paul. "I don't blame you. Nikita didn't actually kill him, but he might as well have. He sold him for a little salt. Nikita caught Benjamin sleeping in his barn. The boy was hungry, so he gave him some bread and milk. As he was eating, Nikita handcuff him. He then put him in the wagon and brought him to the police in Gorodok. There he was tortured and later killed. Nikita is now very careful. You can enter his house, but you will not find him. He hides in the barn in the straw. When he goes out, he carries a Russian rifle and walks his property at night."

Paul serves them three fried eggs each. It becomes quiet except for the chewing and the scraping of forks on plates. It goes down quickly with milk, and torn chunks of fresh bread mopping up runs of egg yolk.

"Thank-you," says Matus as he pushes back from the table and pats his stomach. "You've been a good friend and saved our lives twice tonight with your eggs and your warning."

"I trust you to keep our visit a secret," says Grishka as he reaches for Paul's hand. "If we are successful in finding Nikita, you may say you think he was killed by Jews seeking revenge for Benjamin's murder. Other Nazi collaborators can expect similar treatment. We can no longer stand by and watch our families be murdered without there being retribution."

"Good luck in your mission," Paul says as he shows them the back door. "My only regret in you getting rid of Nikita is that his son might move into his place, but I don't think he has the courage to live out here alone. Let me warn you, Nikita is ready and waiting for you. He sees spooks all the time. He watches the comings and goings at my house and is aroused by any disturbance in the neighborhood. The dogs let us all know when someone is moving about. You were smart coming here; you have given the dogs a chance to quiet down. If you are quiet, you can go next door without getting them started again. I don't know if you can surprise him. Last night I heard his gun go off. I don't know what he shoots at - probably anything that moves. Be careful."

Paul blows out his lamp before he opens the door and whispers good luck as he grips their hands. Matus and Grishka stand in the shadows of the trees and wait for their eyes to adjust to the darkness.

Their muscles twitch with excitement and fear as they slip through the shadows, slide around trees and are careful not to be caught by the light of the moon. They see no sign of Nikita in the house or walking about and assume that he must have retired to his barn. They station themselves on each side of the barn door and wait for Nikita to make his rounds.

It is not long before the door creaks open and Nikita carefully steps out. Matus is ready, and the ax swings down taking off an ear before it stops in the nape of his neck. There is a scream of pain and surprise and the spewing of blood. Grishka jumps to grab the rifle and the magazine of bullets, and they never touch the ground. Two more blows of the ax and Nikita's moaning stops.

"Now we have a rifle, and we will soon have more," says Grishka. "Tomorrow, they will be talking in the villages about what happened to Nikita, and they will know why. Word of the ax murder will buzz through the countryside, and this will warn them not to go to the Nazi police, to keep their mouths shut, and not to report guerilla activities, or they die a horrible brutal death. We want them to remember Nikita, so they will never again trade a Jew for salt."

"And now we will get the salt and whatever else we can find," says Matus. "This army has a belly. I'll take the mare out of the barn, and we will load her with what we can find."

They clean out the kitchen cabinets and the root cellar and are able to find food for a month along with cooking pots, utensils, another ax, a pick, and a shovel. Matus saddles and bridles the horse and they proceed to load her down with the bulk of the weight being flour and potatoes.

"We should take the milk-cow too," says Matus.

"Why," says Grishka. "Don't we have enough? I'm anxious to get away from this place. We got a bloody mess here, and I don't want daylight to catch us going home. A cow can be noisy and draw attention."

"Don't worry about noise," says Matus. "I can keep the cow quiet. I have a way with cows. This cow will give us milk now and meat for the winter, and most important it will keep you from eating my horse. I can tell you were thinking of a meal when you saw her. This horse will be good for making quick hits on the enemy and for gathering intelligence. I can't risk somebody getting hungry and eating my horse. My Sarah is as important as the gun we just got. Besides, the cow can carry more flour and potatoes."

"So it's Sarah already," smiles Grishka.

"Don't be jealous - you can have the cow," offers Matus.

"Then I will call her Jessica," says Grishka rolling his eyes. "I will save her for Fogel. He likes cows."

"So where is Fogel?"

"Lost, I am sure," says Grishka in a sigh of exasperation. "He jumped off the truck. He will show up, sooner or later."

"Later, I hope. He can turn a situation upside down in a second."

They spend the next few days in the forest making a camp and storing provisions. It's decided that all guerilla operations will happen at night, and the day will be spent sleeping and staying in the forest. With their new digging tools, they begin construction of an underground bunker by digging out the side of a hill. They are taking turns standing guard with the gun while the other three excavate their new home. Matus is swinging the pick, and Hirsh and Grishka are shoveling dirt.

Ele is squatting on top of the hill, holding the rifle and searching the forest for any sign of movement.

"With all the wheat we have stored, I must build an oven for baking bread," says Hirsh who at eleven was working with his father as a blacksmith. From that trade he learned to tinker and fix anything made of metal including guns.

"And who can make bread?" asks Matus between swings of the pick.

"Hirsh makes excellent bread," says Grishka.

"You people never stop with your stomachs," says Matus. "The minute you're full of potatoes, you are thinking of bread - next you'll want to eat my Sarah."

"Quit being paranoid about your horse," says Grishka. "When we eat the cow, start worrying about the horse."

"I know you will never eat your Jessica," says Matus. "Her lips are too sweet."

"If I don't rescue my wife soon," says Grishka. "Jessica will be tempting. She is the only female we have."

"That reminds me," puzzles Hirsh. "When I milked the cow this morning she hardly had any milk. Did either of you milk her?"

"No," says Grishka. "That's your job. No one has done it for you."

"She's not drying up, I got plenty of milk yesterday," says Hirsh. "Someone milked her when she was down next to the stream, where we left her last night."

"You're crazy," says a skeptical Matus. "Who? Who could have done it?"

"I don't know," says Hirsh. "That's what worries me. Somebody, and I don't know who, milked her."

No one has an answer for the missing milk. They stop for lunch and eat last night's potatoes and drink the milk they've kept cool in the stream. They are wondering if their camp has been discovered, and if they should find a new spot.

After lunch Matus takes the gun and becomes the lookout. He's hardly settled into his spot when he's on his feet motioning for them to be quiet. He runs down the hill to where they are and whispers, "I saw somebody out there. He didn't have a uniform, so it's probably a peasant. I don't think he saw us, but he might have. We've got to kill him or find a new place. We'll spread out and see if we can find him."

"I'll circle around him and try to get behind him," says Grishka, as he takes off running.

With Matus in the middle and the other three spread out, they walk in the direction of the sighting. Carefully picking their way through the underbrush, they hear a noise coming toward them and freeze in their tracks and wait. Suddenly Grishka appears with a tall, thin, curly brown haired teenage boy walking behind him.

"It's Jeremy Springer," says Grishka. "Sabitai and Michael Springer are out there somewhere. Michael is the one that milked the cow."

"I found the cow last night," says Jeremy. "We thought it belonged to a peasant. We didn't know you were here."

"I'll light a fire and cook more potatoes," says Hirsh. "We have guests for dinner. Maybe somebody could steal a chicken."

"No need," says Jeremy. "We have a goose. I'll whistle and my brothers will bring it."

In a few minutes they are exchanging hugs and greetings with Sabitai and Michael and planning the next guerrilla action. After a festive meal of cooked noodles, goose and potatoes, Grishka takes the rifle and leads his growing platoon through the woods to Leo's house. They are fortunate in that the peasants are scattered out among farms and don't live in villages. They only have to confront Leo who is isolated from his closest neighbor by three hundred meters.

Grishka and Matus are at the front door with an ax and the rifle. The other five have surrounded the house and are armed with knives, hatchets and clubs. When everyone is in place, Matus and Grishka kick open the front door and step in. They find a startled wide-eyed Leo sitting at the table with his vodka.

"Give me the four rifles and ammunition," demands Grishka in a deep commanding voice.

"Please, don't kill me," begs Leo with his hands above his head. "I have no rifles."

"You have them," corrects Grishka as he pushes the barrel tip under Leo's chin. "Six months ago, I was here peddling. You told me about the wolf you shot and the rifles you have. You were quite proud of them."

The back door opens and Jeremy and Sabitai step in with their hatchets. Leo hears a tapping on the window and sees two more faces behind the glass and looks for mercy in Grishka's eyes.

"Don't worry, the gun is just a joke," comforts Grishka. "We won't waste a bullet. Bullets are precious. Matus will chop on you with an ax - first a hand, then a foot and so on until we know where the rifles are. You choose. What do you want to lose first - your balls or your left hand? We'll stop cutting whenever you want to tell us where the guns are. First question - answer yes or no. Are your balls worth four rifles?"

"I only have three," pleads Leo. "Honest to God. I swear by the Virgin Mary, there are only three rifles. Come I'll show you."

Grishka and Matus follow a nervous Leo up the ladder to the loft, where he reaches into the straw on the underside of the roof. One by one he pulls out three shiny rifles and five wooden boxes: each with a hundred rounds of ammunition.

"They are the best of the Polish rifles," admires Leo as he watches the excitement in Grishka's eyes. "They were once used to kill Germans. They were taken out of the hands of our dead soldiers."

"Very good, we will put them to good use," says Grishka as he retreats from the loft while Matus, Sabitai and Michael inspect and load their new weapons. "You've made a wise decision. Now tell me, who else has these guns?"

"Andrei," says Leo with some satisfaction.

Grishka knows exactly where Andrei lives and has visited him many times as a peddler. He smiles into Leo's eyes and says, "Your home and your family will be spared, if you continue to cooperate with us. Tell your neighbors we are armed and will take revenge on anyone who collaborates with the Germans or endangers the life of a Jew. We know who our enemies are. Homes will be burned. Collaborators will be shot. We can no longer stand by and watch our families and friends be slaughtered."

They walk a short distance through the fields to Andrei's house. It's Matus' turn to be the bully. They kick in the door and are in the bedroom with a flaming torch before Andrei can get out of bed. The peasant opens his eyes to see four gunmen in the flickering smoky light.

"Andrei, get up!" demands Matus as he puts his rifle in the frightened man's face. "We come for your rifles - all fifteen of them. Give them to us immediately."

A stunned Andrei stutters, "Please brothers, I only have seven. Come, I'll show you. You can kill me if you find more."

Andrei still in his nightshirt pulls on his boots without tying the laces, and they follow him straight out the back door and ten meters from the house.

"Get the shovels out of that shed," instructs Grishka. We will dig here," he says, pointing to a large stone.

After a few minutes of digging, Jeremy and Hirsh uncover a long wooded box covered with yellowed canvas. They pull off the canvas and open the box and find seven shiny rifles soaked in oil.

"They are in perfect condition," says Hirsh, who repairs guns and anything mechanical.

"There are six hundred rounds of ammunition," says Jeremy holding up a box of shells.

They strap the extra guns and ammunition on Sarah and take another horse from Andrei to carry sacks of flour, potatoes and beets they have collected from the two peasants.

Sunrise greets them as they reach their base camp in the forest. Hirsh builds a fire, while Sabitai butchers the goat.

"Tonight we will feast and celebrate," says Hirsh.

"It will take more than a feast to get over the sadness that reaches down in my soul and grips my guts," says Sabitai, as he vigorously cuts and pulls the skin off the goat.

"We must find some joy in living, even if it is only drinking clean water and breathing fresh air," says Hirsh. "And that my friend is quite wonderful. Life is to be lived as well as remembered. Sometime in your life you will have to bury the dead and the guilt for being a survivor, and we will survive. After being trapped in the ghetto, never has this forest and the rawness of nature meant more to me. You know, this forest is our mother, and we have returned to it. Can you taste its fresh sweetness or is the bitterness of the ghetto still on your tongue?"

"Of course I'm bitter, says Sabitai. "After living on top of each other in our own shit and starving with only death to look forward to. We watched the minutes of our lives and our loved ones slowly slip away from us."

Hirsh smiles and says, "We jumped off the back of the death wagon, and suddenly there is life, freedom and fresh air, and now guns and revenge."

Chapter 9

The Search for Salvation

18 November 1942, Midnight in Gorodok, Poland, on the edge of town.

I am trying to locate a spot that I remember to be centered between two bushes and a tree - a treasure that can save my life. Without it, I am out in the cold, doomed to beg scraps, risk capture, and die from exposure or a bullet. For two nights I have dug in this area with no success, so this time I say a prayer and spit in the dirt for luck. If I fail, I swear that no matter how miserable, and sick I become, adrift in this no-man's-land between Nazis and Russian Partisans, I will never give up and go back to Krasno as my brother did.

I mumble as I dig, "It has got to be here. Where else can it be?"

I swing the pick into the ground with a thud, and pull back on the handle with a crunch as the ground is a bit frozen. In a month it will be impossible to dig as this field will be rock hard frozen. After loosening up the ground with the pick, I shovel the black dirt out with a spade. I do this in three different places and find nothing.

Three hours pass with no luck. I can longer hold back the heartbreak and frustration. I fall down helpless with my knees in mud and pound the cold wet earth with fist that send vibrations up my arms and shake the tears off my face. Then I become silent with exhaustion. I sit quietly trying to collect myself as I search for a peaceful spot in my mind. Anger begins to leak through the superficial, self-imposed calm, and suddenly burst into a raging river of emotion. I spring to my feet and shout at the moon and the passing clouds, "God, I will live in spite of you. They will not beat me. I am not ready to die!" Dejected and beaten, I look down into the empty holes - holes that have sucked up the last bit of energy and left me limp and defeated.

I beg in a pitiful whisper, "Please, someone, anyone - help me. My God, who will help me?"

There is no answer, no other sound. I am alone. Anyone who might care enough to help is just as helpless or dead. I am startled by voices and the bark of a guard dog and know it's not the divine coming to my rescue. My hysterical performance has been noticed. I grab the shovel with one hand and the pick in the other and dart off into the dark and predawn fog. I feel like a fool for screaming at the moon and digging until dawn. I run until my lungs hurt, and I'm forced to walk and catch my breath. I hear a dog bark and find the strength to run again. Finally I reach the safety of the forest and fall down in a thicket. Thank God no one followed me.

Exhausted and frustrated, I despair over my dismal situation. I can't risk going back to dig again. Without bullets or a gun, the partisans will never accept me. Without a weapon, I am useless, pitiful and alone. Where have the damn bullets gone? Did someone see me bury them? Again tears of frustration well up in my eyes, and then I remember that fate has smiled on me. By some miracle, I am alive when so many are dead, and I am free when most Jews in Europe are slaves. I then laugh at being free. Free to starve to death and to be shot on sight. Free to be homeless and roam the countryside alone. I have nothing - everything has been taken. How much longer can I survive? Eating is a matter of luck and charity. I'm tired of being a beggar. What can I do?

I decide to give up looking for the bullets and leave the area before I'm discovered. I have been visiting the same peasants too often. I can't become predictable. The bounty on my head could tempt one of my patrons. My old grammar school at Bakshty is only twenty kilometers away, so I'll go there. The students and parents liked me, especially the way I taught math.

The next morning I start walking toward Bakshty through the forest and fields. At noon I come to a small cottage and knock on the door.

A smiling, grey haired grandmother opens the door. There is love and a delight of recognition as she says, "I know you. You're Rebeka's son, Yehuda. I haven't seen you in ten years. I am Zosia. Don't you remember me?"

"Yes," I smile. "Your hair has gotten grey."

"We all get old – if we're lucky. Please come in. When your family lived here years ago, I was the maid. You were such a smart boy. You could add and multiply numbers in your head like I've never seen. I lived better in your mother's home than I have anywhere. Your mother was like a sister. She was kind and loving and gave me everything I needed. Your father's relatives in America sent him the money to buy his farm. Two years later they wouldn't let a Jew buy land. Lucky, he bought it when he did. I am glad you were able to grow up on a farm. You learn so much that they don't teach in books."

Two steps into the house, she turns to me like she is again the maid of my childhood, and starts scolding me. "Boy, you are filthy. Have you been sleeping in the mud? Take off your clothes, before you get my house dirty. I'll wash them while you take a bath. I am so happy you have come to see me. How did you know where I lived? You don't know, but you have come to the right place."

Already I know I'm in the right place. While I take a warm bath, and shave, Zosia is washing my clothes and drying them in the oven. Once I am out of the bath, she cuts my hair. Soon I am clean and dressed and feeling no longer like a beggar, but a new person about to begin a new life.

"Listen," she says with a smile of excitement. "A nice Jewish girl is hiding in the barn. She wants to join the guerillas. Can you help her?"

"Yes," I smile. "I know where they are, but they won't take her or me without a weapon. A soldier without a gun is useless. The Partisans need guns and bullets, and I need a gun to be one of them."

"I have no guns, only bread and soup. Would you like some?"

Impatient to go to the barn, I say "Yes, but when can we see the lady? Can I take her soup?"

"Not now. Tonight - when it's dark. I'm afraid someone might see you and start asking questions. I don't know how to lie - I never learned. People can see right through me. We must be careful, so they don't ask questions that I can't answer."

I spend the afternoon resting and waiting for night to come. When it's finally dark enough, Zosia takes a cup of soup and some bread and leads me to the barn. I open the barn door and hang the oil lantern on a hook, while Zosia calls, "Come out, my darling. I have soup for you."

In the dim corner of the barn, I see her crawling out from a big heap of wheat straw. Her clothes are faded and her black

94

tangled hair is covered with yellow straw. Using both hands, she shakes and combs the straw out of her hair. She turns toward me and walks into the light, and suddenly I see who she is.

"Hanah," I shout as I embrace her.

With tears in her eyes, she returns my affection with a warm tight hug and a kiss on the neck that sends a tingle down my spine. Never have I had such a welcome from such a beautiful bright woman. I am enchanted and dazed by her warm presence.

"How did you escape?" I ask in a cracked voice as an undefined emotion builds and bellows inside me and sends shivers through my body. "I heard something about you a few weeks ago."

"Excuse me," interrupts Zosia. "I must return to the house with the lantern. You will be safer in dark."

"Thank-you for bringing Julie to me," Hanah says as she hugs Zosia's neck. "You are so wonderful and good to me."

Zosia is quiet. She smiles with a twinkle in her eye and knows she made a good match. Just like a good cake - she has mixed the ingredients, and now it must bake.

Hanah turns back to me and takes my hand and leads me like a puppy across the barn to her hiding place. We sit in the straw and talk while she drinks her soup.

"I fled the Krasno work-camp about ten days ago," she says. "I heard about your escape from your brother David. I was working as a maid for the Germans. They lived in the cottages adjacent to the ghetto. There was only one row of cottages between me and the bridge that crossed the river in to the forest. I often looked down that street and to the forest on the other side of the river. Freedom was so close that I often thought of running away as I cleaned the cottages, but this day the urge to run became irresistible. As I'm sweeping Hans Reem's room, my broom hits something heavy under the bed. I bend down and see a stash of guns - three rifles and six pistols, and I know it is time to leave. I decide to take the two pistols Hans has promised. Hans is sympathetic, and said he would help me escape. Without thinking anymore about it, I quickly pack the pistols along with some food from his kitchen into a small canvas bag. I find a man's uniform in the cottage that fits me well enough and put it on and chop off my hair. I'm sure I don't look exactly like a soldier, but it's better than wearing my ragged clothes. Maybe the guard at the bridge will just see a uniform and won't notice who's inside. Some new troops had just arrived - I'll pretend to be one of them. As I'm about to leave, Hans comes through the front door and sees what I am doing. He's glad I'm trying to escape, but sad I'm leaving. He tells me to wait while he gets my younger brother, so he can come too. He says he wants to marry me, and that he will soon desert the army and join the Russian Partisans, and we will be together. It's all too much for me, and I blush with embarrassment. His confession of love is a surprise, and I am flattered. But the fact that he has my life all planned repels me. I must escape from his plans as well as the camp. I just want my life back and the freedom to choose what I want for myself. I've come to think of him as a protective brother. I know he would never let anything happen to me, but I had never seen the passion of love in his eyes - only concern. Maybe my leaving brought his love to the surface along with the fear that he might lose me forever. In a few minutes he returns with my sixteen year old brother and dresses him in a uniform. He then has us wait another hour until dark. He gives us some bread and cheese, and we drink some red wine. He tells us the Nazis will be defeated at Stalingrad. He says it will be the first nail in Hitler's coffin."

"Yes, I think he's right," I add. "Hitler is losing thousands of his best troops and the myth of Nazi invulnerability. It will be a psychological blow as well as a physical one. I like Reem, he is a good man. He was the first German solider that was kind to us. He said he had been wounded in France and had just spent two months in the hospital. He saved my beautiful cousin Elizabeth from the Gorodok ghetto. He sent her to live with his mother in Vienna. They sent him here to fight the guerillas, and now he wants to join them?"

"Yes, she says." He's very sympathetic to the plight of the Jews, even though he is considered Aryan. His father was Jewish and his mother German. It's the mother's race that determines if one is Jewish, so Reem was considered German and drafted into the Army. If his mother had been a Jew instead of his father, he would have been sent to a concentration camp. It's all so crazy - this accident of birth."

We are caught up in an insane nightmare orchestrated by a madman," I add with a grimace. "How did you escape?"

"So Reem kisses us goodbye and wishes us well. I am feeling vulnerable and afraid. I look to him hoping that he will force us to stay or that he will say he is coming with us. I'm thinking I can't do this alone. He looks at me sympathetically, and our eyes meet. He kisses me again, but this time on the lips. I think it might be the last kiss of my life - I see my life passing before my eyes. I have an intuition that I will die trying to escape. I give into his love. The kiss is long and passionate. I can tell he wants me. He must think I love him too; because when our lips part, and we step back and look at each other, he is speechless and tears are falling from his eyes. I'm overwhelmed by the kiss too, but my kiss is more for the love of life than it is for him. I'm crying as I leave him, because it feels like I'm leaving life behind and walking into death. I am certainly leaving my protector and walking into God knows what."

"I am crying for myself and my brother beside me. I don't want to die. As we march down the cobblestone street toward the bridge and the Nazi machine gun, I realize that we are much too thin for our baggy uniforms. I know the guard will see that we are too thin to be soldiers. Tears stream down my checks as I anticipate my death. We don't know what will happen. I keep telling myself that somehow we'll get through this. We are too young to die."

She stops, takes a sip of soup, and reflects before she continues, "Something about us must look suspicious, because the bridge guard points his gun at us and commands us to halt. My brother stops and I run past him across the bridge into the trees expecting to be shot. It doesn't happen, for some reason the guard doesn't shoot. Maybe he was too busy dealing with my brother. That's the last time I saw my brother. He must still be in Krasno. So that's the only reason I'm here - the bridge guard decided to let me live."

"Who could murder such beauty?" I smile in admiration. "He had to know he was looking at a woman. No man has eyes that sparkle like yours. You are too shapely and beautiful to be a man. Clothes alone could never make you look like a man."

"You are too kind," she says modestly. "But you haven't been around a woman for a while. My hair, my clothes, and everything about me are a mess. But thanks to Zosia I am clean. If soap could only wash away ugly memories."

"You mean losing your parents and your friends?"

"Yes of course, but also my innocence."

"We've all lost that," I say sympathetically as I kiss her beautiful almond shaped eyes and reach around her as she snuggles into my arms.

"I was raped more than once," she says looking at the ground. "My mother and I were raped at the same time - together in the same bedroom. Remember what it was like two weeks after the invasion. Put yourself in my place and you will understand why I hate Germans."

I can see the pain in her face as she continues. "Two S.S. men are knocking on the door. When we are too frightened to answer - they shoot off the lock and come in. They come straight to the bedroom where I am sleeping with my mother and father. They grab my father and throw him out of the house and barricade the door. I can see they intend to rape my mother. When my mother was in public she often turned heads - she was a very beautiful woman. They saw her on the street in the late afternoon and followed her home. From what they say, I understand that they planned this for several hours over a leisurely meal in a nearby cafe where they find courage in the local vodka. They are ripping my mother's night gown off when they see me hiding behind the bed. The older one takes his pistol from my mother's head and points it at me. I can see in their eyes that they want me too. The younger one grabs my arm and pulls me up across my bed. He's plump bellied and looks to be about thirty five. He has a squat ugly body and the face of a panting animal."

"Have you ever had sex?" He asks.

Shaking and freezing with fear, I shake my head no. "Then I'll show you what an S.S. man feels like," he says as he pulls off his boots and unbuckles his belt and drops his pants - exposing his skinny white legs. He takes everything off but his white undershirt."

Tears are coming to her eyes as she continues, "The older man is already on top of my mother when the younger one rips off my clothes. "You are more beautiful without your clothes," he says. He rolls on top of me and pokes me in the neck with his hand gun as he thrust his organ at me - pushing harder and harder, finally forcing himself in me. It's hurting. The pain is unbearable. Instinctively I pushed on his chest trying to get him off of me and find my hands covered with wet blood. With a shriek of horror, I realize it is my father's blood."

The soldier slaps me in the face with his pistol and says, "You had better be good to me, or I will blow out your brains."

"I freeze with fear and he no longer looks at my face. He's bouncing up and down on top of me forever. I think it will never end. I must have passed out from the pain, because I don't remember everything. When they finally leave, my mother is sobbing and terrified. By the front door, we find my father bloody and beaten with two broken ribs. I begin having convulsions and throwing up. I bathe and clean myself, but still I can smell him in my hair. It's like the stink of a strong perfume. It's the smell of a fat, sweaty, dirty, alcoholic body. Even in the ghetto, where baths are precious, I never smelled such a body odor. Underneath a heavy dose of cologne, I can smell alcohol and cigarettes coming out of his skin as a fermenting stink. I smell it now as if he were here in the barn. If I were blind I could know him by his revolting smell."

"I'm sorry," I say as I hug her with compassion. "I wish I could have saved you from it."

She looks into my eyes and thanks me with a hug and a kiss on the cheek and asks, "Will you help me kill them? If I give you a gun, will you kill them for me?"

Hanah in 1939

Chapter 10

Love and Salvation

November 21-26, 1942, In Zosia's barn.

"Here's the gun," she says. Like a sacred object, Hanah slowly offers up a Browning automatic in the palms of her hands and says, "Take it. It's yours. You served in the army and know better how to use it. I have bullets too."

My jaw drops in disbelief that I am holding a weapon in my hand. Speechless and in awe of the gift, I hold up the gun trying to see it in the darkness. After all the struggle and doing without, here is the ticket to survival. I grab her by the shoulder with my free hand, pull her to me, and give her a kiss of gratitude, a smack on the mouth with such force that it startles her.

I smile and beam with a happiness that I haven't felt in years as I admire the pistol, and say, "This gun will save us. Now I know we will get through this. It's for sure. No one has ever given me such a gift. It is the gift of life. I think - no, I know it. I love you my darling, Hanele."

She returns my love with an equal joy bursting from her smile and sparkling in her eyes. With affection and concern, she combs my thick black hair with her fingers and says, "My Julie, thank God you've come to me. I need you so much."

We kiss and roll over in the straw and snuggle in our own private cocoon. For each of us it's unique to be holding another person and to feel their warmth and caring. So for now it is enough to hold each other and be close. Wrapped in each other's arms, we fall into a secure blissful sleep that we know is fragile and precious. I wake in the morning before she does. I am aroused from my toes to the top of my head. I'm short of breath with my palms sweating. Every part of me is tingling and standing on end. But how can I think of making love without a marriage. Such a girl as Hanah, if not for the war, would have gone to her wedding a virgin. She has been educated to be a doctor, and from a good family, and a prize for any man. Did I dare ask her to marry without a ring or her parents blessing. I have no money, no house - nothing but these body shaking feelings. The story of her rape is still turning inside me and breaking my heart. She is damaged goods. I feel so bad for her. In normal times, no one would have a woman who had been raped. Now the old morality is gone.

She wakes and smiles into my eyes and says, "Good morning Julie, my darling." She takes my hand and kisses the back of it and talks to me as we lie side by side in our bed of wheat straw and look up into the long fingers of golden light coming through the cracks in the barn ceiling.

"I dreamt of my father last night. We were all together, your family and mine. He liked you," she says with a smile. "That is a big compliment - my father never liked the men I brought home. He was strict with me. My first outings with men were always chaperoned and my father never wanted the chaperoning to stop. It was only after a lot of protest and years of whining that I was able to go out by myself. When I was in at the

University, my anatomy professor fell in love with me. He was five years older, the age I am now. Everything was wonderful and perfect except that he was Polish and Catholic. My father was furious. He shook me by the shoulders until I was senseless and threatened to cut my throat. I was shocked to see such a mild mannered man become so big and ferocious. I had to swear never to see the man I was in love with. This same Pole later warned us that the Nazis were registering Jews. "Don't go to this registration,' he said. "They will murder you."

Mother didn't believe him. She went to the registration and never came back. None of them came back. They gathered up all the Jews they could find and had them dig their own graves. They shot them down with a machine gun and buried them."

After a pause she adds, "I loved my mother. I do miss her. I can still see her on her knees digging in the dirt. She liked to plant flowers. I will always think of her when I see a rose."

She pauses and tears come to her eyes as she thinks about her beautiful, sweet mother, and is silent for a few minutes. I kiss her tears, and she presses herself to me. Finally she collects herself and swallows the lump out of her throat.

She puts her finger over my lips to prevent me from speaking and says, "As you can see my father was determined that I would only marry a Jewish boy. He wanted to keep me as his princess until he found the perfect prince. You are such a prince, my Julie, with your education and wonderful family. Our parents would have loved each other. We would have had a beautiful wedding with music, family, friends, food, wine, and dancing. There would have been a honeymoon, a house, presents and loving adoration. I would have been a doctor at the hospital and you, a professor at the university. It would have been a perfect world. But that world and our parents are all dead. We have lost everything that we valued. We are both like young broken birches that must mend themselves and grow straight again. As we grow old and strong, we will always have the twists, the gnarls, and the scars where we were broken."

"What are you saying?" I say as I grab her hand.

"I've lost my purity. I have no dowry or even parents. You have no job, no promising future and are homeless. In spite of everything, we are going to be married and celebrate our joyful honeymoon in this old barn. We have absolutely nothing but our love for each other. This marriage is the one thing Hitler will not take away from us. We will take off our coats and lay them on the straw and make our wedding bed."

How do you know that I want to marry you?" I ask with a teasing smile.

She stands up to my tease, laughs at me and says with a tease that becomes serious, "Because my darling, if you don't, I will take the gun back, and you will be out of the barn and in the cold. You see, the gun is my dowry. My husband will be the one with this gun. Do you understand? When I go to the partisans I must have a husband, or I'll be tortured with propositions. I've been raped by the Germans. I'm not ready to be raped and passed around among the Russians. I am not going to be the communal whore for a bunch of guerilla fighters. When this war is over, you will be free to leave this marriage or stay forever. If you chose to play the part of my husband, you will tell them that I am your wife and your lover. I won't go to them without a husband, and they will not take you without a gun. So I need you as much as you need me. We are the perfect match. Do you have any other stupid questions?"

"Yes, will you marry me?"

"Yes, my Julie," she says with a warm kiss on the lips and the beaming, blushing smile of a new bride. "We will be married here in this barn on this beautiful Sunday morning. Take off your coat and lay it on the straw, and I will place my coat beside it, and this will be our honeymoon bed."

We take off our coats and make the bed. She quickly takes off the rest of her clothes and is standing naked before me.

"My God, you are beautiful," I whisper.

"Don't be so slow about getting into bed," she says as she lies down on her coat. "It's freezing in this barn. I'm cold without you."

Never have I undressed so quickly. Never have I seen such a beautiful body. Never has God been so good. I lay down beside her, cup her full, firm breasts in my hands, and shower her body with kisses. I'm in unrestrained bliss.

Slow down," she says." Remember that I am you wife. There is no need to rush; I am here for you always."

Chapter 11

Leaving the Nest

26 November 1942, 10 kilometers west of Gorodok

By some miracle our honeymoon has lasted five joyous days, and neither I nor Hanah want it to end. The barn has become our first home, and more home than either of us has had in a year. In a lovers trance we frolic in our own blissful world. We caress and kiss as we lie intertwined in our honeymoon bed. We comb each other's hair with adoration, and groom one another like monkeys. We are completely spontaneous, accepting and comfortable with each other.

We are smiling and cuddling in a leisurely lunch as we feed each other fresh bread and cheese. Between kisses we are startled by the sound of gun fire and bullets striking stones and boards of our barn followed by the sounds of running boots and shouting. Frozen as if shot, with the gun blast ringing in our ears, we are stunned to silence. Hanah dares not even chew the lump of bread and cheese - it becomes an obstruction in her throat.

Finally Hanah swallows and finds her voice. "My God! They're here," she exclaims in a terrified whisper. "I can't believe they found us. What can we do?"

Bliss evaporates. The sparkling glow of love is replaced by the gut wrenching fear of being tortured, raped, murdered, or returning to the hell we have just escaped. Life again is consumed by apprehension and fear. Protectively, I pull her close and hold her as we both listen for the next bullet and the barn door to open with gunfire.

After consoling her and covering her up with straw, I grab the pistol and say, "Stay here - I'll see what I can find out."

I run across the loft of the barn and peek out the large crack in the hay loft door. I can see eight police men in black uniforms, armed with rifles. They are running away from us, single file down a twisted cow path in the direction of the large farm, Hermanishki. Before I can get back to Hanah, Zosia has opened the barn door and let herself in.

"Did you hear the bullets?" Zosia asks as she tries to catch her breath. "When will it ever end? The police are out collecting taxes. They want twenty-five percent of what we have. The bastards think they're better than God - he only wants ten percent. The collectors were on the way here, to the barn to get what I have, when they were distracted by some Partisans passing through. The Partisans have been busy trying to get provisions before Nazi's get everything. Both sides have their hands out. We're being picked clean. Unless we hide something, there will be nothing to feed ourselves. Anyway, the police have gone for today, but they could be back this way tomorrow. I'm so afraid they might find you. Please hide and be careful, my darlings."

"Then we must leave tonight," I say looking to the sky for help then back to Hanah. "It's time we made our way to the Partisan center. It's about twenty kilometers away."

"First you will both come in the house," Zosia interrupts. "And take a bath and have a meal at my table. I'll wash your clothes and dry them in the oven one last time. You will leave here clean and with a full stomach. I'll pack some food for the journey. Now tell me the truth. Am I a good matchmaker?"

"Yes, yes," says Hanah laughing at the beaming pride of her hostess who has just baked the best cake of her life. She hugs and kisses Zosia's self-satisfied smile. "Thank you my darling Zosia. I will never forget you as long as I live."

"Thank you, dear Zosia," I say "You've saved our lives, given me a wife and a honeymoon, and helped put some flesh back on these bones. I had forgotten what kindness was."

"Julie, you will always be my baby boy," says Zosia returning the hug with a kiss. She then turns and affectionately presses her hands on each side of Hanah's beautiful face, kisses her hard on the lips and says, "And you Hanele are my new daughter. I will miss you both. Please come back to me and bring me some babies. I would love to be the nanny to your babies."

Well after dark, Hanah and I leave our honeymoon bed hand in hand, clean and well fed. The moon is falling into the tree tops and the stars are bright in a clear sky. Dim lights flicker in the small cottages. We imagine families sitting around the fire and going about a normal life. A life we no longer feel a part of as we are just voyeurs passing through. She squeezes my hand as we walk by an attractive cottage, and we both think one day we could be such a family and have our own home. For now there is a sense of freedom and security of our invisibility in the blackness. The night belongs to the guerillas and those brave enough to walk it. We are comforted by the fact that at night the Nazis post sentries and lock themselves in the towns and leave the countryside to whoever wants it.

We slip through the shadows, favoring the woods and fields and avoiding the roads as much as possible. I know exactly which way to go and what to do when we get there. As we become comfortable in the darkness, our gait becomes quick and light with an occasional skip. For the first time in years we are thinking past surviving the next few hours and even of a future together.

Hanah looks me in the eye and asks, "What will you do when the war is over, my Julie? Will you leave me, my love? I won't try to keep you, if you must go."

"Never, never will I leave you, my darling. You are so smart, beautiful and sexy. And I love your Gypsy eyes. After being married to you for a week, I know I will love you forever. You couldn't drive me away with a stick," I say with a laugh as I kick a rock like it was a ball. "I'm going to take you to America. We will go to Texas on the first boat we can find-even if I have to tie you up like baggage."

"I will follow you anywhere my love," she says with a noticeable lack of enthusiasm. "But why Texas? I never thought of going to Texas - even for a visit. I have thought of Palestine, Canada, New York, Argentina, but never Texas."

"I have lots of cousins in America," I say, still being positive. "They will sponsor us, give us a place to stay and help us get a start. My father lived in Texas for ten years and became an American citizen."

Skeptical, she asks, "If it's so great, why did he come back?"

"For love. He came back for my mother. They were childhood sweethearts. After ten years, he was still in love with her. But she wasn't like you - ready to follow her man to the ends of the earth - and there were problems with her age. She was only sixteen when he left. Her father was not ready to let her go."

"I may be like her more than you think," she teases.

"Anyway my father got caught up in what was happening in Gorodok and put off going back, and then the door was shut. He couldn't go back. So I almost grew up as an American."

"Don't worry", she laughs. "You are just fine like you are. And if you were in Texas, you wouldn't be here with me and you would have missed out on the best sex of your life."

"I wouldn't trade all of Texas for the honeymoon we are having," I say as I turn and kiss her.

Puzzled she asks, "Are we still having a honeymoon? The bullets back at the barn, did they end it?"

"Only a bullet to the brain will end our honeymoon," I say as I squeeze her hand and point to the silhouette of a roof top. "Do you see that hut over there in the field?"

"Yes, it's a flax hut - the peasants use it for storage."

"That is our new honeymoon cottage," I say with a grin of anticipation. "We will spread our coats and make a honeymoon bed - you have taught me something I will never forget."

With a quick stride I am walking a step in front of her. Unable to wait I pull her into a run, and we run hand in hand a hundred meters across the field. Out of breath, I stop and open the door, and let her into the empty hut. There is a dirt floor and no window. I take the ladder up to the loft and she follows. I help her off with her coat and lay it down on the attic boards, and then I take off my coat and lay it down beside hers. We sit down on our wedding bed and take off our shoes. As I unbutton her, the backs of my fingers can feel her breast loose in her shirt, and a quiver of excitement runs through my chest.

She pulls off her shirt, and I kiss her breast and feel the nipples erect in my lips. As I nurse her, she begins unbuttoning me and stroking my face and hair. Without leaving her breasts I kick off my pants, and she roles over on top and kisses me madly all over my face, ears and neck. I can feel the strength of her spirit radiating through the darkness and know she is smiling. I am sure she is the most wonderful woman on earth. I kiss and caress and know every inch of her. My ear is wet and tickling as she massages me with her lips. I reach down and feel her wetness. She grabs me and pulls me to her. As we fly through the doors of ecstasy, we are silently praying, "Please God, let us be together, always."

Chapter 12

Family Reunion

27 November 1942, Before sunrise in a flax hut ten kilometers southwest of Gorodok.

Hanah and I are snuggled in, intertwined in deep sleep on the attic boards when I hear shouting, laughter, and the sound of horses and wagons running through my dreams. I am not sure if it's a nightmare or reality. I shake my head and listen again and hear a crash at the door. Trapped with no way out - the walls are closing in. It's too close to breathe. I want to look out, but there are no windows or even a crack in the wall. Hanah is trembling in my arms.

"We're surrounded," I say gripping the pistol. "They're trying to get in the door. It's bounty hunters. Somehow they know we're here. If we're going to die, we will kill at least one or two of the bastards."

"Julie, Julie, Hanele come out," we hear someone shouting. "It's me, Grishka."

"And Ele Lidzki," says another voice.

Too stunned to know what's happening, I help Hanah down the ladder. By this time there are several men in the hut with guns and an oil lantern. One man grabs Hanah and another me, and we are hugged and kissed.

"Old Zosia said you would be hiding around here," says Grishka. Letting go of me and stepping back, he says "I hid in this same hut five months ago. I knew you would be here."

"We have no time to waste," says Ele. "We can't let daylight catch us. We just left some Nazis, who are going to be mad as hell when they discover a month's rations are missing. We've got to keep moving. Like angry wasps, they'll be out in force blitzing the countryside - moving much quicker than our wagons."

"Hurry," says Grishka waving us out the door. "You are coming with us to the guerilla headquarters in the Naliboki Forest."

Quickly we follow Grishka and Ele across the field to a rut road. We can see five wagons waiting in the dark. Each has a cow tied to the back of it. Each wagon is manned by a rifleman and a driver holding the reins.

"Come, you two will ride with me," says Grishka as he helps Hanah up into the lead wagon. "Hanele find a seat in the back. Julie, you ride shotgun with my rifle."

Grishka and I climb up into the wagon seat while Hanah finds a place on a sack of flour behind us. Grishka gives his horse a swat with the reins and we are off at a trot.

Hanah and I are feeling safe and grateful that we have been saved by a big brother. How are we so lucky to have been rescued by Zosia and now Grishka?

"I thought I saw Hirsh in the wagon behind us," I say. "Who else is with you?"

There are the Springer brothers; Sabitai and Jeremy. Michael is back at camp. There is Ele, Hirsh, Matus and myself. That makes six Jews, and we have three Russians

POW's who escaped from Monderno. Before we joined up with the Russians, there were twenty-eight of us - all from Gorodok. The Russians have scattered us about, so we are half Jewish. It's maybe for the best, we have all the languages covered and the Russians get along better with the peasants. But to tell you the truth I don't completely trust the Russians, and they don't trust us. It's a marriage of convenience."

"What about the Polish partisans?" I ask. "Do you have anything to do with them?"

"Nothing, says Grishka. We have both been shooting in the same direction, but at some point I think we will be shooting at each other. The Poles don't give a damn for the Russians or care much for Jews either. They don't trust Stalin, and they don't want him in their country. They think he will never leave. So that's why some Poles have collaborated with the Germans. They would rather have the Germans than the Russians. The Polish partisans are in an impossible situation. They must drive the Germans out but keep the Russians from coming in. And we Jews are caught in the middle trying to stay alive the best we can."

"So brother, what have you been doing since we jumped off the truck?" asks Grishka. I thought I would see you months ago. Where did you go? I was thinking you were dead, and then I heard rumors that you were alive."

"Well, you were almost right about my death," I say. "I was captured by a bounty hunter and taken to Krasno."

"Krasno," repeats Grishka. "You were lucky to get away from there. Now twenty-nine of us have survived the jump from the truck and have joined the partisans. And you are the last to come to us. Welcome home, brother and sister. Welcome to the family - the only family we have left. Your new home is on the marshy islands of the Naliboki Forest. The road in

115

is knee deep in mud which is good for keeping the German trucks and tanks out. You will soon understand why no one has ever lived here until now. You will be looking forward to the coming winter, when the ground becomes frozen hard and there are no mosquitoes."

Chapter 13

Acceptance

27 November 1942, In the Naliboki Forest, 25 kilometers west of Minsk.

I am holding on to the side of the wagon to steady myself through the bumps, as Grishka hurries the horses along. Even though my fingers are finding fresh splinters in the wagon wood pushed up by bullets, I am feeling safe and at home with Grishka's Guerillas. Hanah is half-asleep and affectionately snuggled into my side. I squeeze her and a chill of joy runs through me. Home will always be with Hanah.

"If you are tired, lie down on the flour sacks in the back," offers Grishka. "We're going to ride the rest of the night. It will be dawn before we reach camp.

"Thank-you, but no," I say. "There's too much excitement to sleep. I've never felt more awake and alive. This is exactly where I've wanted to be for months. Now that I'm here, I won't be excess baggage - not for a minute."

"Then I have a job for you my friend," grins Grishka. "You hold the reins, and I'll sleep. I've been up for two days. It's an endless job - finding provisions for well over a hundred men."

"Don't forget about the women," says a sleepy Hanah.

"I never forget about women," smiles Grishka as he kisses Hanah on the cheek. He gives me the reins and retires to the flour sacks.

I am ecstatic. It reminds me of when my grandfather handed me the reins for the first time. It was my seventh birthday and a rite of passage. I remember the chill that came over me and the power I felt in my hands. Then as now - it's a position of privilege and trust. It finally feels like I'm doing something useful.

The wagon wheels keep falling into holes. I wonder how Grishka can sleep through the jolts. I soon hear him snoring above the rattles of the wagon. Hanah puts her head in my lap and falls asleep. I am left alone without a light on an empty black road. Only the tree line shows the road. I search the darkness with my eyes and ears and let the horses find the way. I think of the rifle beside me and remember using one like it when I was in the Army. How long would it take me to grab it and shoot? Then I remember and put my hand on Hanah's loaded pistol in my coat pocket.

As I search the dark, looking for the way, my eyes become heavy. I keep blinking to keep them open, and begin to wish I had taken up Grishka's offer of sleep. In my stupor, I begin to see faces from Krasno floating out in front of me. All week, I have been haunted by bloody nightmares of my family's murder. I am slowly drifting into the horror of last night's dream. I am again walking through graves as far as I can see - holes in the black earth filled with bright red blood. I find myself lost - looking and calling for my brothers and sister. But there is no answer.

I begin talking to the empty road and to the trees soaring above. "Martha. Where are you? Where are your babies and your beautiful blossoming Shoshana? Ez! Brother. I want to hug you and feel your sweet breath warm on my face. I love you my dear David and Sarah. Please, come to me. My God! Where are you?"

The faceless darkness answers. "We are here," I hear my sister, Sonia say. "Lying in a pool of blood in the bottom of a deep grave. Many others are stacked on top of us."

"I heard voices," says Hanah as she hugs me hard around the ribs. "What's happening? Have we reached the camp? Are you OK?"

"I was dreaming and talking to myself," I say. "I'm worried about my family in Krasno. All week I've had nightmares about it. Tomorrow, I must go back there. I promised David I would rescue him."

"My poor darling,' she says with a hug. "I'm worried too. I will go with you."

"Too late," says Grishka getting up from the flour sacks. "They're dead - murdered a week ago."

Hanah begins sobbing and is joined by Grishka and me. Grishka sits in the seat beside her and holds her in his arms. We are all hugging and leaning on each other and choking with grief.

"God! Why?" I shout with tears running down my cheeks. "Where are you, God?"

"Dead," says Grishka. "He died with everyone else. The Nazi's killed him. There is no God. If there were, how could he let this happen? I've given up God for bullets."

"Damn the filthy bastards," I say. "Nothing will ever be the same."

For the longest time we are motionless and too choked-up to talk. We just sob and hold each other and stare into the dark. It's all silent except for the rattle of wagons and the clip-clop of horses. In our silence, we feel warmth and strength in a nest of togetherness. We realize how precious we are to each other.

The road becomes muddy and the horses strain to pull through it. I crack the whip and Grishka yells to keep them going. I can see Hanah is worried that we are going to be stuck. I don't welcome the thought of getting out into knee deep mud and pushing a loaded wagon.

Finally Grishka breaks the silence with, "We're heavy, but we're going to make it. Camp is only a few kilometers away, and good, strong horses are pulling us. You know how much I like a good horse. They took all the best horses. Now I'm slowly getting them back. Last night I got this beautiful, big horse from the police chief. He was so gracious to leave it behind. We had come to the house to kill him, but found only his horse. Maybe he heard us coming and ran into the woods. We took what we wanted and burned the house and the piano he took from the synagogue. Anyway it's his horse that's tied to the back of the wagon, and I haven't had a chance to ride it and make it mine. From just looking at him, I know he's fast, and he can win some races. And if anyone is foolish enough to bet, I'll make some money. I'm going to untie him and find out what he can do. Just keep the wagon on the road. See you in camp."

Grishka crawls to the back of the wagon, unties the horse, puts one foot in the stirrup and jumps onto the black stallion. He immediately digs in his heels and darts off into the woods at a gallop. The horse is as black as night. Together they move over the ground with the shadows of the clouds passing beneath the rising moon. He stays low, leaning into the horse's neck to avoid branches. He finds a trail where the ground has been packed down by passing platoons of Partisans and turns into it. He whips the horse with the reins and pushes to top speed. He rides like Greek gods on winged horses. Every man wants to fly, and this is Grishka's way. He is making a reckless escape from the problems of earth. Flying among the clouds, he doesn't give a damn about any threat to his life - so much of him is dead already. But he still feels something when he flirts with death. That's why he keeps risking everything. It's a way of reassuring himself that he is still alive. He arrives in camp at full gallop, pulls up the reins and comes to a quick stop. As he dismounts, he notices Major Katkof coming toward him at a determined stride."

"Are you crazy? Where's the thrill in an insane race through the woods in the dark?" Major Katkof asked as Grishka's horse snorts to a stop. "Is it not enough to be shot at every night? You are pushing your luck and mine."

"What good is luck, if you don't push it? I like pushing luck - especially when it means cheating death. Death has cheated me out of everyone I care about - my wife, my little boys, my parents, almost everyone I know," answers Grishka. "So you can see why I want to cheat death as much as I can. If I cheat him for the rest of my life, I could never get back what he has taken from me. Of course I'm going to die and don't give a damn if I do. I just want to live long enough to kill another Nazi."

"Yes, and I want you to stay alive to keep us fed and show me around this part of the world," says Katkof, "I can't be without you - you are my eyes and ears as well as my bread basket."

"Don't worry, I'll be around. I'm doomed to live," says Grishka as he turns away from Katkof and walks toward his dugout. He is passing the kitchen hut when he hears a hoarse, fractured voice coming from the open door.

"So Moses, where are the chosen people?" grunts Yorgo, the head cook who is bent, wrinkled and baked red from the stove. He gives away his drunkenness as he slurs and spits out his next sour sentence. "Where is the damn meat and flour you promised? What's chasing you? Why did you come back alone? Are your people dead, my brave Jew? He laughs. "Did you get them all killed?"

"Don't worry about the brave Jews," barks Grishka. "I got the damn food - now you'll have to get off your drunken ass and cook. We'll have a bellyful tonight. I got five cows, five pigs, two hundred pounds of salted pork, five pounds of butter, fifteen sacks of fresh flour, and five sacks of salt, among other things. If you're so damn brave, come with me on the next trip. You'll know what hell we go through to keep vodka in that belly. Yes, we even got vodka for you. You can start your damn fires and cook some breakfast. Look, the wagons are here."

"You must be joking," the wide-eyed cook says. "Our peasants don't have anything to give us."

"Yes, Where did you get all this?" asks Major Katkof as he walks up to our wagon and looks in.

"We took it from their peasants. Yesterday this was provisions to be delivered to the S.S. Company guarding the railway station at Molodeczno. The peasants are all collaborators there."

"And who is this guy driving your wagon," asks Katkof? "Introduce me to the pretty lady."

"I am Yehuda Adelman and this is my wife, Hanah," I say as I put down the reins and climb down. "We have a gift for you - a Browning automatic and bullets," I say as I pull the gun and ammunition out of my coat and hand them to Katkof."

"Very good", says Katkof as he admires the pistol and turns to Grishka. "Tell me about your friends."

"Yehuda is a good strategist - very smart," says Grishka. "He graduated from the university and became the headmaster of a grammar school. He specializes in languages - he can speak to anyone in this part of the world. In school he has taught German, Polish, Russian, English, Hebrew and Yiddish. He has been in the Polish Army and knows the backwoods as well as me. I trust him with my life."

"You might have to," says Katkof. "Tell me about Hanah."

I can speak for myself," says Hanah. "I've been to medical school and worked in clinics, but I am not yet a certified doctor. I know enough to be of help to your doctor and I don't mind carrying a gun or washing clothes. I am at your service."

"Welcome," Katkof says as he reaches up to the wagon and shakes her hand and turns to Yehuda on the ground. "I'm sure both of you will be good Partisans, but in separate units. Husbands and wives are not allowed to serve side by side. Yehuda, you will be blowing up trains with Ele. Hanah, you will be a medic attached to Grishka's unit. You will sleep in different huts and can have holidays together. Good luck and don't take any foolish chances. And please, be more careful with yourselves than your daring commander on his big black stallion. Like Grishka, you will soon become indispensable. I don't want to lose any of you to foolishness and stupidity. Now unload this stuff while we get your breakfast going."

Tears are welling up in my eyes as I watch the Major turn away and disappear into his hut. Side by side there are tears of happiness and disappointment. I am happy to finally be accepted into the Partisans, but what will I do without my Hanah? What cold emptiness. How can I sleep without her snuggled into my side? I feel like half a person.

Chapter 14

Sonia and Rose

18 November 1942, before sunrise in the synagogue at Krasno Compound in eastern Poland

Lights flash around the walls of the sleeping synagogue as Sonia opens her eyes to a crash - like a bed being turned over. Startled, she hears boot-stomping and shouting, "Out Jew! Everyone, outside and into the trucks. Quick! Now! Move! Get out you bastards! Now!"

"Quiet," she whispers to two year old Rose, "Quiet my pet, not a sound."

In spite of her coat, Sonia can feel the cutting cold of the early morning pouring through the open door along with the black choking stink of spent diesel fuel. The vibrations of a convoy of trucks shakes the floor and races through her arteries as she dives under her bed. She silently lifts up the small trap door in the wooden plank floor that husband Pesach made to access the crawl space. Carefully she slides the door away, and in a matter of seconds she throws in a couple of blankets, dives head first into the blackness and pulls two year old Rose in after her. Pulse throbbing and fumbling in fear, she reaches for the trap door and pulls it back in place with a quick scrape across the floor, finishing with a low thud that shudders through her stomach.

Fear subsides slowly as her squinting eyes adjust to the cold darkness. Slivers of light penetrate occasionally through cracks in the planks. Already the cold ground is biting her wherever her body makes contact. She folds up a blanket and sits on it. She places Rose in her lap, and wraps the other blanket around them. The sleeping Rose is a little bundle of heat that Sonia squeezes as she rocks back and forth to keep warm, soothing herself as much as her baby.

After all the promises of no more killings - Hitler's mobile killing units have come again to finish what's left of the Gorodok Jews. Too frightened to move, and with tears gushing from her eyes, - she dares not make a sound. After what seems like hours of commotion and crashes, the trucks finally leave her with a cruel empty silence.

Much later, after a long stillness that almost lulls her to sleep, she is startled by a door slamming in the room above her and the sound of heavy boots clunking slowly across the floor. The boots stop directly above her and suck her breath through the floor. A rapid pulse pounds between her ears. Have they seen the trap door? They could be standing on it. Who is it? Scavengers, bounty hunters, S.S., or police - all are deadly. She guesses the boot steps belong to a local policeman scavenging for whatever. The steps finally walk away, and panic relaxes into worry. She wonders what happened to her Pesach. He went over the fence two days ago with the hope of joining the Partisans. Thank God he left before they came. There has been no word of him and nothing from the others that have escaped. She worries herself through the day about Pesach and how to save herself and Rose. She is growing old from worry. Where will she go when she crawls under the fence? Who will risk being shot to help her? If she escapes the death squad, will the police, the S.S., or the bounty hunters find her first? She feels her face folding up and hiding in wrinkles. Her body is numb from shock. The deep lines in her forehead reach down into the brain and touch scars that will always hurt for her mother, father, brothers, grandparents, and everyone she knew. How is she alive when everyone else is dead? She wonders if her image is alive in any other brain. Is anyone she knows still alive? Will she ever see her reflection in another pair of loving eyes? Is there anyone on earth who knows her? Where is Pesach? My dear Pesach, please be alive.

She is thinking the longer she waits, the safer it will be for an exit. She must at least wait until dark. But if she waits too late, she will be waking people up. And they could be angry about getting out of bed in the middle of the night and less likely to help her out of the cold. Finally there is no daylight coming through the cracks in the crawl space. Hungry, thirsty, tired of waiting, and desperate to escape - she pushes the floor boards away. She places Rose on the floor and climbs out the crawl space and welcomes the fresh air of night and the chance to stretch her cramped muscles.

She makes her way out of the synagogue and to the perimeter wire in the pitch blackness. The long day in the crawl space has given her eyes plenty of time to adjust to the dark. Thank God the moon is covered by clouds. She pushes up the wire and crawls under the tall fence, and is greeted by sharp coils of prickly barbed wire.

She places one of her blankets into the tangle of barbed wire and starts shoving Rose through a hole she is making by pushing the blanket against the wire with her arms and shoulders. Halfway through, the baby starts screaming and Sonia feels blood dripping on her right hand. She can see that Rose's shoulder has been cut. By extending her arms she is able to get the baby through to the other side. Baby Rose is hurt, terrified of being alone, and screaming at the top of her lungs. The baby's screaming is grating on Sonia's nerves, and panic begins to seep down her throat. She tries to remain calm as she pushes the blanket against the wire to make a hole big enough for herself. The heavy wire pushes against her and pricks her through the blanket. She ignores the bleeding in her hands, wrist, and shoulders. It takes all her strength to push through the fence. Finally, she reaches Rose. She pulls the crying child into her and comforts her into quiet as she walks quickly away.

She knows someone must have heard them, and she doesn't want to take the time to extract the blanket from the barbed wire. But when they find the blanket tangled in the wire, they will know what happened and the dogs will be able to pick up her scent. Damn, why did she leave it? But there is no time to go back. In her mind, she imagines the authoritative barks of guard dogs and wonders how soon they will come, and if they'll be able to sniff her out. She quickens her pace as panic takes over. The only relief from the panic is to run. Rose is heavy in her arms and Sonia is gasping for breath as she forces one leg in front of the other in a desperate attempt to get away. Like a knife the cold is stabbing at her lungs. Each step is a supreme effort of will, and every muscle hurts. It's only the adrenaline of panic and her determination to save Rose that keeps her moving. Exhausted, cold, and unable to go another step, she decides to try her luck at a small farmhouse back from the road in the middle of a field. She barely has strength to get to the front door.

Desperately, she pounds on the door and a curious, older woman pushes her head out the only window on the front of the cottage.

"Who is it?" The woman shouts.

"Dear Babushka, please help me and my baby. I am Easser's daughter. I am trying to get to Gorodok."

The Babushka looks at her and exclaims, "Sonia! I know you. Your husband is a shoemaker. Once he made me a good pair of shoes. I still have them."

She leaves the window and unbolts the door. Her brown eyes are big and sympathetic as she says, "Come in, quickly. Sit here and stay away from the window. This is not a good place for you. My neighbors are all collaborators. Even my son is a policeman. Oh, My God. Your child looks half dead. You can wash her cut in the basin. I'll heat some water. You must be hungry - I have left-overs. I'll fix you something. Please, call me Laura."

Sonia is relieved to be sitting down in a warm house. She is too exhausted to respond or listen. But the widow Laura needs no response and fills up the silence with chatter and loving concern as she puts soup, bread, and milk on the table. It's a feast Sonia's eyes aren't use to. The knot of fear in her guts subsides at the sight of the food. She gives into Laura's mothering and hunger takes over. Never has bread tasted so good.

After eating, Sonia cleans up their cuts and scratches while Laura prepares a bed in the pigsty. Soon Laura pokes her head in the back door, and with oil lantern in hand she says, "Come, I'm ready for you."

Three steps from the house Laura opens a gate to the pig pen and takes the mother and child into a small stone shed that lacks the head room to fully stand up. An old iron stove without legs is propped-up on a pile of brown rocks and is lighting the place with a flickering yellow glow. The dirt floor is matted with dirty straw. Laura has thrown several old blankets down on a pile of black and brown straw she has raked up from the floor between two tangles of nesting pigs. Sonia falls down on the blankets with Rose. She is too tired to object to the filth and stink of her noisy neighbors that are squealing, grunting and even snoring. Laura throws two more dirty blankets on Rose and Sonia, and then piles dirty straw on top of that. When she is through, the hiding place looks so much like a vacant bed that Laura worries the pigs might want to lie on top of them. The stink of ammonia is so bad that Sonia buries her burning nose in her coat to try to overcome it. She does her best to keep her soup from coming up. She begins to make peace with the smell, thinking that no one would believe a human could be hiding in such filth. The smell wouldn't let them come close enough to find out. In spite of everything, Sonia and Rose sleep.

19 November 1942

Sonia wakes to the sound of a loud male voice coming from the house.

"Mama, all the neighbors know you took them in. The dogs followed the scent here. I just talked to Matthew, and he saw a woman and a small child come here last night. The only reason the police aren't here is because you are my mother. I begged them to let me take care of this. These Jews are criminals - escapees from Krasno. I can get two-hundred marks for them. It can mean a promotion. Look, they shoot people for not cooperating. Please, let me save your life, Mother. Tell me where they are."

"OK, Michael. May God forgive me, I will tell you, but you must not mention this to me again. This whole matter makes me sick in my stomach. Do you promise?"

"Yes, yes of course," Michael says.

"Say, I promise and as God is my witness."

He rolls his eyes and holds up his right hand and says, "May God be my witness, I promise never to talk about these two Jews ever again. Now, where are they?"

Sonia, who can hear all this in the stillness of the morning, is trembling as she waits for Laura's answer. She is thinking, thank God, Rose is still sleeping.

Laura is silent as the reality of this young mother and her baby being murdered sinks in. How did her son get mixed-up in this? She frets, makes a grimace, and looks at her offspring in disbelief. How did he become a Nazi? Where did she fail him?"

Michael takes her by the shoulders and shakes her and, says, "Mama, look at me. I want them. Now!"

She pulls away from him and screams, "Stop! I'll have no more of this. If your father were alive, you would have some respect for God's ways. May God have mercy on your soul, son. Please, you must go to church. Tell me you will take me to church on Sunday, and I will tell you where they are."

"Okay Mama," he says as his eyes roll over in the top of his head in acquiescence and then resignation. Under his breath he asks himself, "Why will I always be the little boy in your eyes?" Finally he whispers, "I'll go to church on Sunday. Now, where are they, for Christ sake?"

"She and the baby left here at daybreak. She went across that field toward Krasno. There's a small hut in that direction not far from here. You know the one by the stream. She'll probably stay there until dark. Please, don't bring her back this way. I couldn't bear to look into her eyes after I betrayed her."

"Thank you mother, you are one of a kind," he says as he runs out the door thinking of the marks that will soon be in his pocket, and the promotion to sergeant.

Before Michael is out of sight, Laura shouts, "Remember your promise to take me to church."

Laura is soon in the pigsty desperate to get Sonia moving. "Sonia get up. They say you are the only survivors of Krasno, and they need to kill you too. They want no witnesses. They know you came here last night. But I told my son that you had gone. They could still be watching the place. Here's some bread and cheese. Take it and run toward Gorodok. I told him you were going to Krasno. Crawl out of here and stay low until you reach the woods. Good luck to you my darling."

"I have friends in Gorodok," she says as she kisses her protector on the cheek. "Don't worry about us, we will be just fine."

Sonia is rested and strong again. The fresh air feels good in her lungs. She walks quickly with deliberate steps through the forest. She knows each step is taking her closer to the comfort and loving care of her Nadia in Gorodok. They were neighbors for ten years and never quarreled. The families were close. Sonia helped Nadia care for her two teenage sons from the time they were small. Nadia helped with Rose's birth. "They are people to be trusted," said her husband, Pesach. When the Jews were herded into the ghetto, they brought everything they owned to Nadia and her husband, Vania. She had given Nadia all their furniture, silver, dishes, clothing, and even their wedding rings - everything of value.

"I hope I will be able to return it all to you after the war," Nadia had said. "I will keep it safe for you."

If there is anyone in the world that will help her, it is Nadia. Sonia is becoming tired of trudging through the fresh snow with the weight of Rose in her arms. Again exhausted and spent, she reaches Nadia's house just as night falls and softly raps on the back door.

Nadia is a large, blonde, brown-eyed woman in her mid-thirties with the stubborn strength of a survivor. She wipes her strong man-like hands on her apron, unlatches the door and cracks it just enough to see out. After a few moments of hesitation, she opens the door wide enough for them to enter and says, "It's you Sonia and the child. Oh my dear. Rose is bleeding. What has happened? Please come in. You must be freezing. Are you hungry?"

As Nadia closes the door, an exhausted Sonia stumbles in like a drunk and deposits Rose on the table with her blanket and flops into a chair.

"Vania," calls Nadia to her tall, lanky, sour faced husband. "Help me. Let's warm them up and give them something to eat. Boys, bring me two blankets."

Sonia takes off Rose's clothes and wraps her in a dry blanket and rocks her in her arms. Nadia washes out Rose's bloody shirt and places it in the oven to dry. Vania doesn't move from his chair by the fire. He doesn't say or do anything.

After a few minutes of being busy in the kitchen. Nadia puts a bowl of soup on the table. As Sonia starts to feed Rose, she notices the tablecloth is hers and that the shirts and pants the boys are wearing are Pesach's. Even the simple spoons, knives, and forks were part of a set she had given Nadia for safe keeping. Sonia's embarrassment grows as she notices other things around the cottage that are hers that were left in Nadia's attic for storage that are now being used and abused. The only sound that can be heard is the cracking of the fire and the scrape of Sonia's spoon striking the bowl as she feeds herself and Rose.

Nadia brings a basin of water and helps Sonia wash Rose by the fire. They clean her wound which is puffy and red and starts to bleed again. Nadia plays nervously with Rose, keeping her eyes down and avoids looking at her old friend.

Finally the embarrassing silence is broken as Sonia takes a deep breath and speaks in a nervous voice that reveals her desperation. "Nadia, you know I have nothing, because I have given you everything," she says as she tries to still Nadia's darting eyes with a steady gaze. "You have been my best friend. I came here confident that you would help me. You can have everything I left here except for the rings. I must have the wedding rings to sell, so I can buy food and clothes for Rose. Just give me the rings, and everything else is yours."

There is a tense silence as Nadia exchanges glances with her husband. Finally Nadia says, "They're gone. We sold them a few months ago. I am terribly sorry, but we were hard pressed during the eight months since you left your house to live in the synagogue."

"To tell you the truth," says a cool, calculating Vania as he gets up from his chair and searches Sonia's eyes. "We thought you were dead. We heard everyone in Krasno was killed." He laughs at himself, throws up his hands and continues, "We never believed you would come back. How could you be living? You should be dead. When I saw you come through the door, I thought you were a ghost come to haunt us."

"Where do you intend to stay?" asks Nadia, as she hands Rose's dry shirt to Sonia.

Sonia's eyes drop to the floor and find Rose looking up at her. Too upset to speak, she dresses Rose and wraps her in a small blanket. Finally Sonia finds courage in Rose's smile, stands up and says, "Kumoc Alexander, my father's neighbor. He is a good man - he will help."

Without saying another word or even looking at them, Sonia, with Rose on her hip and tears in her eyes, opens the door with her free hand and goes back out into the cold. She hears the door shut and lock behind her and doesn't look back.

Anger seizes her and gives a burst of energy to her stride as she goes in the direction of Kumoc's house. Snow is falling and her shoes are sinking down into it. Weighed down with sadness, her tiredness returns - each step is an effort. She resists the temptation to lie down in the soft snow and sleep - to rest, if only for a minute. Slowly her mind clears from the double shock of being deserted by her best friend and losing all hope of ever recovering her possessions.

As she approaches Kumoc's house, she changes her mind and makes a left turn and goes to the river. She is too tired to think and is acting on instinct. She crosses the bridge and goes to her old friend Piortr, who helped her the last time she escaped the death squad.

Three raps on the door bring a response. "Who is it?"

"Sonia and Rose," she shouts through the door.

The door opens and Piortr says, "Come in quickly and don't bring in the cold." He hugs them both and takes Rose from Sonia and walks to the fire that gives a yellow glow to the timbers and stone of the old cottage. "I'm so glad to see you - especially the little one. She has grown so. I was worried that you were murdered along with the rest of them at Krasno."

"Somehow I escaped again. It's so good to see a friendly face. Thanks for letting me in. I think they are looking for me. You are risking your life, you know."

He laughs, "That's nothing to risk - not much of my life left. They won't waste a bullet on me; and if they do, I'll only reach Heaven a day sooner. I'll make you a bed by the fire - you'll be warm as toast. They won't be around tonight. Before the sun rises, I'll put you in the cellar."

20 November 1942

Just before daylight, Piortr gently shakes Sonia. Startled and ready to flee, she grabs up her baby before she realizes where she is. Without saying anything, she relaxes and smiles at her benefactor. Rose snuggles into her mother's arms and does not wake. Piortr helps Sonia up with her burden and motions for her to follow him. The entrance to the basement is a trap door in the pantry. Piortr lifts it up, props it against the pantry wall, and walks down the steps, with Sonya following with the baby. He hangs his lamp on a nail protruding from a post at the bottom of the steps and helps Rose into a cellar filled with potatoes, beets and carrots. In one corner are a fermenting vat and a still used to make vodka from potatoes.

"I'll fire up the still," he says as he picks up some wood and places it under the kettle. "I can make some vodka and keep you warm at the same time. And if you feel like a drink, go ahead - I have plenty." He laughs and continues, "But there will be no vodka at all if the Germans or the Partisans find it. Some people court one side or the other with their vodka. I don't want any of them in my house - drunk or sober. I don't want to become involved in another war or the miserable twisted souls fighting it. I've had my war, World War One. Too many people were killed. And for what? We are just fighting it all over again. I've been in the army, and as a child I heard the old men talk of their wars, but this is the first time I've known women and children to be hunted down and shot like stray dogs. I'll try to keep that from happening. Anybody would do that."

Sonia is feeling very lucky to have Piotr as a friend and is wondering why there can't be more like him. She gives Rose some milk as he builds the fire.

"There, it's done," he says. "There's plenty of wood to keep the fire going. I'll leave you some bread and cheese. You should be safe here. I won't check on you until tonight."

Piortr carries three bags of potatoes up stairs, drops the door down, and places the potatoes on top of the trap door to camouflage it.

* * *

At daybreak, the Gestapo kicks in Kumoc Alexander's door and throws him up against the wall in his nightshirt.

"Where are the Jewess and her child?" asks the Gestapo Captain as his black gloved hand goes for the helpless man's throat.

Struggling to find his voice beneath the hand gripping his voice box, Alexander says in husky whisper, "You are mistaken, I know nothing of this. What woman are you talking about?"

"You know what woman," accuses the Captain. "She lived next to you for twenty years. Her father was your best friend."

"But that was before I knew he was a Jew, he says squinting trying to keep the tears out of his eyes. "Today I wouldn't befriend a Jew. I don't even want to know a Jew. Please let go of my throat. I can't breathe."

"Maybe he's telling the truth," says the Lieutenant.

"No," says the Captain. "He's lying. Take a hammer to the walls, rip up the floor, poke around in the yard - I've seen them hide in holes. I won't have this stray bitch running around loose. I want no witnesses to Krasno. This woman must be found and shot this morning."

136

Turning back to his prisoner, the Captain says, "We will search for fifteen minutes, and if we don't find her in that time, you will be shot."

"Save your life," begs the Lieutenant. "Don't be a fool and die for a Jew."

"I have done nothing," pleads Alexander. I haven't seen this Jew or any other Jew. There are no Jews here. Believe me; I will never speak to Jew again. You can kill all you like, but why kill me. If I knew where a Jew was hiding, I would tell you."

"Then why are you protecting this woman?" asks the Captain. "We have reliable information that she came here to this house. If she is not here, then where is she?"

"I don't know, believe me," says a tearful, terrorized Alexander. "I'm a Catholic. Why should I help a Jew? Sure the man lived next door, but that was all. I never thought of him as a friend. He was just a damn Jew. I occasionally had a word with him about our fence line or exchanging labor, but I hardly knew his family or this woman you speak of. Don't shoot me. I believe in Jesus Christ, the son of God, the Holy Catholic Church and the Virgin Mary. I'm not a Jew. I've done nothing. There is no Jew in my house. Look, try Piortr's house on the other side of the river. Maybe she's there."

The Captain puts his pistol in the middle of Alexander's forehead and pulls the trigger. He is thrown straight back with eyes looking at the ceiling as blood fills up the eye sockets, and spills on to the floor.

"Why did you shoot him?" asks the Lieutenant as he grimaces and swallows to keep his breakfast down.

The Captain is surprised at the question and shows no sympathy for the Lieutenant's weak stomach. He is indifferent to the dead man at his feet. Finally he breaks the silence with a low husky voice, "I hate liars and cowards. He was groveling in the dirt. Let's go. It's over here, the Jewess is somewhere else. We will cross the river and go find this peasant, Piotr."

* * *

"Everyone knows I hate Jews," says Piotr as he sits at his kitchen table and smokes a cigarette with the Captain while the Lieutenant and three solders poke about the place. "The Jews killed Christ. I always hated them for that. If a Jew ever comes here, I will capture him for the bounty and tie him up like a goat. I could use the money. Search the place if you like. If you think I'm hiding Jews - shoot me. I'm dying anyway. Look at this hand - how it trembles. I can't keep it still. Each day is only pain and hurt. I can hardly walk for my rheumatism. I'm the only one left here. My family is all dead. There is no one to help me with the chores. My farm is going to hell - it's dying with me. How can I live here by myself? Do you think I'll make it through the winter? I don't have enough fire wood. I'll die tomorrow anyway. You might as well kill me - I'm tired of hurting."

"You aren't worth killing," scoffs the Captain getting up from the table. "Sergeant, grab the potatoes in the storeroom and put them in the truck. No point in wasting potatoes on a dying man."

Sonia hears the voices and footsteps over her head, and panic jumps from her stomach to her throat. She is praying, "Please God, don't let them see the trap door."

Above her Piotr is standing on the basement door with his hands on two bags of potatoes, saying to one of the enlisted men, "You grab the big bag and I'll take these two smaller ones." He is careful to let the soldier walk away first before he moves the potatoes hiding the door. When Piotr reaches the front door, another soldier takes his potatoes and jumps into the back of the truck.

"Remember the reward," says the Lieutenant from the front seat of the truck. "We are giving two hundred marks for these two Jews."

Piotr is breathing a sigh of relief as the truck drives away. He is wondering how an army that's fighting a war can afford to send a truck full of men out for even an hour hunting down a mother and a baby. All these machines and manpower are going to waste. He could put them to work on his farm that's falling apart for the lack of attention. If he ran a farm or any business in such a manner, it would be bankrupt overnight.

Back in the cab of the truck, the Lieutenant is trying to hide his sarcasm as he asks the Captain, "Why didn't you shoot him? He could have been lying too."

The Captain smiles at him and says, "Whenever you are trying to control a population, you must shoot a few people so they will respect and obey you. You are young - you will learn. Kumoc was a groveler. I hate weak people - they must be eliminated. Piotr was different, strong like a rock. He made me think of my grandfather in Bavaria. He lived near Munich on a small farm much like this one. Anyway, how can you intimidate a man who has no family and doesn't care if he lives or dies? Piortr has no fear of death. What's the fun of killing someone who is ready to die? Besides, I've already shot somebody today. A soldier's job is to kill the enemy. I've done my duty. I've killed one miserable groveling son-of-a-bitch."

"Kumoc had a good, well-kept farm," says the Lieutenant. "Some German will be lucky to get it."

Piotr waits until his neighbors are sleeping and then takes his sheep dog for a walk around the property. It is only then that he dares open the door to the cellar. He climbs down the steep steps with a lamp in his hand. Sonia stands up and stretches her legs. Rose is asleep on the blanket.

"How is the baby?" he asks as he holds the lamp so he can better see her.

"I think she is feeling better. She has just gone back to sleep," says Sonia with a warm smile. "You are so kind to take us in. How can we ever thank you enough?" she asks as she puts her arms around his shoulders and kisses his cheek.

"You just made me smile - no one has done that in a long time. Come upstairs," he says as he turns to climb the steps. "I have some soup on the stove and there's hot water for you to bathe."

"If you don't mind," she says as she follows him up the steps. "I think I will bathe before I eat. We still smell like Laura's pig-pen. I want to wash our clothes. Maybe you have something I can put on while they dry."

"Yes I have a warm nightshirt that will do just fine. I'll go to bed so you can have some privacy. The place is yours - I'm going to sleep. Tomorrow I will try to find the Partisans for you. I don't know of anyone else that can help you. The price on your head is twice the normal rate. Every bounty hunter in the area is looking for you."

21 November 1942

Before sunrise Piotr puts his guest in the basement. He hitches his horse to the sleigh and heads south toward the Partisan headquarters. The sun rises on a cold clear day. Piotr's face is wrapped like a mummy with small slits for the eyes. He keeps to the fields and back roads until he is well south of Gorodok and into the territory of Partisan control. He's been traveling for two hours and thinks he must be half way there when he spots a column of men walking single file on the road. Suddenly he is surrounded by six horsemen that he knows to be Partisans. One of them grabs the horse's reins and stops the sleigh.

"Where are you headed old man?" asks one of the horsemen.

"I'm looking for help," answers Piotr. "I'm hoping it's you. There is a young Jewish woman and her child hiding in my house outside of Gorodok. The Nazi's have doubled the normal bounty and are searching for her. They are the only survivors of the recent massacre at Krasno. Can you help us?"

"We know about her - perhaps we can help," says the spokes-man for the group. "We heard there was an outbreak of typhus at Krasno and everyone was infected. Does she look healthy?"

"Typhus? That's Nazi bullshit," says Piotr. "That was their excuse for killing them all. I know typhus, and she is not sick. She's strong, beautiful, and healthy as a horse."

"Then tell us where you live."

"It's simple to find," smiles Piotr. "I'm two kilometers this side of the river from Gorodok. Coming back this way from the bridge, it's the third farm on the north side of the road."

22 November 1942

At noon, a lone horseman with a rifle on his back rides up to Piotr's and bangs on the door.

"Who is it?" asks Piotr.

"It's Major Katkof, I talked to you yesterday. I've come to see the girl.

"Come in," he says as he opens the door. "I will take care of your horse later."

"Now to the point," he says as he places his rifle in the cor-ner and takes off his coat. "I don't have much time. Here's a stick of candy. Take the child for a ride in the sleigh. Do something, anything. Just leave for a couple of hours. I must be with the woman alone."

"What if she doesn't want to see you alone?" questions a concerned Piotr.

"Then I can't help her, and she will die and maybe you too."

Reluctantly Piotr says, "Come, I will take you to her."

Piotr opens the trap door and calls down the stairs, "Sonia, one of the Partisans is here to see you."

"Then send him down," she answers with enthusiasm.

"He wants to see you alone. So bring Rose up here and I will take care of her for a while."

She carries Rose to the top of the stairs and places her on the floor apprehensively. Her eyes dart nervously from one face to the other as she studies the two men. She hugs Rose and says, "You're going to play with your uncle Piotr."

Piotr holds out the candy. Rose smiles and takes the old man's hand. Katkof follows Sonia back down the steps, and Piotr shuts the trap door behind him. Sonia motions for him to sit. She takes the chair across from him and waits for him to speak."

"My name is Katkof. I am a Major in the Russian Army. I have been here for more than a year organizing the Partisan Army that is growing stronger every day."

"Yes," she says as she turns to him. "I would like to be a part of it."

"What can you do? Do you have a weapon, money, food, or anything of use? We have a rule that no one can join us empty-handed. We are not an orphanage but an army. Everyone must carry his own weight."

"I have always done my part. I have no money, no weapons, no food, nothing at all. I have only these two hands, and I am strong. I'm a hard worker - I can clean, wash, cook, sew, carry water, and chop wood."

"It looks like you know how to be a woman," he says as he looks into her eyes. "I could use a woman. I haven't been with a woman for more than a year. You are rough around the edges, but still beautiful. If you could spend a little time with me today, I could make you a Partisan tomorrow."

Sonia becomes quiet. After several fretful minutes, she speaks in resignation, "Just tell me what to do."

"You have a child. You know how to make love. That is all there is to it. Just think of me as your husband."

She doesn't move, so he becomes instructive. "I am spreading my bearskin coat down on your bed. You will take off your clothes while I take off mine. We will then lie down on the bed together."

"Just like that?" she asks in disbelief. "It's going to happen?"

"Yes," he answers. "Just like that. Now we will turn our backs to each other, take off our clothes and get in the bed."

She finishes undressing first and lies down on the black fur of the bearskin coat and pulls a blanket over her. He is muscular, husky and hairy with a deep scar across his stomach. He leans over and with his large hands neatly folds the blanket down to her waist. Apprehensively, she holds her arms at her side and lets him look at her. She is full breasted in spite of her thinness, and she is hard with defined muscles. Her skin is a bit grey and lacks color but still has the tightness of youth.

Katkof notices everything about her is tight and nothing is sagging or out of place. He finds her beautiful in spite of the hardness and definition of her muscles. He sees that she is cold and pulls the blanket back up to her neck. Everything is perfect for him except for her eyes that are vacant and staring right through him. He wants to shake her so that she will look at him. He wants her to love him or at least be affectionate. He wants her to want him. How can he do that? He is realizing that it's affection not sex that he needs most. No one on earth gives a damn for him - not the men in his command or his wife in Moscow.

Slowly he comes down on the bearskin and kneels beside her. She is so still and stiff that he doesn't know how to begin. He puts his hand gently on top of her head and pulls her long black hair up through his fingers and up to his nose. The hair smells clean and fresh. He starts to tremble as a shiver runs through his body. God, he loves women so much he wants to cry. Cry because they are so wonderful, and he has been without them for so long. He smiles, laughs at himself, and puts his hands on her shoulders and massages the tightness in her neck.

"Oh," she says as some of the tension leaves her shoulders. She is still sore from carrying Rose and the ordeal of her escape. His hands feel good on her muscles in spite of the fear in her chest.

"Roll over - I'll do your back," he says pleased with her response. "I'm good at this. I had a grandfather who made me massage his legs every night. I'm especially good with legs and feet."

She is becoming relaxed and no longer flinches to his touch. He works his way down her back, through her butt and down her legs to her feet and finally her toes. Finished, he places a blanket on her and wraps himself in another.

He gets up and opens a bottle of vodka from Piotr's stock. He turns it up and takes a swallow. He closes his eyes and inhales.

"The old man makes good spirits," he says on the exhale. Most of the stuff they make around here is bitter. I've had to spit out some of it. But this brew is smooth and goes down easy without a bite. He's got a gold mine here. You know, it's good to be in a house - even if it's only the basement. Here, drink this," he says kneeling back down to her."

"No thank-you," she says.

"Just a sip - it will warm you up. It's good. A little vodka helps the digestion. The peasants drink vodka for all kinds of aliments - it's good for you," he says as he puts the bottle to her lips. "Today we drink it just to relax and to forget about the war."

He puts it to her mouth, and she swallows, sputters, and gasps for breath.

"See, I told you it would warm you up."

She uses the back of her hand to wipe the excess off her face as her eyes look at the floor.

"Go ahead, have one more - make it a big one," he laughs as he puts the bottle to her lips, and again it runs out the corner of her mouth. "It will relax you. You need relaxing."

Like a child taking medicine, she swallows another mouthful with a grimace and says, "It's making me dizzy. I'm falling asleep."

"No," he laughs, as he pulls her chin up so their eyes meet. He kisses her gently on the lips and pulls back and searches her face for approval. He kisses her again, and they fall down into the bearskin coat.

She is frightened of his building passion, but allows him to kiss her breast. She now knows she can't stop it. It's happening. She closes her eyes and thinks of Pesach, so she can get through this. She knows she must please Katkof or she will die, and she is frantic to live - to live for her baby, for her Pesach, and to live for herself and to keep tasting life even if it is bitter. This may be the only chance to show that she is useful. He could be her protector and save them all. Pesach would understand - survival is more important. She has not one single ruble or anything else to bribe him with.

Katkof is thinking of his wife a thousand miles away. He can't ever remember feeling as passionate as he is with this docile, timid woman. She is deep, complex and beautiful. Is she his for the moment or longer? He doesn't want it to end. He is already thinking of another time.

Finally he is exhausted. They lie together under the blanket holding each other. He is holding on to the moment - savoring the memory. She is holding on for her life, and Katkof is her life jacket. Together they doze off.

Katkof wakes up first, hears the rumble of the old man upstairs and shakes Sonia. She opens her eyes and looks at the ceiling, and then at the floor as she gets up and starts to dress. He puts on his pants and wishes he didn't have to go back so soon. He has already stayed too long. Together they dress and clean up. She is feeling almost comfortable with him as he embraces and kisses her good-by.

Katkof climbs the steps and pushes open the trap door, looks down at her, and says, "Be ready to leave early tomorrow morning. Grishka will be your company commander. He will pick you up on the way back from his assignment. Your job will be to cook, wash clothes and help guard the camp. You will be part of the support troops. I'll see you soon."

He closes the basement door and turns to Piotr with a handshake and says, "Thank-you my friend, we have two more brave Partisans. I have also made friends with your Vodka. I hope you don't mind me taking a few bottles - it is excellent."

"Help yourself, take all you want. I only use it for my rheumatism. Thank you for helping us. And please, get these damn Nazis out of here."

Sonia is sobbing in the basement trying to clear her head of her sex for life bargain with the Russian devil. Now that the deal is made, when will it stop?

23 November 1942

It is not yet light when Grishka pounds on the door. "Piotr, it's Grishka."

"Come in," says Piotr. "Warm yourself by the fire. It's been a cold night to be out."

"The Partisans' must eat in any kind of weather," he says as he knocks the snow off his boots and stoops through the door. "I'm out gathering provisions again. Can you spare some potatoes?"

"Grishka!" Sonia exclaims as she steps away from the fire to hug him. "Thank God you've come for us."

"My darling Sonia, I'm glad to see you that you're alive. I think you and Rose must be the only survivors of Krasno. For the life of me, I don't understand why Katkof is taking you in. He is not sentimental. It is not like him to be generous or sympathetic to Jews or even to Russians. He is all business. Emotions never get in his way. He has never taken in a woman by herself with a child and no weapon. What did you give him? You must have bribed him with something."

Sonia and Piotr silently look into the fire. Finally Sonia says, "I gave him a ten ruble coin that I had sewn in my coat."

Grishka looks at her skeptically and changes the subject with, "In Krasno, did you see anything of my wife?"

Sonia looks into his eyes with sympathy and says, "She was so very depressed, the last time I saw her. She was still mourning the death of her boys and wondering if you were alive. She had lost the will to live and no longer cared what happened.

She made me promise to take care of you, if she should die. She must have been murdered with the rest of them."

"I have bad news for you too," he says with tears in his eyes as he pulls her into another hug. "Pesach was shot and killed by our Partisans. The same people I've been gathering food for killed our Pesach."

"How did it happen?" whispers a stunned Sonia.

He can feel her sobbing on his shoulder as he speaks. "It was done on our doctor's orders. He said that anybody from Krasno was infected with typhus and must be executed. Katkof pulled the trigger."

Chapter 15

Grocery Shopping

December 1942

Heavy fighting continues in Guadalcanal. Rommel is retreating to his final corner in North Africa. The US has been in the war one year. The Luftwaffe flies in meager supplies to the German troops trapped at Stalingrad. The first nuclear reaction is initiated at the University of Chicago. Gasoline rationing starts in the US.

16 December 1942, in a village near a large German garrison on the outskirts of Minsk

A large lopsided moon upstages the stars and throws the heavens out of balance as it slips up through the crack between earth and sky. Hanah finds the brutally bright light an unwelcome intruder. Instinctively she pulls back into the shadows of the trees.

Hanah hasn't relaxed for a moment on her first night out with Grishka's guerillas. She is a stranger here and not yet accepted or proven herself to be useful. She and the others are huddled on the banks of a frozen stream in a wooded ravine on the outskirts of Minsk. Like most military operations, it's hurry up and wait. Even though she's saddle sore from the long ride, she's now ready to hurry again and do something to be warm. For hours she's been wrapped in her coat and blanket, half awake, in a silence of cold, musky men. They don't risk talking or dare lighting a fire as they wait for the village to put itself to sleep. She tries to ignore the cold biting her nose, fingers and toes. She bends over and pulls her blanket tighter about her. In spite of the pain of frostbite and being away from her Yehuda, she can still smile and think herself privileged and lucky to be free and at last fighting back. By a miracle she has escaped the Nazi net that has eliminated most everyone she knew.

Crash, plop, splash goes Ele's ax as it breaks through a thin place in the ice to the cold creek water. Hanah takes a turn with the dipping gourd as it is passed around. After a quick drink, she brushes the water away from her mouth and blots her lips to keep them from chapping.

They wait on the edge of a village of collaborators who are holding stockpiles of meat and dry goods less than two kilometers from the German's garrison at Minsk. Traveling at night and on horseback, skirting around villages, and slipping quietly through the forest, it has taken Grishka's company all night and most of a day to cover the sixty kilometers of snow from the swamps of Naliboki. After a few hours rest, they are now ready to help themselves to the German food stocks. In the distance, Hanah can see flares shooting up into the sky and bursting into fire balls that throw a ring of daylight around the forest surrounding the garrison.

A flash from a bright flare causes Grishka's black beard to shine as he stands, holds up his hands for attention, and speaks in a husky voice just above a whisper. "Every day we have more mouths to feed, and we need to stockpile for a blockade that we know is coming. Our troops are out of meat, salt and flour. If we return empty handed, we could be the next meal. These peasants feel safe, because they are so close to German protection. Tonight, they will know there is no safe place for collaborators. Now a word for the new recruits: the enemy is not expecting us to be so brazen as to come here under the noses of so many Nazis. So we will surprise them. Don't give anyone a chance to grab a gun. If we are quiet and careful, we won't have any trouble. These peasants are used to being shoved around - just let them know you are the boss. As long as you are holding the gun, they will obey you. We now have the night to ourselves, and soon we will own the day. Whatever happens, I don't expect the Germans to leave their barricades until morning. It will be like going to a well-stocked market, and they have everything we need."

"Then they have women?" interjects the gravel voice of tall, bug-eyed Fogel. A twisted smile creeps across his long bony face. The large left eye set clearly below the right gives a lecherous wink to the group as he waits for an answer.

"Yes, plenty of women. Beautiful, sexy Russian girls," says Grishka playing off Fogel's joke. "But for you, Fogel, there are only pigs."

After the muffled laughter dies down, Fogel looks dreamy eyed and ready to embrace the imaginary lover cuddled in his arms as he continues in a soft voice, "I love pigs too - they're so squirmy and squealing, and they give you all they got. When I was a young boy..."

"Enough! Time is of the essence" says Grishka holding up both hands for silence. "Fogel, after you lead us in, it will be your job to put a dead pig into each wagon. Wrap your pistol in a blanket to muffle the sound and shoot her between the eyes. And when you go in to scout things out, take Hanah with you. Send her back to us when you see things are clear. When we move in, Hanah will position herself halfway between you and us, so she can keep us both in sight and pass on your stop or go signal. We will try to stay about fifty meters back. You will keep waving us on as we go. All the while be looking for cows, horses, pigs and dry goods. First we must find six wagons and harness them up with the peasants' horses. Each platoon will be responsible for two wagons. I want them filled to the brim with meat, flour, cheese, butter, beans - whatever you can find. And tie a cow to the left corner of each wagon."

"One question," asks Fogel as he uses his rifle as a crutch to stand up.

"What?" ask Grishka expecting the worst.

"When will I have time to be with my pig?"

"When it's cooked," says Grishka rolling his eyes and holding up his hands to stop the laughter. He has lost his sense of humor as he commands, "Hush, quiet! You're getting too loud. Now go - it's time to work. If things go wrong, disperse. We will regroup south of here in the village of Shalyk. Stay in the shadows, walk quietly and be alert."

"Why do you keep doing this?" asks Sabitai.

"Doing what?" asks Grishka acting naive to the question he knows is coming.

"Sending Fogel in first." says Sabitai as he watches Fogel and Hanah disappear into the shadows. In fact - putting up with Fogel at all."

"Like me, he's a peddler. He knows this country like the back of his hand. He's quick, good with a gun, an excellent horseman, and he never panics."

"The guy's too crazy to be afraid."

"We are all crazy. Think of it. We fight a war against the most mechanized army ever - with trained troops and the best of everything. He laughs and continues. "And what do I have? It's funny to say it. A homemade bomb, a few shells in an old Polish rifle and Fogel." Grishka laughs again, "Let's hope we will find sanity when the war is over, but for now, a man must be crazy and do the impossible. Look, there is no one better at making war than you my friend, but you are too valuable to lose. You are the man to take over if something happens to me. I can't put you at risk by sending you in first."

Sabitai pouts, "If you won't listen, I'll speak to God. "Please God", begs Sabitai. "Don't let this joker get us killed." After a pause, he turns back to Grishka and continues, "Now you've seen the way he eats his soup - it seeps out the corners of his mouth and drips into his beard and onto his clothes. He's just that sloppy with everything else. I don't trust him to do anything right."

"But he cleans himself up after each meal," says Grishka. "Somehow he survives."

Sabitai is in a defeated silence.

"Trust me," says Grishka putting his arm around Sabitai's shoulders. "If there is anything he can do, it's this. Everyone has his niche, and Fogel has found his."

"He's had so many close calls," says Sabitai. "He should be dead already."

"Yes, we should all be dead," laughs Grishka. "None of us has had as many chances to die. Unlike a cat, Fogel has ninety-nine lives."

"Then he's on number one hundred," grunts Sabitai.

"Then it will soon be your turn to play the fool," smiles Grishka. "Someone must keep us laughing through this tragedy. I say Fogel, and everyone smiles. We all need to laugh - some of us have forgotten how. Fogel has a talent for throwing things off balance and then bringing it back together. He's clumsy like a clown doing a tightrope walk. The rope shakes and jerks and the clown waves his arms wildly about, but he doesn't fall off. At the end of the act, when he jumps off the wire; he lands on his head, does a somersault and stands up with a big wide grin."

"Fogel certainly keeps me on my toes," says Sabitai. "So much so I'm becoming a ballerina. I'm always wondering how he's going to screw up and what I have to do to save myself. It's a dance I'm tired of doing."

"That reminds me," smiles Grishka. "Because there's this mistrust of what he is doing, he keeps us thinking and ready to act."

Sabitai laughs and says, "Shit. If ever the Russians want to court-martial me - please, Grishka, be my lawyer."

Now well into the village, Fogel gives the all clear signal to Hanah, who relays it on to Grishka. The company moves single file in two columns quietly through the shadows on either side of the road. Rifles are raised with bullets in chambers. Intermittent flares keep throwing an uncomfortable strobing light on the two moving columns.

Grishka waves Sabitai's squad toward a cottage on Sabitai's side of the road. The first front door is kicked in and swings open to a quiet warm room lit yellow by flickering fire light. Sabitai steps in to find three half-grown children, the parents and a grandmother all under blankets lying around the brick stove in the main room.

"Search for weapons, tie and gag them," instructs Sabitai. "Hush, not a sound out of any of you. If anybody moves, everybody will be shot and the house burned. Understand? No mercy for collaborators."

"You, Papa," orders Grishka as he uses his rifle to poke the pudgy, wide-eyed peasant in the belly. "Put on your coat and come with me to the barn, and hurry - your ass depends on it."

In back of the cottage, Fogel has found a shed full of pigs. With his pistol muffled in a blanket, he is quietly shooting them in the head. One at a time, Hanah drags the half-grown pigs out to the road on a small sled. Across the road, Ele and his platoon are opening a barn.

"Look, we won't have to go far to find what we need," says Ele. "It's all here - flour, corn, and dried beans. Harness the horses and hitch up the wagon."

In quick order everything is done, and they are on the road. Grishka has it down to a science. Each of the six wagons is loaded with dry goods and one of Fogel's dead pigs with a reluctant cow tied to the wagon and trailing behind. Hanah is driving and Fogel is riding shotgun in the last wagon behind Sabitai's.

Hanah is silent and fuming. She wishes her friend Sonia was here. Finally, she can stand it no longer. Like the relief of constipation, she fires the question like a bullet, "Why, do you make jokes about women and pigs? Do you know the difference?"

Fogel laughs, "Wasn't it a good one? Don't you like jokes? Somebody needs to make jokes - for God's sake and mine. This is the grimmest group, I've ever seen. Everybody forgot how to laugh. But it's not only laughing I want. I'm just trying to remind our commander that we have needs - even the lowest ranking soldier, like me. And that we are all human beings. Just because he has a girlfriend that is taking care of him, he thinks everyone else should be happy too. Well, we're not. I need a woman. God damn it, I need a woman! Can you understand? I'm tired of just existing. Who can be alive without laughter and a woman?"

Indifferent to Fogel's needs, Hanah lets her anger pass in silence. Finally after she cools, her curiosity gets the best of her and she asks, "Who is Grishka's girlfriend? Do I know her?"

"Sonia Essers," says Fogel with a role of his eyes. "Need I tell you? It's obvious," he says with a grand gesture. He realizes he's not getting through, so he continues, "Look at it for yourself, she spends more time in his hut than hers. I see it in her eyes - she worships him. She would do anything in the world for him. Wake up. It's right in front of you. Maybe you don't want to see it."

He pauses and thinks a minute before he decides to prick her with an insult. "You're the typical educated, intellectual, scientific type, so you only understand books. I'll write it down, draw you a picture, and put it in a book - then you'll understand. Look, they have both lost their families. There's no reason for them not to be together."

"Except that they've had their hearts ripped out," says Hanah with compassion. "Sonia has lost everyone except her baby. Grishka has lost his wife and two boys and has no blood relation alive. They're both still grieving. There is too much sorrow there for the joy of love. No," says Hanah shaking her head. "He's like a big brother to her."

"And a big dick to her," Fogel adds emphatically. "It's possible to be both. Right?"

Hanah, offended and exasperated, takes a breath to relieve her anger and continues. "Yes, it's possible, but not likely. Grishka wouldn't take advantage of his position."

"He's the one on top, if you're talking about position. In such a position, with such a woman, he'd be a fool not to take advantage. Grishka is no fool, and don't think he doesn't take advantage. Everyone is seduced by power and uses what power he has to get what he needs."

"I will never believe that about Grishka."

"Believe it," says Fogel with a shake of the finger. "And she is not so innocent. She's using Grishka as a shield to hide from Major Katkof - who's crazy about her. She's frightened of him. You know she had a thing with Katkof before she joined us. I heard him talking about it when he was drinking. It was like an initiation fee. As long as she is with Grishka, she thinks Katkof will leave her alone. Can you believe what our old Russian buddy did to her? First he shot her husband in the head, and a week later he fucks her."

"Enough," says Hanah. "I don't want to know all the gossip."

"Don't worry," says Fogel. "You won't. Not even I, with both ears to the ground, know everything." He pauses and looks at her with desire and continues. "I always thought Yehuda was a smart man. He was always an excellent student. Until now I didn't know his intelligence went beyond the books, but now I see it does. He has my profound respect. The man is a genius."

"Are you making fun of us?"

"No," says Fogel with a wide admiring smile. "I'm complimenting you and him on his choice of a woman and the wisdom of bringing a lady such as you to this womanless hell."

Hanah bites her lip and doesn't respond. She knows the conversation will never end, and it's getting too personal and vulgar. She knows that Fogel will continue talking even without her participation. She takes a deep breath and lets go of the tension and tries to relax into quietness as she watches Fogel take a sip of vodka. The argument has been exasperating for her. Both are tired to the point of being simple. She is thinking this argument is a waste of precious energy.

They are following close on the heels of a fat brown milk cow that is being jerked along by a rope tied to the wagon in front of them. Fogel is mesmerized as he watches the cow's hypnotic hip movement and the large udder swinging between her legs. They are both drifting into mindless relaxation. Fogel is just a few nods from sleep. Like after a big meal, Hanah is feeling full and satisfied with the night's work. She is impressed by the efficiency of the operation and thinks nothing could be more perfect on this first night out.

A loud piercing screech breaks the silence and is followed by a scream from the horse.

"It's our pig. He's alive and running around the back of the wagon," shouts Hanah. "Do something.

Fogel turns in his seat, draws his pistol and starts shooting at the pig. Hanah tightens up the reins in an attempt to control the frightened horse. Immediately, flares start flying and mortar shells start dropping - the Nazi's are awake and are shooting off multiple flashes making the world bright as a summer day.

Despite Hanah's efforts, the startled horse charges for the woods and the wagon wrecks as the front wheels fall into a snow filled ditch. Hanah and Fogel are thrown clear of the wagon. The horse breaks free and pulls the harness through the woods and out of sight. None of Fogel's bullets have hit anything critical enough to impair the mobility or the screech of the pig, which is still trapped in the wagon. Flares are lighting up the sky above them and mortar shells are hitting all around. Shell fragments are striking their wagon ripping through the canvas. Hanah finds her rifle in the snow and crawls toward the other side of the road. Fogel runs about twenty meters, dives for the ditch, and lands on a groaning Grishka who has just claimed the spot.

Without seeing his face, Grishka knows the man on top of him by his size and smell. He pushes him away as he screams, "You drunk, clumsy, stupid bastard."

The other wagons are being pulled off the road as their drivers dive for the bushes. They hug the ground and hold on to their hats as mortar shells continue to explode around them. The frightful bellowing of cows and whinnying of horses joins the piercing shrieks of the pig. It all makes a chaotic chorus that is joined by the whistles, booms, crashes, and the screams of sirens. A quiet starry night turns to pandemonium complemented by the appearance of a peculiarly lopsided moon.

All the wagons are now in the cover of the trees except the one abandoned by Hanah and Fogel that is still stuck in the ditch with its ass end in the road and its pig still protesting in shrill agonizing screams. Besides being the cause of this ruckus, Fogel has the added worry of having left his rifle in the wagon. The consequences of returning to camp without one's rifle are well known. The Russians will not be sympathetic or want to hear excuses. Fogel will be court-martialed and shot the day he returns. So he can never go back to camp without his rifle.

"For God's sake, you stupid bastard, crawl to the wagon and get your damn rifle," orders an angry Grishka, still wincing from Fogel's bad landing. "And do something with that damn pig."

"I'll go," volunteers Sabitai.

"No, this is Fogel's mess," shouts Grishka. "He's making us all look like fools. I'd rather see him die in action than shot by a firing squad. I don't know how to report this trouble. I don't want to report it, and I won't have to say anything, if he can get his rifle."

Fogel gets ready to meet God. If he stays or goes - it's all the same. He's a dead man. Maybe this is God's way of telling him to stay away from pigs.

Like a snake, with his belly hugging the frozen ground, he wiggles out of the ditch and across the icy gravel road toward the disabled wagon. Fogel's wagon is on a serious tilt with its front end in the ditch and a slowly spinning right rear wheel dangling in the air.

"He will be the death of us," grunts Sabitai.

Mortar shells are dropping on either side of the wagon. Everyone is waiting for the one that will hit in the middle and blow it all to bits. Somehow Fogel gets there alive. Up on his knees and reaching over his head, he fumbles at the tailgate. Finally the tailgate opens and out leaps the pig - diving over Fogel's right shoulder. The shrill squeal turns to a solid grunt as he hits the road and is off squealing through the woods. Fogel grabs his rifle and dives to the ground crawling. He is barely ten meters away hugging the bottom of the shallow ditch when a mortar shell hits the wagon. The blast is followed by soft and heavy sounds of debris hitting the ground. Sifted flour is thick in the air and blowing around in swirls of silence. All is quiet except for the faint cries of a dying cow. Fogel doesn't move even to breathe. Finally he takes a deep breath of flour and coughs and sneezes. He clears his lungs and spits. He is content to be still and caress his precious rifle as he becomes white with flour. He is cherishing the peaceful moment, when he finds the toes of two boots in his face. He looks up and sees Grishka shaking his head.

"With all the flour on you, you look like you belong to a bakery. Fogel, have you ever thought of being a cook?"

"No," says Sabitai. "He looks more like a bagel, ready to be baked. Please, don't cook. Who could eat it?"

"Fogel," says Grishka shaking his head. "I would make you ride your cow home, but she's dead. It's a wonder we all aren't dead. I don't know how to punish you. If I were a Russian commander I would just pull out my pistol and put a bullet through your stupid head, but I don't have bullets to waste and too many Jews are dead. The Russians will shoot me, if they find out that I let you live - so don't go bragging about this catastrophe and how we got through it. I know how you like to talk, but don't. This is one joke you can't tell. If you say anything, I will do my duty and shoot you between the eyes. That is a promise. The same goes for anybody who talks about what happened tonight. This is just between us. Fogel, take my horse and ride up ahead. You'll be the lead man until we get to Shylic. The rest of you guys get your wagons back on the road and let's get the hell out of here. Hanah, you lie down in the back of my wagon and get some rest. You might have some wounded to tend to before we get home."

For hours there is only the clip-clop and snorting of horses and the squeak, rattle and bump of wagons. The first streaks of dawn are reflecting gold and purple on the horizon.

Everything is so quiet," says Sabitai with disbelief. "Like there is no war. No guns, no Germans - nothing. No one ever came out of the garrison. No one is in pursuit. Do they think they killed us all?"

"They won't know until the sun is up," says Grishka. That's when the rats come out of their holes. Since the battle has turned against them at Stalingrad," says Grishka. "They've lost their confidence, courage and the sharpness of the winning edge. They can no longer believe in Hitler. They are a wounded bull - it's time to cut off their balls."

"Look up ahead, it's Fogel," says Sabitai. "He's signaling us to stop."

"I saw some people crossing the road," says Fogel as he gallops up and draws up his reins. "They went into the woods over there. You wait here until I find out who they are."

"Yes, check it out," says Grishka. "We've had trouble here before. This place is good for an ambush. Don't go back up the road - circle around through the woods."

Fogel swats his horse with the reins and is off leaping through the woods. He finds some tracks in the snow and soon sees two small figures stumbling through the knee-deep snow. He pulls his horse up in front of two children.

"Stop or I'll shoot!" commands a voice from the bushes. "Drop your rifle. Put your hands on top of your head and come down from your horse slowly."

Fogel obeys by dropping his rifle in the snow, slipping off his horse and turning toward the voice. He sees no one but a snow covered bush.

"Who are you," the voice asks?

"I'm just a poor peasant - looking for a cow that got out of the barn," says Fogel as he sees a boy who looks to be twelve come up behind him and pick up his rifle and admire it like it's a most marvelous thing. A younger girl is hanging behind the boy looking shy and afraid.

"Be careful, it's ready to shoot, "says Fogel leaning toward the boy in an attempt to instruct him.

That's far enough," says the bush.

In a split second Fogel decides it's time to act. He lunges for the boy, grabs the gun, hits the ground and puts two rounds into the talking bush.

"Stop! I give up," the bush screams in panic. "Don't shoot. I give up."

A large muscular man of about thirty steps out from behind the bush with his hands on top of his head and says. "I'm trying to help these kids. I knew their parents. The man pauses, studies Fogel and finally says, "We looking to join the Partisans."

"You've found them," says Fogel.

"Sorry," says the man sheepishly. "I thought you were a bounty hunter or collaborator. I haven't seen any friendly people with guns. These kids are Jewish. They survived the massacre at Minsk."

"Put your hands down, and go get your gun."

"I have no gun," says the man.

"What, no gun. You had me fooled. But you almost got yourself killed. Can you find a gun? You need a gun to become a Partisan."

"Yes, says the man with hesitation. "I keep an army rifle under my bed."

"I admire your courage," says Fogel holding out his hand. "I really thought you had a gun. What's your name?"

"Merlitz," says the man taking Fogel's hand.

"Forget the gun," says Fogel admiring the man's size and feeling his strength in the handshake. "You're so damn big - they will take you without a gun. You'd make a good Partisan. You and the kids come with me. If Grishka likes you, we will get your gun. Oh, call me Fogel."

"OK, Fogel," Says Merlitz. "We will follow you. Show me where to sign-up, I'm ready to be a Partisan."

"Me too," says the boy. "My name is Taicia. This is my sister Betty. Just before father died, he told us to run, hide, and try to find the Partisans."

"Taicia, my man, you're lucky," says Fogel. "Most people don't ever find us. And then we can't take everybody in and still fight a war. We will see what Grishka says. He has a big heart - I think you will be of use, and he will say yes. You've gotten this far - God must be on your side."

Fogel mounts his horse and motions for the boy and girl to climb on. With his foot he gives Taicia the stirrup and holds out a hand, and the boy swings in behind him. Merlitz places the girl in the saddle in front of Fogel.

"Follow me out to the Road," says Fogel. "The kids are cold. I'll put them under some blankets."

Fogel kicks his black horse in the ribs and they leap off toward the wagons with Merlitz trotting behind.

"What have you got here," asks Grishka.

"Taicia and Betty, survivors of the Minsk Massacre, they are traveling with this man, Merlitz. He is hoping that we will take them. He also wants to be a Partisan.

"Here, put them in my wagon," says Grishka as he reaches out and grabs them from Fogel. He accepts the boy with a hug and tears well up in his eyes. Hanah takes the girl in her lap and rubs her limbs to make her warm. Never have children looked so beautiful.

"I can see why this man wanted to save you," smiles Grishka. "You are so perfect and precious and bright. Who could let you die? Don't be afraid - you are safe now. Nothing can harm you. We'll find a place for you in the next village. I know some people there. I will give them a pig and they will take you in and treat you as their own. Don't worry. In a few days I'll come back and get you. I will tell the Russians that you are my own children. They like me, so they will like you."

"Are you my new family?" ask the girl with hope.

Grishka feels warm inside as he looks into her crystal clear innocence and wipes a tear from his eye. He leans over with a smile bursting from his heart and says, "Yes, Betty. Call me Papa."

Chapter 16

Katkof and Sonia

16 December 1942, 9:00 PM, At a Partisan camp, Naliboki Forest

A large lopsided moon rises through the leafless trees, pushes its long bright fingers across the snow into the swamp's blackness and pulls at Sonya's emptiness. All day she loved in a trance, as she smiled, skipped and floated as carefree as a snow flake. She blinks and blots a love tear and hopes she will see her Grishka soon. She must tell him how the depression has lifted, and of hopes to go to Palestine. She wants to be lying next to him with Rose on her other side. The thought of Rose brings guilt up into her throat. She left Rose to sleep alone with her nightmares.

She needs Grishka for more than comfort. She needs a defender. Will she survive Katkof? He won't take no for an answer. Damn! Why did she ever sleep with the bastard? Now he wants her every night, forever. And she never wanted him for a minute.

Ever since she washed the dinner dishes, she's been carrying his army rifle that's becoming as heavy as her eyelids. She wasn't ever issued a gun, but Katkof gave her one of his and put her on the command post for the entire night. The usual watch is four hours, but she is doing twelve as punishment and persuasion. Somehow he thinks this sort of intimidation will force her to submit.

Every day she washes, cooks, cleans, tends children, and is up before dawn, feeding fires and men - then falling down exhausted at night. Her life keeps time with chickens and babies.

She never stood watch before. Or even shot a gun. Who could stay up all night after such a day? The hell with him - maybe she will just lie down and go to sleep. Does he dare do anything? Whatever Katkof does, he will have to answer to Grishka, who because of his strength, leadership and expertise in feeding them is the most valuable Partisan in the camp. An angry, fearless Grishka would kill him regardless of consequences. But her protector is not here, so she won't take a chance or do anything to aggravate Katkof. He is too insanely drunk and beyond reason.

Katkof has been too afraid of Grishka to do anything to her. But tonight, he has found courage in vodka and is trying to bully her to bed. Stand watch or come to him - that's the choice he is giving her. If she falls asleep on guard duty, according to military law, she can be shot on the spot.

Damn him! Why can't she just pull the trigger on him before he kills her? No, she can stay up all night without blinking even once. She stayed awake for three days when she escaped with Rose. What is one night - thirty-six hours or however long it takes for Grishka to get home? She can do it, by God. No one is stronger than she. She will beat the son-of-a-bitch Katkof like she beat the Nazis, at whatever game he's playing. Just wait till Grishka gets home; he will put an end to Katkof.

Fifty meters away, she can see a hatless Katkof stumble out of his hut. As he gets closer, she can see him, red faced, sweaty, with his hair matted to his head, and a bottle of vodka poking out of his coat. He looks red enough to have fallen in the fire. Sight provokes the smell she knows is coming - alcohol oozing through his skin and stinking in his breath. She is becoming nauseous as he approaches. If he tries to kiss her, she knows she can't help but throw up.

"You look tired, my darling, "he says with tender slurred concern as he blinks his red swollen eyes and holds out his hand. When the hand is refused by a nod of the head, it closes into a fist.

"Come with me," he pleads. "The hut is warm for you. The covers are turned down. I have cheese, fresh bread, caviar, fruit, chocolate and even a good red wine. I've been saving everything for you."

You should share it with the others," she says trying to stop his advance. "Everyone is hungry tonight. No one has had enough to eat. Besides I've had my treat. Grishka bought me all of that the last time he went out."

"Fuck Grishka," he spits. "I'll kill the son-of-a-bitch, Grishka. Grishka! I don't want to hear his fucking name! Ever again! Grishka is dead. Or soon will be. Like a small street kid, Grishka's out trying to pick the pocket of the big bully. One day he will get caught and hanged. He won't survive the jobs I'm giving him. Like tonight, he goes up against the garrison at Minsk. Twenty men against two-thousand. Do you really think he's coming back? Forget him. He's gone. He never existed. That's an order. Understand? Forget him!"

"Please," she says with forced composure. "Go to bed and get some sleep."

Don't die," he says in a sad whisper. "I didn't save you from the bloodhounds for this. It's suicide. I won't let you kill yourself. You can't stay up all night. Please, I can't live without you. Come to bed with me. If you stay here..., you'll fall asleep, and I'll have to shoot you... As a soldier and son of Mother Russia, I must obey her. I love Russia as I love you, but I must do my duty. Don't make me kill you!"

"Don't worry," she says sympathetically. "You won't have to kill me, because I won't fall asleep. I too, love Mother Russia, so I am going to stay here and do my watch as my commander ordered. Don't worry about me. Go to bed."

"Not without you my darling," he says with a cock-eyed twisted, rubber faced smile. "You don't understand the danger you're in. You don't know how sleep will slip up on you when you're not looking, and bam - you're dead as a door nail. You'll never wake up, if you go to sleep."

"Go to bed," she says firmly. "You're drunk."

"You go to bed," he shouts. "As your commander I say forget any other orders. Come to bed now. That's the order."

"As my commander you can order me to fight, make preparations for battle and do many other things, but private relations are my own."

"It's too cold out here," he says with a shiver of disappointment. "I'm going back in and sit by the fire and eat something and drink my wine." He steals a wet kiss from her cheek and turns away.

With revulsion, she tries to wipe away his slobber and smell of alcohol. He doesn't look back but keeps moving toward the open door of his hut. She is left with his stink in her nose, but she won't let herself throw up - food is too precious to loose.

A chill runs up her back and stops in her head. Her face becomes twisted in worry. How close is death? Is this guy crazy enough to shoot her? Will Grishka get back in time? Should she run? No, he would find her and have an excuse to execute her.

Fright for her life and worry for Rose are keeping her awake. She couldn't sleep if she wanted too. She has flash backs to the work camp and a guard that wanted her. He dragged her by the foot underneath the barracks. She bit his ear, pushed him off, and was able to get away. This dilemma will not resolve itself. And there is no one in camp who can help. Anybody who's well enough is off foraging for supplies or blowing up trains. There is no one here who could stand up to him. She thinks of leaving her post and getting help, but that would be desertion of duty and a firing squad.

She laughs and whispers, "If the Germans don't shoot me, the Russians will."

The moon is falling in the sky. Soon it will be daylight. People will be moving around, and she will be somewhat safer. She is beginning to think Katkof has passed out when she sees the door of his hut open, and spilling yellow light onto the snow. Katkof starts out with a stumble and wobbles toward her. He is even more drunk than before.

"Come here!" He shouts. "You God-damn whore. You fuck-ing bitch. You had better be awake, or you're dead."

Instinctively she pulls back the bolt and puts a bullet in the chamber, points the rifle at him, and aims to shoot. Maybe if she can hit him in the leg, she would be able to stay away from him until Grishka got home. She has him in her sights. Her finger pulls at the trigger, but it won't budge. She pulls again, but nothing happens. The gun won't fire. In a panic she freezes.

He grabs the rifle by the barrel and yanks it away from her. "Hah! Caught you sleeping," he shouts with gleeful meanness.

"No! I wasn't sleeping," she protests. "Who could sleep with you lurking about? I haven't even blinked. Give the gun back. I haven't finished my watch."

"You're finished," He shouts. "You neglected your duty. You fell asleep, and must be executed," he says coldly as his finger shoves off the safety, and pulls the trigger. The bullet shatters her skull, as she falls back into the snow.

Chapter 17

The Ambush

January 1943

Soviet Troops launch an all-out attack at Stalingrad and renew attacks at Leningrad and the Caucasus. The Russians have Germans trapped in a pocket west of Stalingrad.

January 3, 1943, 20 kilometers west of Minsk

The midmorning sun is a diffused orange glow in the grey sky. A winter storm has left the earth frozen, flat, and knee deep in wind swept snow. It is still and quiet with no sign of a human. Suddenly the silence is broken by grunts of Grishka and slaps of the whip as he drives his horse through the pristine whiteness. The large black stallion puffs steam from flared nostrils. Hooves slash at the snow and eyes bulge as the horse strains to outrun Grishka's whip.

Except for an island of dark woods in the distance, the world is white. The fresh snow is marked only by a narrow trail that he knows was made by Katkof's horse. Grishka's attention is distracted by the sting of tears freezing on his red cheeks. He blots his face and pulls the fallen scarf tight about his head, so only the slits of his eyes are exposed to the bite of the cold. As he wipes the blur out of his vision with the back of his glove, he sees a horseman in a fur cap and coat leaving the island of woods three hundred meters in front of him. In a matter of seconds, Grishka pulls his rifle up on his shoulder and puts his finger to the trigger. Half the trigger finger has been cut out of the glove on his right hand, so he feels the cold steel shooting through his hand. The crack of the bullet bounces off the trees and dies in the vast silence. The horse in the distance falls head first, throwing the rider out in front. Katkof lifts up out of the snow and begins dragging himself toward the cover of his broken horse. Without moving the rifle from his shoulder, Grishka pulls off two more rounds. Katkof flinches twice as he is shot.

Grishka rides up, pulls up his reins and swings down from his horse with his gun pointed at the crumpled body. Cautiously he approaches Katkof who is motionless and face down in the snow with his horse spewing blood, snorting and trying to get up without the help of a damaged rear leg. For a second Grishka's attention is distracted as he turns to the damaged animal and pulls the trigger. Another crack of the rifle puts an end to the horse's efforts. His stallion jerks at the reins that are still in his left hand. Two more steps bring him to the body sprawled on the snow. Grishka is anxious to see if Katkof is still breathing. He pokes the black bear coat in the ribs with the point of his rifle. He jabs harder, but there is no response. Seized by anger, he turns him over with a kick of a boot to see the dead frozen face of his Sonia.

Grishka's black eyes open as he pushes the straw out of his face and sits up in a shiver, trying to shake loose from the chill of his dream. He pulls the army blanket tight about him. His eyes stare into the darkness of a cold barn. Breathing thick heavy steam and exhausted from a restless night's sleep, he is still thinking of Katkof and poor Sonia. He wonders if he will ever see Katkof again, or if time will allow the luxury of looking for him. Did he run back to Moscow? Was he transferred to another unit? The Russians are stupid and indifferent to his whereabouts.

It's not yet daylight. He begins seeing the sleeping, snoring bodies of the troops spread out about him. Like him, they are tired enough to sleep until noon. The nightmare has been a good alarm clock. Hot off of a supply mission, they are tired and short on sleep.

In the far corner of the barn he spots a lump in a blanket that he knows is Hanah. It makes him think of harsh, bureaucratic rules that allow husbands and wives to be together only on holidays and this is not a holiday.

Together with Ele's help, Grishka hopes to execute an ambush of a German convoy transporting supplies from the big railroad junction at Molodeczno to the garrison at Gorodok. An attack on the Gorodok Garrison is planned for next week. If they can keep Gorodok from being supplied, it will be easier to overrun.

Grishka has chosen to attack the convoy where the road runs between two hills. It is Sunday morning, so the response will be slow in coming from the German garrisons. A platoon of guerrillas is stationed several kilometers away on either side of the ambush site to make sure the road is clear and to delay German reinforcements. There are five guards in each of the eight German trucks that must be eliminated.

Ele is asleep with his curly blond hair spilling down his thick neck. Like Grishka he grew-up traveling about the countryside with his father. They bought up bundles of flax cotton, sacks of wheat, corn and flour that they would then resell to retail merchants. In 1939, Ele was drafted into the Russian Army and trained to be a sapper (an explosives expert). When the Nazis killed his parents, he and his brother Michael fled the ghetto and ran to the forest. They became the first guerrillas to help Commander Kuznietzov get arms and organize. Ele was given a platoon with the assignment to blow up trains moving east.

In school, Ele was a handsome blond with sleepy blue eyes that winked and got many girls. With such a gift, he was not a serious student. He had trouble with math, Polish, and German, so his classmates helped him. Now as an explosives expert, it's Ele's turn to be the teacher.

Grishka nudges Ele and says, "It's time to go to work, Mister Sapper."

Ele scratches the straw out of his hair, yawns, rubs the sleep out his eye, and says, "OK, comrades, get up. It's time to get moving. We must be in the woods before the sun catches us." Ele then turns to Grishka and asks, "Should we mine the road? I could blow up the first truck, and the convoy would have to stop."

"No," says Grishka. "I'm afraid to disturb the area around the road. They might see some evidence of our presence in the snow. Blowing up a truck could blow up the whole thing, and we would lose much needed guns and ammunition. Our marksmen are good enough to shoot the drivers and the tires. Like you suggest, we will disable the first truck and the last, then they will be trapped with nowhere to go. They won't be able to turn around or go forward without going in the ditch. And they won't be able to jump the ditch because of the steep incline of the hills on either side of the road. While they are floundering in panic, we will be on top of both hills shooting down at them. It will be like shooting ducks in a barrel. Save the explosives until we get what we need, then blow it up."

"OK, boss. Whenever you've got something to zap let me know."

"I wish you could zap me back to sleep," sighs Grishka.

"Ah, you want to go back to sweet dreams?" asks Ele. "That's where I was - with my Sarah."

"No sweet dream," grunts Grishka. "A nightmare. It was Katkof again."

"Yes, that's a nightmare," says Ele as he gives Grishka a hug about the shoulders and a slap on the head. "Don't worry; it's making you an old man. Crow's feet are growing in the corners of your eyes. He will get his, but you might not be the one to do it. The vodka will get him, if nothing else does. Let it go. Better to not have it on your conscience."

"No, it will clear my conscience," says Grishka, putting his fist to his chest. "I will wear his execution like a badge."

"Don't worry about badges, you have plenty," says Ele. "No one has been more heroic. Someday, he will pop up, and we will get him. Until then, let it go. Don't be consumed by this revenge. Too many lives depend on you. You need to be in the here and now. Think of what's happening at this moment. Dream of the next battle plan and how we can get through this war alive."

"There is so much hurt. By now you would think I would be numb to it, I don't know how I'll get through the pain of this war," grunts Grishka.

"One day at a time," consoles Ele. "Today we've got to rob a convoy."

"Yes," says Grishka. "After we get everything out of the trucks we can carry, blow up the bastards. Blow them to hell and back."

Grishka stands up, stretches, puts his hands in his coat, and surveys the movement in the barn. He slept in his clothes and overcoat, so there is no need to dress. Most everyone is up, and like him ready to go. In spite of the nightmare, Grishka is rested and ready to work. Like every other day in his life, it's work or don't eat.

"Everything we do has to do with supplies," grins Grishka as he reaches out to the troops in the barn. "It was the same before the war - several of us were delivering supplies to farmers. Now, it's Russian Partisans. So what's new? Today with Ele's help, we're going to blow up supplies, but not before we take something for ourselves. New boots, clothes, guns, bullets - we will have them. Our target is the convoy supplying the Gorodok garrison. Every other Sunday they bring in a load from the railroad junction at Uratishki. They will be coming into our ambush about midmorning. The best location has already been spotted by our scouts, Chazanovich and Matus. They will lead us to the spot and show us the way home. Like the fox, we will not go back the way we came. Remember, whatever happens, don't use the same trail twice. As you know, German garrisons are all around us. So we will stay in the woods with the scouts watching our front and rear. Wish us luck on our first offensive action. But we will be more than lucky - we will be ready for them. We want to be in place before daylight, so get moving and be quiet about it."

Matus leads the way into the woods on a black spotted grey gelding. Grishka follows behind him on his black stallion. Thirty foot-soldiers are following single file with packs, rifles, machine guns and mortars. Broad, black bearded Chazanovich is bringing up the rear with his chestnut brown mount pulling a chain of six pack horses.

They cross the road from the Gorodok side of the ambush site and climb each hill from the side opposite the road. After a few minutes the mortars are in place. Hanah is looking down her rifle barrel as the pale yellow glow rises in the grey sky. She looks toward the other hilltop for any evidence of the other troops but sees nothing. She is thinking of her Julie and is tired of the emptiness of separation.

They wait in bone chilling cold. The rest from the early morning hike was welcome, but now they are shivering and rubbing their hands and wishing for a fire or the sun to break through the clouds. Some are hoping for some activity to keep them warm. If only they could chop some wood and build a fire. Hanah is dreaming of a new German coat on her back.

Grishka's mustache is a frozen icicle, but he has no feeling of being cold. His mind is busy with the coming battle and how it will unfold. He smiles and knows the ambush plan will work. Then he worries about losing someone. So often he has felt like a thief who wakes up a dog while stealing a chicken from the coop. The farmer shoots, and the thief runs for his life. That's what it's like scavenging and stealing under Nazis' noses. He is pleased to finally be the hunter rather the hunted.

The sun burns through the haze and lights the world with colors of brown, evergreen, and bright white. Perched on a hill as the lookout, Hanah can see several kilometers of empty road winding like a brown furrow through yesterday's snow. She has been watching the road for an hour, when she sees movement in the distance. She feels a lump in her throat as she blinks the moisture out of her eyes and gives it a hard look. Yes it's a truck. She gives a nervous wave to the waiting troops and hears the clicks of rifle bolts pushing shells into their chambers. A shiver of excitement chills down her back as she crouches down and pushes the safety off her rifle.

She can now feel the truck motors rumbling in her chest. She counts eight trucks and five soldiers in each truck with two in the front and three in the back. There are three rifles and a machine gun in the first truck.

Hanah takes a bead on the driver in the last truck and waits for the first shot. Through her sights from the steep angle of view, she can see only the soldier's chest through the windshield as the head is hidden by the roof of the cab. The firing starts, and the glass shatters on her target, the driver falls forward, and the truck hits the right rear of the truck in front and goes in the ditch. She fires at three soldiers leaving the back of a truck and each is hit by several bullets. Two of the trucks are on fire - one explodes setting another on fire. The killing and explosions goes on until nothing moves. All the trucks are burning or disabled. Grishka gives the word to approach with caution. Hanah is left on the hill to watch for German reinforcements.

"These poor bastards are Lithuanians," says Grishka as he pulls a pistol from a limp hand. "They got these suckers to fight their war. If you find someone alive shoot him. We can take no prisoners. Load up the horses with ammunition and machine guns. Put on their coats. Grab their boots. Tie the laces, and put them around your necks. Put a pistol in your pocket. I want every man carrying two rifles - one on his back and the other in his hands. We've made too much noise, and they've had time to radio for help. So hurry! Get moving!"

Hanah keeps a lookout while the looting is done. The silence is occasionally interrupted by shooting a survivor. That is something she would rather not do. It is one thing to fire at a figure from a distance and another to execute a helpless man from a meter away.

She sees no sign of enemy reinforcements when Grishka signals her to join the others. She comes off the hill into a mangled smoking battlefield. The fight and the looting have left things looking like a trash dump with red fire and black smoke. The looters have taken everything but the garbage. Most Lithuanian bodies have lost their clothes and boots and are now lying naked and sprawled in the mud. Her unit is moving toward the woods loaded down with their booty. It reminds Hanah of peasants leaving the flea market with their goods in peaceful times. She feels the soot filled fire on her face and smells bodies burning in trucks. The fire pops and crackles with dogs barking in the distance. It's a wild, chaotic gruesome scene. She feels the horror, guilt, and pride of winning a battle. As she trots through the wreckage of trucks and bodies, she trips over a dead man and discovers the body is wearing boots that appear to be her size. She hesitates and inspects her pitiful feet and decides to wrestle the boots loose from the limp bloody legs. She then pulls off the soldier's coat, grabs his pistol, and wraps up the gun and boots in the coat. With the booty under her arm, Hanah runs to catch up. She looks back to see trucks coming down the road as she enters the woods, and they are far enough away that they look like toys. Frozen in her tracks, she watches their progress. In a few minutes they are big enough to be real. The flight response kicks in, and she runs up the hill toward the others.

"They are here," she shouts to Chazanovich who is scouting the rear on a chestnut brown pony that seems too small for the husky rider.

"I'm keeping an eye on them," grunts stoned faced Chazanovich. "I think we are safe enough. But run up ahead and tell the others not to slow down. The Lithuanians don't have the Nazi's courage and won't leave their trucks to chase us, but who knows."

Matus is leading the way with the pack horses as they double time through the woods. Mortar shells are landing about them. Several trees with rocks and dirt explode fifty meters behind Hanah.

"Damn!" screams Chazanovich feeling a pain in his shoulder. "I'm hit. Damn."

"Are you okay?" She asks? "I can help you. If you weren't behind me, I would have been hit."

"Don't stop!" shouts the wounded man as he discovers blood running off the tips of his fingers. "Run! Keep moving! Ele planted a delayed charge - it will soon be going off. They are firing, but not trying to follow us. We'll soon be out of range."

* * *

"One minor casualty and we are home alive," grins Grishka as he enters the commander's hut. "No supplies will reach Gorodok this week. And after we take what we need, there are enough weapons to arm twenty more men."

"Well done Comrade," smiles Commander Platanov as he encloses Grishka's hand with both of his. I will tell the elder to prepare a special feast. I want to take a look at your booty. We have men waiting for these weapons."

"I want to thank you," says Grishka with a pause. "For letting me do an offensive action."

"You are welcome," smiles Platanov. "And I thank you for doing an excellent job. Tomorrow after you rest, we talk about where to go next for supplies. It's time to go grocery shopping again."

Chapter 18

The Best Laid Plans

February 1943

The battle of Stalingrad comes to an end with the surrender of the German 6th Army. Nuremberg, Berlin, Vienna, and Munich are heavily bombed. The battle of Guadalcanal is won by the US and becomes the first major achievement in the Pacific offensive. General Eisenhower is selected as the Allied commander in Europe. Shoe rationing goes into effect in the US.

8:00 PM, February 1, 1943 in the Partisan camp in the swamps of Naliboki.

A hundred bundled figures huddle with their ears in their collars and backs to the wind on a hard snow blanket in the dark of a moonless night. Their hands reach for the warmth of several lively fires. Hot oak coals crack and spit red and orange across tired bearded faces. Yellow tailed flames swirl and spark up into the blackness to join bright stars in the clear cold air.

Shouting to his audience, with hands on hips, the short stout Commissar stands above the crowd on an empty ammo box. In spite of the cold, the Commissar's open army coat is pulled back to proudly display the authority of the black captured SS uniform. His top button has broken loose to expose a sagging double-chin that vibrates and sways with shakes of self-importance.

"As Commissar of the Communist party, I am your commander," he says as his black leather fist smacks his black shirted chest. "It's not a title I take lightly. I am proud of our recent ambush of the Uratishki convoy and the destruction of the Gorodok Garrison. The Nazis are also impressed and have stepped up their efforts to eradicate us and fortify themselves. In order to survive, we must do something and quickly. On every mission we play hide and seek with the enemy. They have increased the number of police and paid agents. They are building sandbag bunkers around their Garrisons, and use only stone and brick buildings at night. Last month, a platoon of fifteen Russian partisans was ambushed and killed by Nazis from the Naliboki garrison. Because of that I have increased our efforts to identify and assassinate enemy agents and have pressured locals to cooperate with us. Tomorrow morning, I personally will lead the attack on Naliboki with a battle plan of my own making. Naliboki is choking us like a bone in the throat. The garrison must be destroyed. Commander Platanov has approved my plan, and we are ready. Lieutenant Nathan and his twelve Jews, who are native to Naliboki, will be our guides and lead the way in. Once inside the city, the Jewish platoon will kill the guards and slip into the town hall where the Nazi barracks and headquarters are located. Grishka's men will be outside shooting them as they flee the building. The rest of us will be outside the town ready to move where and when reinforcements are needed. We will catch them on Sunday morning, full of vodka and sleeping with their whores. Enough. Go, get some sleep, and be ready to move when the order comes. We must attack while they are in bed. Be rested and ready, comrades. Long live the revolution."

The Commissar buttons his coat and steps down from his perch. Like a turtle his head slips down in the collar of the coat. Suddenly he is smaller and less than ordinary, but he is still feeling his importance. He walks with an aloofness and swagger that parts the crowd and discourages personal contact as he marches toward Commander Platanov's hut. The commissar salutes the guard and Platanov as he walks in.

"Long live the revolution," says the Commissar, expecting echoes that don't follow.

"Have a seat," greets the Commander in a calm voice. "The plan is fine except for one thing. Grishka's unit is just back from Gorodok and is not yet rested and ready for front line duty."

"Nonsense," scoffs the Commissar. "He's been back eight hours."

"It's been four at the most. Why are you so intent on using the Jews on the front line," asks the Commander?

"Grishka's got guts and Nathan knows the town."

"I guess that's reason enough," sighs the commander." But I would recommend that you hold Grishka in reserve and take Orlov's unit into the town with Nathan's platoon."

"As you wish," says the Commissar as he puffs up his importance.

"The sapper Ele is with Grishka's unit," adds the commander. "He could be of help."

Good idea, the sappers could come in handy," sighs the Commissar showing fatigue from maintaining his rigid posture and a facade of importance. "If there is nothing else, I will go take a nap."

"Yes there is something else," says the commander in a low serious voice. "Two Naliboki police men have been persuaded to come over to our side. They will station themselves inside the city hall. When the action starts, they have promised to throw grenades in the outside bunkers and help you into the building."

"Excellent," says commissar. "I know who they are. It will make our job much easier."

"The policemen must be protected," continues Platonov. "If you retreat, you must take them with you. Their families have been evacuated. There is one more thing. The men and weapons you are taking are very precious to Mother Russia. They are my friends, my sons and my daughters. Please, take care of them. Grishka is our umbilical cord. He has never failed to feed us, please, may his unit come back intact."

"I will do my best," says the commissar with confidence as he rises and salutes.

They leave at midnight with four scouts out in front - Matus, Fogel, Olif and the gypsy, Rassa. Four Russian riders from Orlov's unit are watching the rear. The infantry marches in single file with the commissar following behind on horseback. The world is frozen and white with no sign of life on the road or in the forest. They are soon on the outskirts of Naliboki. Going through frozen fields and backyards, Nathan and his men lead the way in with Orlov's platoon close behind. The commissar stays behind with Grishka's troops, who make ready to ambush any fleeing Nazis. Sabitai Springer's new platoon is stationed on the other side of town to block a Nazi retreat in that direction. Everything looks good for success.

The town hall is a four story masonry building with a clock tower on the front center that can give a bird's eye view of the town. In the steeple's covered opening above the clock, a single Guard is on watch. Sandbag bunkers are in place on the ground at the front and back of the building.

Nathan's platoon makes ready to enter the city hall with four men prepared to take over the bunkers so they can defend it from the outside and shoot any fleeing Nazis. Across the street in the shadows, two of Nathan's men with rifles in hand steady themselves against the stone wall of the post office and take aim at the guard in the clock tower. On Nathan's signal they fire and drop to the sidewalk. Hit, the tower guard slumps over the rail. Rifle shots are followed by flashes of machine gun fire from the bunkers that are quickly silenced by grenades thrown down from windows of the building. After several minutes of explosions and gun fire, there is quiet.

"On your feet," instructs Nathan. "Run for the windows that has just been opened."

Nathan is the second one to dive through a window. He finds himself in a hall full of gun smoke and lit dimly by a single gas lamp. A bullet smashes into the wall above his head. He drops back into a doorway and hears two more shots and the groan of one of his men as he comes through the window. He jumps out of the doorway and fires two bullets into a half dressed policeman shooting his way down the hallway. The man stumbles and falls face down. Nathan fires another bullet into his head to make sure. He waves the rest of his men through the window as he and Sergeant Simon cover.

"It's Hershel, a friend," says a voice from the dark.

Nathan turns and sees a Policeman he knows.

"Nathan, I'm the one who opened the windows. My partner, Luther is covering the staircase in the back of the building.

The guy on the floor shot his way past me on the front staircase. So far we've killed five. Four more are on the top floor."

"Do you think they will give up?" asks Nathan.

"No," says Hershel. "They want to die heroes. They have plenty of guns and bullets. I have a plan. First you must know that there is a hallway around the perimeter of each floor, and the rooms are in the middle. That's the layout of the first three floors. It's just one big room on the fourth floor. The room has a door at the top of each set of stairs. We will work our way up each staircase. A policeman will be at the top guarding the door. We will shoot him out of the way and throw a grenade in from each end."

"Good plan," says Nathan. "You take these three and join Luther on the back stairs. We'll keep a man in each bunker to guard the outside. Jacob, you climb the tower and keep an eye on things. The rest of us will go to the front stairs. Quickly, before they decide to come down."

Nathan reaches the third floor. Everything is quiet. Apprehensive, they climb the last set of stairs. As they reach the landing between floors, the door at the top opens with a burst of fire. Nathan's lead man is hit and collapses on the stairs. Nathan and the others fire over the still body into the door, splintering it and knocking out two panels.

Nathan charges up the stairs and throws in a grenade through a blown out door panel. There's an explosion. Then there's a second explosion on the other side of the room. He opens the door into the smoke. He sees Hershel on the other side of the room silencing a groaning man with a single shot. A smoldering mattress is turned over and stomped out.

"That's all of them," says Hershel. "They thought they were better than us, but we won the argument. How many did we lose? I heard some gun fire on your side."

"We have two dead," reports Nathan with a sigh of sadness and relief.

"Where are the rest of your troops?" asks Hershel. "They should be moving in now. I don't hear anyone outside. Send somebody back to get them."

"Maybe Jacob in the clock tower can see something," responds Nathan. "Steven, find Orlov and see what's going on. It's time they moved in and secured the place."

The building vibrates with an explosion in the street on the front. Two more explosions hit on either side - breaking some glass.

"Go for the basement," shouts Hershel over the sounds of shells hitting around them." This roof could come down."

Three kilometers west of the village, the scouts have found the Nazi artillery unit that is firing on the City Hall. Grishka's men are moving on it from the rear, on the low side of the hill.

"Get a shell ready for the mortar," says Grishka looking over the top edge of his ditch. "We could get lucky and make a hit on their ammo."

"They could get lucky and hit the dynamite I'm carrying," Ele says.

"Then please take it down the ditch a bit," says Grishka. "Listen up everybody. The plan is to lob in some mortars and open fire at the same time."

Grishka frets and hesitates about opening fire on the Nazi's hill top position. How strong are they? How can he charge up hill and take their position? He thinks he can keep them from coming his way, but what else can he do. He's got to make a lucky hit. If not, he's just stirred up a hive of bees.

"Get ready, take aim, fire!" Shouts Grishka as he ducks down in the ditch.

All hell breaks loose. After five minutes of fighting, the bullets are so thick across the top of the ditch, none of Grishka men dare raise their heads.

"Fogel, go get help," commands Grishka. "Tell the commissar, with two more units, we can keep them bottled up, and defeat them"

Fogel crawls down the ditch and into the woods and on to his horse without exposing himself to machine gun fire. He makes his way back to the command post on the outskirts of the village. Shells are exploding fifty meters from the command post. Fogel enters the Commissar's tent and salutes.

"We didn't have enough fire power to take the artillery position," says Fogel. "It can be done with three units surrounding their position. Will you give us Springer and Orlov?"

"I've been waiting on your report," says a nervous Commissar. "It's the only reason I'm still here. Shells are bursting all around me. I had hoped you could put a stop to it. Since you came back with your tail between your legs, I must retreat also."

"We're ready to fight sir," pleads Fogel. "Just give us more men. If we assault the artillery, their infantry will be tied up and can't attack the village. It would be to our advantage to bottle them up outside of town."

"I'm giving it up," says the Commissar as he picks up his black leather bag and walks out of the tent. "Matus, order a retreat. Tell Orlov and Springer to report back here at once. Orlov and I will lead us back home. Grishka and Springer will follow. Fogel, you will order Grishka to retreat."

"What about Nathan's unit?" says Fogel.

"Too risky," stutters the Commissar. "With us in full retreat, the Nazis will be there before you can reach them. Now go before it's too late for Grishka."

Fogel jumps on his horse and forces it to leap through the snow. He wants to go to Nathan, but his first obligation is to Grishka. After a short ride he ties his horse in the woods and crawls back down the ditch to Grishka.

"Retreat," says Fogel. "The Commissar has ordered a retreat."

"Why?" asks Grishka.

"He's a coward," replies Fogel. "Everybody knows it."

"I didn't," says Grishka. "The bastard has risked our lives for nothing. More of our patrols will be ambushed because of this garrison. We will just have to come back and do this again. Let's get it over with."

"We're going to be over with, if we don't get out of here," says Fogel. "If we leave now I might have a chance to warn Nathan that he has no help coming. Don't tell anyone I did it. The Commissar told me not to go."

"He won't know anything unless you get killed," winks Grishka.

"I never got killed yet. But if it happens, it happens", says Fogel with a shrug of acceptance. "I'm to die in the arms of a beautiful woman. God promised me that. That's why I'm not dead. There is no woman anywhere in my life. Because of that I don't give a damn if I die or not. That's another reason why death hasn't taken me."

"Shut up and get out of here," says Grishka pushing on Fogel. "You're too damn stupid to die."

Fogel is on his white and brown splotched Kate. He is pushing her toward the center of the village. As he gets close he sees Steven from Nathan's platoon. Steven is frightened and out of breath.

"I'm looking for Orlov," pants Steven. "Are you coming to help us?"

"Orlov has retreated," says Fogel. "The Commissar has left. Jump up behind me. "We will go and tell Nathan to retreat."

Fogel pushes his Kate into a gallop on the hard snow packed streets. He charges up to an open window, and yells retreat. Four of Nathan's men dive out the next window and start running toward the street. Fogel looks to the west and sees a Nazi squad two blocks away. He kicks his Kate in the ribs and charges off. Bullets are soon flying by him. He hears a groan from Steven and knows he is hit. There is not another sound from Steven. He pulls Steven's arms around him to keep him from falling off and doesn't slow down until he is well into the trees.

Fogel hops down and Steven falls into his arms. He lays him in the snow, slaps his face, and pulls back his eye lids. With sadness Fogel looks at his lifeless body and knows that Steven stopped the bullet that was coming for him. With scoops of his hands he covers him up with snow. There will be no burial until the ground thaws in the spring.

"Too many people dead to think about it," mumbles Fogel as he mounts his horse. "But the man saved my life. Did I know that by riding behind me he would protect my backside? Yes, I did. If I only had somebody in front of me - is that the way I think? I hope not. Too much thinking. I'll go crazy. He's just another dead man. I'll give this death to the Commissar. God damn him!"

Back in the village the Nazis have captured Nathan, Hershel, Luther, and Jacob. They are lying on the lobby floor of the city hall bleeding with their hands tied behind with two machine guns pointed at their backs.

"Throw them in a cell," says the young angry SS captain. "Tomorrow we will hang them. Two Jews and two gentiles will hang side by side in the village square. When they're almost dead, we'll cut them down and hang them again the next day. We'll do that for a week. Make them last a week. When they're finally dead, let them hang another week. Everyone must know what will happen if they betray us or take up arms against us."

Chapter 19

Plan B

3 February 1943, In Commander Platanov's hut at the Partisan camp in the swamps of Naliboki

Orlov and the Commander are seated in front of the stove. Platanov is stirring the coals with a stick as he speaks, "I hope we've seen the last of the Commissar. I don't think he will show his face here again."

"It's a crime that Nathan and most of his unit were killed," says Orlov. "They were heroic in taking the garrison. The fact is that we've still must get the Nazis out of there."

"We'll do it by attrition," says the commander. "Just like we did at Gorodok. We'll cut off their supply line. There is only one road in, so it will be easy to do. They'll bring trucks in on Thursday as always. We'll set up an ambush. It might take a month, but we will be rid of them."

Chapter 20

Blowing-up a Train

April 1943

The last German troops in Africa surrender in Tunisia. Ten American POW's escape a Japanese prison camp in the Philippines to tell of the Bataan Death March. The Red Army attacks to rid the Crimea of German forces. The Warsaw Ghetto uprising continues.

16 April 1943. At a farm house
20 Kilometers southwest of Minsk.

It is eight o'clock and dark when I knock on the door of Nikita's farm house. Thank God for the first breath of spring. A month ago I would be knocking snow off my boots instead of mud. But I am still tired and cold enough to curse the door for not opening. I look behind me and see Ele and the others waiting in the shadows. I become apprehensive as I wait for the door to open. What could be wrong? Is he OK? I clinch my fist and bang harder. Where is the old bastard? Is he too deaf to hear me?

"Just a damn minute," I finally hear a voice say. "You woke me up. For Christ's sake! Don't knock the damn door down. No Vodka. It's finished. Go away."

"It's Yehuda."

"Yehuda? I didn't think you were coming," Nikita says as the door unlatches and swings open. The yellow light of his hand held lantern shows off his yellowed night gown and the faded blue eyes studying my face. "You said late afternoon. I thought you were dead. I didn't know who was knocking. Why make me worry?"

"We ran into an enemy patrol," says Ele stepping past me into Nikita's light. "We were able to avoid them, but we had to hide until dark."

"Come, quickly, before the neighbors see you."

"Only four of you?" asks Nikita as he bolts the door.

"I thought there would be more. You need only four to blow up a train? Hey, why not blow up the police station?"

"We'll do it," yawns Ele. "Soon enough."

"It can't be soon enough," scolds Nikita. "They're always here looking for taxes and taking what they want. Yesterday was too late to blow up the bastards. They've taken everything."

"You still have your land and your life," I add as I make a blanket bed on the floor.

"Your life? My life?" laughs Nikita. "What is a life? A life is worth nothing as long as gangsters come into my house, rob me, and call it taxes."

"Amen," says Ele. "Thank you for your hospitality, but we must say goodnight. If we don't get some sleep we will have to stay another day. Please, wake us at one o'clock."

"You're lucky they didn't take the clock," grins Nikita as he puts the lamp on the table and blows it out.

17 April 1943

I wake to see firelight spilling through cracks in the wood stove as it throws a dancing yellow light around the snoring room. Nikita opens the stove and throws in an oak log. While the door is open, he steals some fire with a thin stick and lights the oil lamp on the table.

"Rise and shine," Nikita grunts as he slams the steel stove door.

I shake Ele and say, "It's time."

"There's bread and milk for you on the table," offers Nikita.

I am rested and feel as fresh as the bread on the table. My senses are acute with the joys of perception. The bread is crisp and warm. The milk is cold and thick with cream. My eyes delight in the subtle hues of the cracked polished oak, the flickering candlelight shadows on the yellowed plaster, and the smell and color of simple fresh food.

"Sorry, there is no time to warm the milk," grunts Nikita. "The bread was baking while you slept."

"It tastes as good as it smells," says Ele, taking a bite. "It's so good to wake up to the smell of baking bread. It makes me think of having a home."

The two grumpy Russians take turns coughing and clearing their throats. They wake-up enough to push the bread in their mouths and wash it down with gulps of milk.

"Maybe you got vodka," begs Uri. "I need just a swallow to wake me up and clear my head."

"Me two," grunts Vanja.

Nikita pulls a bottle and glasses from the cabinet and pours a shot of vodka in each and hands the glasses to Uri and Vanja.

195

Uri throws it down with a gulp and a grimace and slams the glass on the table like he wants a refill. Vanja takes several sips and wipes his lips with back of his hand.

"Anyone else," offers Nikita.

"Time to go," says Ele glaring at Uri and daring him to take another drink. "Remember walk quietly behind me single file. No talking, no coughing, no breaking branches or any other noise. On the way home don't stop at any building or house. The Nazis will be looking there in the morning. We must get as far away from the rails as we can and quickly. If there is a problem, we will meet back here tonight."

Like a shoplifter, Vanja grabs the Vodka bottle and shoves it in his coat pocket.

"No more vodka," scolds Ele as he grabs the bottle and slams it on the table. "We have work to do. Why did I train you? A drunk can blow us up. Explosives are dangerous enough when you're trained and have a clear head. Your eyes are blood-shot. I didn't see you drinking last night. When did you have time?"

There's a silence while Vanja tries to make his mouth work and can't. He just looks at the floor.

Ele shakes his head in disgust and says, "Remember, no talking and no noise. Follow me single file. Do as I do. If I walk, you walk. If I run, you run. Let's go."

I grab the machine gun and lead the way out the door. The Russians pick up their packs full of explosives and follow me.

Nikita grabs Ele by the shoulder and says, "Give these boys a bath before you come back. Somebody is stinking like a pig."

"I will," promises Ele. "It's the vodka. They are so saturated they're flammable. Maybe they'll just blow themselves up. Thank you for your help."

"Where did you learn to blow up trains?" worries Nikita. "How do I know you won't make a mistake and blow away my house?"

"That's something I think about all the time," says Ele. "That's why it hasn't happened. I was a sapper in the Russian Army. I was drafted for two years, thirty-nine and forty. I had an officer who taught me everything, even how to dismantle mines and get explosives out of them."

"No dismantling bombs here," says Nikita. "Next time, please leave the explosives outside, way outside. Somewhere down the road."

"Don't worry. You're safe. I promise," smiles Ele as he pats the old man on the back and steps outside. "We've got a train to catch. I'll see you soon. Maybe next time, we'll blow up that police station."

"In that case you can keep the explosives under my bed," smiles Nikita as he waves goodbye.

We have been walking single file for more than an hour. The sound of the engine and then the movement of boxcars can be heard in the distance. Everyone is searching the darkness for soldiers patrolling the rails. We come to a shallow place in the river. One by one we pick our way down the bank and leap from one slippery rock to the next. Vanja slips on a rock and gets his right foot wet. Everyone else is across dry. I hear Vanja cursing under his breath and give him a slap on the mouth. He takes the slap personally and threatens me with his fist.

It's a wooded area, and ground cover is not far from the railway. Ele is able to get within thirty meters of the tracks and still has vegetation for cover. We know the guards to be stationed along the tracks two hundred meters apart. He would like to locate a guard to get the spacing, so Ele can go in between them and plant his explosives. He pushes his head under a tree limb and searches to the left and to the right. He sees and hears nothing. Maybe they've been slack with guards. Maybe the guy is sleeping. Trains are coming every hour. That gives us about thirty minutes to plant his explosives and get away. If he waits for another train, there will be less time to travel before sun-up and more time to be discovered before we plant the bomb. We don't want to be on the road or anywhere near here at daylight.

Ele gives the signal to proceed. He and Uri crawl toward the tracks with their packs full of explosives, while I stay in the trees with the machine gun and move fifty meters to the right and Vanja moves to the left to give cover. With a small shovel, Uri digs a hole in the gravel under the track while Ele prepares the explosives. When the hole is dug, Ele starts placing the explosives in the ground. For an igniter he uses a shompol. This is a thin steel rod used to clean rifles. He will rig the shamapol into the fuse, so it sticks above the tracks. When it is pushed to the fuse by the train's wheels, everything will explode.

I spot a figure coming out of the shadows about eighty meters up the track from Ele and not far from where Vanja should be. Still holding his rifle in his right hand, the man puts his arms above his head and stretches like he just woke up. Staying in the shadows, I move up the tracks to where Ele is working and position myself to fire. If I pull the trigger all hell will break loose, no train will be blown up and they will be killed.

I am breathing heavy as I watch the man stretch his neck and then relieve himself. Do I have time to move through the woods and come in behind him with a knife? What is Vanja doing? Should I stay here or not? What good is it to shoot the guard, if the unit is wiped out?

Finally I see Vanja running out of the shadows toward the guard. With one swift move he grabs the Guard around the head and cuts his neck. The man shakes violently and falls to the ground. He is thrashing and groaning as Vanja drags him into woods. Vanja stops and stabs him twice more to quiet him. I am wondering if I could have done what Vanja did. I have yet to kill a man close up. I've shot at figures in the distance, but maybe it was someone else's bullet that knocked them down.

Nervous and sweating, Ele and Uri have also been on alert. Ele exhales his tension and thanks God for Vanja. He is good for something. Before he is through, Ele can feel the vibration of a locomotive on the rails. It has taken a long fifteen minutes to plant the bomb. A lifetime has passed before my eyes. Trying to be calm, Ele digs up a clump of grass and plants it on top of the shompol as camouflage.

Ele and Uri crawl back to the woods. As soon as he is in the cover of the trees, Ele gets up and takes off in a run with the rest of us following. The rumble of steel wheels on the tracks can be heard in the distance. No one worries about breaking branches or the river with its steep slope and falling rocks. Ten minutes pass and everyone has lathered up a sweat.

"It didn't go off," says Vanja. "It's all been for nothing. I've risked my life for nothing."

"Shut-up and keep moving," scolds Ele. "It will happen. Yehuda you've got to keep up. Slow running is going to kill you. Don't stop in any of these scattered buildings. That's where the Nazi's will be looking. Don't stop anywhere or you're dead. Just keep running, no matter how much it hurts. We've got to be twenty kilometers away from here before sun-up.

Behind us, there's an explosion. The sky lights up like daylight. We can see each other's shining faces. Then we hear the clatter of machine guns. We laugh, embrace and watch the fireworks. It's better than a New Year's celebration. Overcome by the spectacle and self-satisfaction, we forget about escaping.

"Enough," prods Ele as he collects himself. "Get moving. They'll soon have dogs on our trail."

It's early evening when we reach camp. Ele reports his success to the Commander, who gives us two days off. It will take the Nazis at least four days to repair the tracks.

I am thinking of Hanah. It's time for her to be in her hut getting ready for bed. She squeals with surprise and pulls me inside and locks the door. Her eyes light up and she throws herself into my arms. She nibbles my ear while I kiss her neck. Her strong beautiful body pushes and flexes against me.

"I'm so glad you're alive," she whispers with a warm breath in my ear. "I love you so very much."

18 April 1943

Our assignment is part of an ambush. At daybreak our platoon is dug in on either side of a road in a wooded area. We are waiting on a German supply convoy en route to Minsk. When we open fire on the moving trucks, they are expecting us. They answer with a barrage of heavy machine guns. We can do nothing but hug the ditch. The drivers step on the gas and accelerate out of range. We have two casualties - a Russian boy and Frauma Tanfel. Frauma is an attractive twenty-one year old nurse, who lived in Hannah's hut. Her twenty-two year old brother, Jakov, belongs to another platoon. Their story was similar to mine. They had escaped the mobile killing squads in their village by not showing up for work the day the Nazis loaded everyone in the Synagogue into trucks. Now Frauma is lying in the wagon covered except for her head. I hear her brother crying nearby. I am looking at her face that has become very thin. Her nose is more pointed than I remember and her lips are white. I am remembering how sweet and compassionate she was.

We choose a hill overlooking the forest. At her open grave are three honor guards including Jakov. Our platoon leader, Lesnov orders the guards to give three salvos from their rifles. We are hungry for revenge. The grave site is the beginning of our cemetery.

Chapter 21

Sasha and Vanya Lesnov

June 1941 to February 1943

22 June 1941, Hitler invades Russia
2 February 1943, The Germans
surrender at Stalingrad

The Lesnov brothers are Jews serving in the Russian Army at the Fort of Brest, Poland in June of 1941 when it is attacked by the Germans under the command of General Von Brauchirsch. After an artillery duel, the Germans order an air strike that is effective in destroying half the fort, but does not discourage the Russians. Under a flag of truce Von Brauchirsch demands the Russians surrender. When they refuse, the General orders in his giant artillery pieces. Lieutenant Vanya Lesnov is astonished as he sees the huge artillery guns being put in place. They are pulled by many horses and the ground trembles with their advance. Vanya understands that no wall can stand up to this firepower. He points this out to the Commander who knows he can't surrender, when Stalin's orders are to stand fast. He orders Vanya back to his post. When the guns are fired, the

fort shakes as if an earthquake is in progress. Soon the entire
western wall becomes rubble. Sasha Lesnov is a medic who
doesn't know where to start. He can hear the moans of the
wounded and dying and thanks God he is not one of them.
Sasha and Vanya Lesnov were among the survivors taken to
the POW camp at Molodeczno.

By January, 1942, Sasha and Vanya have seen thousands
of prisoners die of starvation. Selections of Jews, Communist,
Gypsies, and Russian activist are made daily in the POW
camp. Those selected are executed in public. The Communist
and officers are hanged. Most of the Ukrainians are nationalist and see the Russians as oppressors. As informers, they
try hard to help the Nazis and gain favor. The Ukrainians get
better rations, clothing and treatment than the Russians. The
S.S. tries to incite them against each other. The more energetic
Ukrainians police the camp. They organize themselves into the
Nationalistic Ukrainian Division. Sasha and Vanya, who are
Jews from Eastern Ukraine, see an opportunity.

"We are going to pretend to be nationalistic Ukrainians and
join the division," says Sasha. "We will have more freedom of
movement and opportunity to escape. With better rations we
might survive and have the strength to run away."

"But will they believe we are not Jews," asks Vanya.

"The Russians thought we were Catholic Ukrainians, so
why shouldn't the Germans believe us. We are Ukrainians,
who also happen to be Jews. Come, my brother, put on your
best Ukrainian accent and be a patriotic nationalist."

Together they become part of the group and are benevolent
policeman to the Jews.

In March, 1943, an order is given to clean the camp and to
prepare for an important visitor, General Vlasov, the famous
Red Army defector who is organizing the Ukrainian Division

to fight for an Independent Ukraine. The Russian prisoners are placed behind the Ukrainians who meet the General with jubilant shouts of "Hurrah." He has a captive audience.

The General is a large striking figure at forty-five. He is six foot-six with black curly hair and foxy brown eyes. He is standing on a wooden platform surrounded by elite S.S. officers.

He gazes quietly at the two electricians who are connecting the microphones. He adjusts the microphone up to his face with the experience of a performer. He appears to be a consummate politician. With hard expressionless faces, the prisoners wait meekly to hear about the war.

He begins quietly in an earnest tone," The heroic German army has advanced more than a thousand miles. I was injured, my army destroyed and I was taken prisoner. The desertion of hundreds of thousands of Russians, Ukrainians, Tartars, and Asians are greater every day. The Germans have freed most of the Ukraine from the Communist and Jews. They are both miserable bedbugs who suck your blood and exploit your hard labor. Now our liberators ask you to fight for the heroic Wehrmacht, who have freed all of Europe from the plague of Communism. Do you want forced collectivism of your farms?"

"No!" shouts the response.

"Should we fight for Stalin's dictatorship and slavery?"

Again the answer is, "No!" Thousands of POW's answer, "Hurray. No, no to the Communist!"

Vlasov shouts, "Don't listen to the subversive slogans of Molotov and others. I, General Vlasov, have come here to free you Ukrainians who want to fight the Bolsheviks. We are fighting for a free Ukraine. We will be free of the Polish yoke, free of the Soviet yoke, and free of the Jews. Our famous hero Brogan Chmelnicky started the job three hundred years ago. He cut the throats of our oppressors. He destroyed sixteen hundred small towns and villages of the hated Jews. Now is the time to finish our patriotic Ukrainian job. Will you join the National Ukrainian Division?"

"Hurray, yes!" is the answer by thousands shouting with applause.

"Liberate all nations from the Jews and the bondage of the Capitalist and Bolsheviks," he shouts passionately. "Ukrainians, Russians, we must fight for our lives, for our families. There must be a new and decent order in Russia. It is our destiny to achieve it."

"Heil Hitler," shouts thousands of hungry prisoners of war.

Sasha and Vanya are among the thousand volunteers. They are checked and rechecked. Their perfect Ukrainian helps them. They are given black uniforms and put in a training camp near Molodeczno, five miles from the POW camp. The first night they slip under the fence and flee into the forest. They trade the uniforms for food and clothes to a farmer in the area and rest in his barn and wait till dark. They are joined by Levik, a Jew who has escaped from the POW camp. Levik grew up in the area and knows the terrain and where the Partisans are. About mid-night, they get word from the farmer that they are being hunted and the SS is not far away. The SS has discovered some Jews among the recruits and has just tortured and hung them. With Levik in the lead they run for their lives. After twenty kilometers, they come to the village of Traby where Levik grew up. This town had twelve Jewish families whose fifteen acre farms had been passed down for generations. The huts are similar to all the houses of White Russian Peasants. There are four small windows and two rooms. There is a large brick oven with a chimney in the corner. The oven is wide enough for the mother and children to lie down and warm themselves in the winter. Levik's heart is pounding from exhaustion and tension. He can't wait to see his parents and show them that he is still alive. The trio comes through the field behind the house at four in the morning. It is as quiet as a cemetery. They find the door and windows missing. The beds are gone and the kitchen is empty. In the corner Levik finds a picture of the family, his parents with his younger sister and brother. He looks at the rooms where he had spent twenty-one years with his family, and the hearth where his mother sang Russian and Jewish songs. He remembers the song about the Wailing Wall in Jerusalem, the city of David. The song is about the Jews crying and praying to God, asking, "When? When God? When will you see our pain and tears?" He runs to his uncle's house and finds nothing but a bloody pillow.

Levik sees light in a neighbor's window and raps on the door. Aleksey is surprised that Levik is alive. He gives them food and tells how the Nazis and police rounded up all the young Jews into trucks and took them to Borisov to dig trenches. They killed the older Jews in the forest. The peasants looted the abandoned homes.

Vanya takes charge of the situation. "Listen Aleksey. We are going to rest here until dark. You, your son, and wife will stay with us. No one will leave the house for any reason. We are Russian Partisans. If you or someone else reports us to the Police, you and your family will burn along with your house. Do you understand?"

"Yes I understand and support you in fighting the Germans," says the peasant. "You might want to know about the local Batushka, head of the Russian Orthodox Church. He grabbed everything from the Jews. They brought him money, sewing machines, clothes and all they could carry for safe keeping. They gave everything expecting to get it back after the war. He has been selling things saying the Jews won't be back to claim them. He lives three kilometers from here. Levik knows where he is."

That night, Levik leads them to the Batushka. His farm is fenced with a large black and tan German Sheppard guarding the property. Levik and Vanya draw their knives as they open the gate. Sasha is holding a large stone. The dog approaches them with a low guttural snarl. They can see that this is a serious watch dog. She comes with a rush. The snarl becomes a blood curdling growl as she leaps at Levik's throat. Sasha hits her with his stone and her jaws snap shut and rip the front of Levik's jacket. The bitch charges again. This time Levik cuts her on the snout and kicks her about two meters away. She licks her bloody snout and retreats to her dog house.

The bishop is now standing in the door with his wife behind him. He is tall, about forty-five with broad Slavic features, with short blond hair framing a bald spot. His trembling face becomes more composed when he recognizes Levik.

"Brother Levik, I was a friend of your family for many years," he patronizes. I have all the clothing and goods of all the Jews in your village. They brought them to hide for them. Take everything you need and give them to your friends."

Trying to control his anger, Levik speaks in a low trembling voice, "My ten year old sister came to you, begging you to keep her for a few days and you threw her out. You took everything from our family and refused to help them."

Vanya puts his knife to the bishop's throat.

The wife screams, "Don't kill him! We have three children. He didn't steal. We couldn't help the Jews. Here are the letters from the Bishops of Vilna and Kovno forbidding us to aid or protect Jews in anyway. They warned us not to expose ourselves and our families to the possibility of a death sentence. It is signed by Bishop Brysgs."

Several other letters and signatures follow that show a tragic Jewish situation with the Church. The Christians are under orders not to give the Jews food, shelter or help in any way. The trio spares the Bishop, takes his food and clothes, and leave.

It takes them another week to find our unit in the forest. Sasha and Vanya are accepted as Russian soldiers. They do not reveal they are Jewish. Vanya becomes my platoon leader and Sasha becomes a medic. Levik is also assigned to my platoon. All are given new rifles and press them to their hearts and pledge to take revenge and destroy the enemy.

Chapter 22

Battle for the Naliboki Forest

July 1943

July - August 1943, The Battle of Kursk in Western Russia was the Germans' failed attempt to regain the offensive after their loss at Stalingrad. It was the largest tank battle of WWII. Two-thirds of the German War Machine was involved. The partisan attacks on the rail lines that were supplying the German offensive played a large part in the Russian Victory. The offensive was delayed by breaks in the German supply lines that averaged over a thousand a month. This gave the Russians a chance to build an impenetrable defense with trenches and mine fields. In July of 1943, the Germans launched Operation Hermann that deployed 52,000 troops and artillery in an attempt to eradicate the Partisans from the Naliboki Forest.

21 June 1943

No night is without a section of the rails being blown up. The Germans are determined to eradicate us and do what they can to protect the rails. They post guards every 100 meters.

Sandbag bunkers are built. Machine guns are placed on the freight cars. Flatbed cars fortified with sandbags run in front of the train. Patrols guarding the tracks are reinforced to ambush our sappers.

25 June 1943

The Germans kill two of Ele's best sappers in an ambush. The next day the command sends a platoon to the same spot on the railway that blows up the station and kills the guards. We retrieve the sappers' bodies and bury them in the hilltop cemetery overlooking the forest. Ele gets replacements and they reorganize. A platoon is assigned to cover the sappers when they approach the tracks. Segments of the rail line are divided between the companies. More sappers go to the tracks. Units are forbidden to go outside the assigned territory, so they won't be mistaken for the enemy. Before each Russian offensive, the whole guerilla army attacks the rails, breaking the line in at least ten places. Without supplies, the Germans have no choice but to retreat.

28 June 1943

We prepare for the Nazi invasion we know is coming. On different islands we dig holes and hide food supplies. We dig more holes to camouflage hiding places for the wounded.

2 July 1943

We have been seeing small reconnaissance planes and wait for our chance. "Look! Directly overhead," shouts Lesnov. "Shoot him down!"

We fire a swarm of bullets, and the light plane falls in the river, a few hundred meters from our dugouts. We hurry to our prize and pull out two pilots. They are begging, "Don't kill us. We are Czech."

We cover the plane with branches and take the pilots to headquarters. Planes keep coming. About midnight I can feel the vibrations from low flying heavy aircraft. The forest starts shaking from the bombardment that continues into the night. Maybe they are trying to demoralize us, and will send the troops in at daybreak. Morning comes and there is no invasion. We relax, have breakfast and are grateful for another day. We hear from the radio that the German Commander claims to have destroyed a division of Stalin's bandits. They have merely blown-up a few thousand trees.

4 July 1943

Except for a few gaps, the Germans have surrounded us. We are ordered to stay in the forest with the tactic of wait and see. The defectors and collaborators are telling the Germans how many supplies we have and how long we will be able to hold out in the mire.

6 July 1943

"The enemy has encircled us," says our Commander, speaking to us from the back of a supply wagon. "Their guns are being put in place. We expect an artillery bombardment to start tomorrow. You are to split up into squads of 5 or 6. Each squad will be given a different coordinate to follow. We will break through the German's blockade at every point on the compass, and they will be confused about where we are. Once you break through the German line, keep going. Make your presence known in the surrounding area. Find targets wherever you are, and hit them at night. We will distract them from their purpose as much as we can. While they are here, we will be there. Keep an eye out for collaborators and spies. There are some among us. Show them no mercy. For that reason each squad leader will be sure that his people are accounted for at all times. If anyone strays from his unit, he must be shot by the squad leader. You will move at night and hide during the day. In four days we will rendezvous in the village of Bakshty."

Hanah and I are allowed to work together. Lieutenant Vanya Leshnov, a stocky, resourceful Ukrainian is our leader. Fogel and 19 year old Jeremy are also with us.

7 July 1943, 5:00 AM

Bombing and shelling begins with the splintering of the pines and the large birch trees. At times the explosions are close and deafening. We are on an island lying in a trench at the bottom of a hill with our rifles ready for the approaching enemy. We have cut branches and replanted bushes to cover and camouflage our short trench. Hanah is resting - snuggled in to my side as I keep watch. About noon, four German scouts approach firing automatic weapons into the bushes, trying to provoke us to fire back. They are five meters away. I can see the tops of their helmets through the roof of our ditch. The bullets are splintering the bushes over our heads. I'm nervous that the gun fire will displace our cover. Our rifles are cocked and ready to shoot, but they don't come any closer. We hug the dirt and wait until dark when we move to an area where the Nazis have already searched.

We choke down flour mixed with swamp water, and wait while Vanya makes contact with the command. He returns with the news that the Germans fired thousands of shells and sprayed the forest with bullets with little results. The only partisan casualties are among the small children who were strangled to keep from crying out when the Germans came too close. He tells of Fizel's beautiful two year old boy that had to be choked to death. In the confusion some German troops were bombed by their own planes. They actually killed more of their own than Partisans.

8 July 1943, 2:00 AM

We must proceed while we still have the energy to make the hike through the bog. At one point we are waist deep in mud. At each step, we are forced to use our rifles to push our legs out of the boot sucking mud. Out in the open bog, between the islands, we are vulnerable and easy targets. With our rifles in the mud, we are defenseless. We have an hour of fighting the bog before getting to the next island. Exhausted, wet and covered in sticky slime, we lay down to rest and listen for any sign of the enemy. The shelling is still going on and the sky is flashing and blasting with artillery, but nothing from the direction we are heading. It is five in the morning when we break through the line in another area of deep mud. The Germans have left this spot in the bog open. We find a rut road and for an hour we walk backwards to confuse the enemy. Daylight breaks our cover of darkness and our guns are still caked with mud and won't fire. We are naked, helpless without weapons, and skittish enough not to talk or make a sound. If we spot anything moving, we are ready to dive into the brush. We walk two hours outside the blockade before we find a stream to drink, cleanup and restore our rifles to working order. Already we are out of flour. By luck we find some berries for breakfast. By noon we are twenty-five kilometers from base camp.

"Look, our next meal is up ahead," Vanya points. "A horse is behind those trees, in the field to the right."

"What do you have in mind," asks Fogel? "You are not thinking of eating a good horse.

"I'm hungry enough to eat any horse," replies Vanya as he pulls out a rope. "Look, his ribs are showing. Not strong enough to carry you, Fogel. He is eating grass like he's as hungry as we are. He's lost his owner."

Fogel moves slowly toward the horse while talking in a calm voice. He e is soon stroking the animal's neck and making friends.

"You keep him happy," Vanya instructs. "I'll tie up his legs, so we can get him on the ground. While you hold his head, I'll cut its throat.

Hanah and Jeremy gather wood and start a fire. Vanya keeps watch while Fogel and I cut up the horse.

In the same way the Tartars make shashlik, Hanah puts sticks through the meat to roast it over the fire. We all wait and drool with anticipation as each one holds his own meal on a stick and watches the juices flame as they drip into the coals. Too hungry to wait for well-done, I pull my meat out of the fire and take a rare seared bite off the end.

"Delicious." I say with a swallow. "Thanks to Fogel, we even have salt."

"I don't like eating this horse," Fogel says. "It was painful to slaughter. The animal trusted me, and I betrayed his trust. He could have been saved, but it's more important to save ourselves. I hope I can find my Kate after the shelling. I left her with a peasant. She is my only female friend."

"Let's don't go down that road again, "pleads Hanah. "We know you are lonely and need a woman, but please, it doesn't need to be a horse."

"I love pigs too," says Fogel with a wink. "Don't you love animals?"

"I am not going to get started with you and how you don't know the difference between pigs and women," says Hanah. "But you could tell us the latest gossip."

Fogel pauses and lets her barb and the laughter die and says "I don't have gossip but a true story of resistance at a death camp that came from my friend, Sol, with the Bielsky brothers. There was a group of Jews that paid for permits to immigrate to Argentina by way of Switzerland. They were told to report to the train station where they were loaded and locked in box cars for five days with little to eat or drink. When they arrived at the death-camp they were taken to the showers and instructed to take off their clothes to be deliced. Many realized they were about to be gassed and refused to remove their clothes or obey any orders. They were huddled in groups searching for a plan of action when the Germans started beating them with clubs, but still the guards didn't gain control of the situation. The commandant became distracted by a beautiful woman disrobing and moved closer for a better view. When the woman realized she had the attention of her guards, she slowed down and undressed with the tease of a stripper and soon had them under her spell. She slowly took off a high-heeled shoe that she slammed into the face of the commandant, grabbed his pistol, shot him dead in the chest and disappeared into the crowd. There was one more shot and the lights went out, and the guards massacred them all with machine guns. The body of the woman was laid out on a dissecting table for the guards to view.

"If there were more of us with that woman's courage and with weapons, many more would be alive," I say.

"That woman only had a shoe," says Vanya. "It was courage and ingenuity that made the shoe a weapon."

"Don't forget her beautiful body," adds Fogel. That's the weapon that turns a man's brain to mush."

"Enough," says Hanah as she stands up. "The meat could be spoiling. You butchers - go cut off the buttocks, the shoulders and any other good meat and give it to me. We can put it in the stream, and it will keep for at least a week. Remember this place, so we can find it again."

"I have it marked," says Vanya. "I have been through here before. We now have food, water and a forest thick with trees and undergrowth, so we stay around for a while. Our job is to be alive when this is over. The Germans will get tired of searching for us, and they still have the pressing problem of the Russian advance. They waited too long to be rid of us, now we are too many, too strong, and too clever."

That night, we go back to the stream and find the meat cold like on ice. After supper, Hanah and I walk up stream and to a private spot and wash each other. We make love under a whispering canopy of pines in a bed of leaves and straw. In a long silence, we looked up through the trees into the stars. Hand in hand, we are very much in love.

"I love you more than anything," I say as we kiss.

"Did you ever tell anyone else that?" she asks with a teasing smile.

"You are the most precious person that has ever to come into my life," I say as I squeeze her hand. "But I was once in love with Zipora, and we talked of marriage. We were both in love for the first time and innocent - we never made love.

"When did you know her?"

It was the summer of 1939 – just before the Nazis invaded Poland. I had my first job in Ozarow, near the German border. It was a place of three thousands Jews, who were tailors, blacksmiths, and shopkeepers. I was teaching Hebrew and Polish, and she taught mathematics. There was a thick forest of trees in the hills behind the town where we took long walks.

"Tell me about her."

"Like you, it was the intelligence radiating from her eyes that first attracted me. She had a beautiful voice and would sing the Polish ballads at parties. I remember her singing, 'Happiness doesn't last long,' in the song "Rosemarie". It's what people had on their minds and a premonition of the September Nazi invasion. We had a few months of happiness – musical, romantic evenings and parties in the forest with food and laughter.

"How did you survive the invasion?"

"On the third day of the war, our town was bombed. Buildings were blowing up around me. The planes came so low I could see the pilots. I saw three young women killed while drawing water at the well, and hopelessly disfigured with their blood spilling onto the cobblestones. Those first dead of the war will always be with me."

"What happened to Zipora?"

"She was killed in the bombing when her house was hit. I couldn't find her in the rubble. Three days later, Nazis marched fearlessly into town on the way to Warsaw with automatic weapons and new grey uniforms. They rounded up all the Jewish men and packed seven-hundred of us into the small medieval red brick synagogue. Five young soldiers were on the pulpit with automatic weapons as a Catholic priest translated and told us to turn in any weapon, even a kitchen knife, and if one soldier was harmed, we would all be killed. Their Captain shouted, 'Get out.' There was a stampede to the door that was too small for the traffic. I was hit in the back by the butt of a rifle as I pushed through. Once outside, I kept running as did many others. We knew that compliance was death. They later found me in a field. A soldier escorted me - probably going to a place of execution. He was proudly marching behind me with his rifle on his shoulder ready to be rewarded for his prize. I threw myself to the left and behind a house, and ran through the garden, into a second house and up into the attic. I waited until dark and let myself out onto the roof and dropped down to the ground and made my way to a nearby marsh. It took me a month to get back to Gorodok, where we were temporarily safe under Stalin."

"Thank God for the miracle that you are alive and here with me," she says as she snuggles into me. "I know we will be together always."

10 July 1943

We have a breakfast of horse meat and berries by the stream. The Germans are busy on the road, so we move through the forest toward village of Bakshty where we are to rendezvous with the rest of the company. When we reach the village, we hear the latest news from the commander.

"The Germans are claiming a triumphant victory," says Commander Platanov. They claim three thousand guerillas killed or captured, and five hundred surrendered. Out of a thousand, we are missing seventy. What they did do is murder hundreds of civilians. They gathered them in churches and barns and burned them alive. The only people they killed were innocent victims. More local people are joining us, because of the atrocities, and the Russian Army is getting closer. The tide of public opinion is turning in our favor."

Chapter 23

Battle for the Rails

August 1943

The US is winning the battles for the Solomon Islands in the Pacific. The Fall of Palermo in the Allied invasion of Sicily inspires a coup d'état against Mussolini. The firestorm bombing of Hamburg begins. Polish Jews mount a futile resistance with a few weapons in the Bialystok death camp. The famous slapping incident happens that results in General Patton being relieved of duty for ten months.

1 August 1943

After the blockade, all battalions return to their bases strengthened by recruits. Our survival has infused us with new vigor and enthusiasm. We survived the German attack and still the Third Panzer Division and the Fourth Army are being diverted from the Russian front to deal with our attacks. Our Partisans are successful in destroying the supply lines as well as tying up troops. It is now easier to do our business. We know where our territory is and where to expect the Germans and the police.

Although the hospital had been camouflaged and buried on an island in the marsh, we find it destroyed. You could be within five meters and not see it, so someone gave away its location. The patients and staff were burned alive when the Germans torched it with a flame thrower. Among those killed were a mother and daughter and two pharmacists. Thank God Hanah was with me.

We had long suspected a Soviet doctor as being a spy. The fact that he was the only survivor of the hospital attack, and that he has fled to a nearby village is evidence enough of his guilt. He condemned two of the Jews who had escaped from Krasno to be shot, because he falsely diagnosed them with Typhus. My friend Pesach was one of these. Matus is able to locate the doctor and bring him back to us. He is immediately shot.

10 August 1943

Ele, reinforced with three new sappers, is waiting in a farmhouse until night to sabotage nearby rails. The four eat a breakfast of sausage and eggs, and then the young sappers Stephen and Antek start drinking vodka. There is eight hours to wait until nightfall. Stephen, out of boredom places the dynamite and fuses on the floor next to his vodka bottle.

"Now let's go over this procedure with the shamapol again," says Stephen. "It will be dark on the railway. I don't want to make any mistakes."

"Don't worry Stephen," says Ele, irritated that his nap has been interrupted. "I have done this many times. It always works. Put the toys up. They could kill us."

Ele is resting on a big upholstered sofa with a large window behind him. He has turned his back to Stephen and buried his face in the sofa trying to get back to his nap. Ele is an officer but treats his men as equals. He knows the anti-Semitic environment and the prejudices in the Russian and Polish recruits. He finds Stephen uncooperative and a hard drinker, and Antek often disobedient. Maybe he would do better without them.

"Put the bomb up," orders Ele without moving from his napping position. "You don't want to put it together until it is time to use it."

"A Jew is always afraid," says Stephen taking another sip of his vodka that wets his black moustache and spills on to his stubbly beard.

Stephen continues to manipulate the parts of the bomb, while the others watch. Ele lies on the sofa apprehensive and thinking he will report Stephen for insubordination. He must get up and put a stop to Stephen. Suddenly there is a blast. The light is blinding. Steel, blood, wood, glass, plaster, and body parts go flying. Ele is thrown out the window with the sofa.

Seventy-five meters away, Anton, owner of the house, is shaken by the blast. He drops his plow in the field and runs to see what it is. As he turns the corner of the barn, he finds the back wall of the house gone along with half of his roof. He looks through the rubble and sees blood and body parts. Outside, on what is left of the sofa, he finds Ele still breathing.

Nervous and stuttering, Anton shakes Ele. "Wake up, we've got to go. The police and my neighbors will soon be here. Please, don't be dead."

Ele doesn't move. Anton in a panic hitches the horse to the wagon and lifts Ele into the back and takes him to the forest. After five days, Ele regains consciousness. After five weeks he can talk, but cannot hear.

15 September 1943

The Russian Army is still advancing. We are disrupting the German build-up by attacks on garrisons, ambushes on the roads, and primarily by cutting the supply lines at the railway junctions and blowing-up the bridges. Stronger sapper groups are organized. Whole partisan companies are used in the most fortified areas.

Our best scout, Matus Simoncholntz, leads our sapper squad. He has found a target twenty kilometers west of Minsk. There are no bushes or trees around. The Germans have come to expect us to bomb the rails in places where undergrowth and trees are thick. Bushes can hide Germans as well as partisans, so we are now operating in open areas. In order to save our energy for our escape, we pack our explosives and heavy guns on horses, and ride on horseback to the village of Belvo and leave our horses with a peasant.

It is a cool night, overcast, humid, with a threat of rain. Led by Matus, the five of us carry our guns and explosives into the tree line between the fields. We can see the crops coming in that we will stockpile for winter. We are doing some harvesting ourselves, since so many of the peasants have been murdered. Vanya Lesnov, being the strongest, is carrying the heavy machine gun. Uri has the ammunition. Channel is carrying the backpack with the explosives. Matus and I have automatic weapons covering ourselves back and rear. After fifteen minutes, we reach the tracks. The clouds are covering the moon, and we are getting a misting rain, so we are less visible.

We can hear a train in the distance and know we don't have time to plant our bomb. We stay in the shadows and watch it pass. Two flatbed cars loaded with sand bags are being pushed in front of the locomotive. It is all boxcars and flatbeds - tanks, food and ammunition. We find a place between the German outposts and set up the heavy machine gun. Channel and I man the machine gun; Uri is ready with the light machine gun. Vanya is digging under the rails while Matus is unpacking and setting the explosives. It takes only a few minutes to place the explosives. Matus puts in the fuse and the shompol and signals us to pack up and be ready to run.

"Another train is coming", says Matus. "I can feel it in the rails. We've only got a few minutes before it gets here. I don't have time to camouflage it."

"They won't see it," says Vanya. "Coming so close behind the other train; they won't be looking for a bomb."

We start running, and the engine comes in view. We turn our heads and take a few seconds to look. It is a passenger train carrying troops. It has no flatbeds in front. They must think the rails are safe, because it is closely following the freight train. But not close enough.

"Run Julie! Run!" says Matus in a whispered shout. "If you're slow, someday they'll catch you."

I can feel my lungs busting as I pick up speed. We are a kilometer from the rails when I'm stopped in my tracks by a deafening blast of dynamite throwing up a flashing thunderbolt and lighting up the sky. For a second we revel in our success. We then break out of our daze and resume running. We are still two kilometers from our horses. Shells, rockets and heavy machine gun fire shatter the ground around us as we run across the fields. .

"Run! Run!" shouts Matus. "Look for an ambush when we get to the road. Be ready to jump in the ditch."

There is no ambush. We didn't give them enough time to cut off our escape. Exhausted and wet with rain and sweat, we reach the safety of our horses. I am shivering in wet clothes as we ride through the damp cold of early morning. We gallop the fifteen kilometers toward the safety of our swamp. At first light the sky to the east is showing purple and pink clouds as we reach the Berezina River that marks the boundary of our swamp. With Matus's help, we have cheated death again. We start to cross the river.

"Stop! Don't cross," shouts Matus. "Look, see that truck parked two-hundred meters away. It is hidden in the bushes. You can see only a little of the top. How did the truck get there? We cut trees down across the roads so nothing could pass. Stay here - it could be an ambush for our brigade, which will go out today to attack the Naliboki Garrison."

Matus jumps on his horse and looks around. He can see some German helmets above the bushes. Instinctively he pulls the trigger of his machine gun with the realization of an ambush.

"Fritzes," he shouts as he lets out his whole magazine in the direction of the Helmets. "Retreat to the other side."

In two minutes we are on the other side. The forest echoes with heavy explosives. Matus covers us shooting at the crawling Germans until his horse is shot out from under him. Wounded, he slides down from his horse and jumps in the river.e throws himself in the river. It is wide and deep and the current is strong. Now we are covering him with the heavy machine gun and with everything we got, hoping he can get past the rapids before they shoot him. The current brings him very close to us.

"I am wounded, help me Julie," he begs.

I stretch out my arms, but he misses my hand and the current carries him away.

"Matus swim over here," I shout as bullets are hitting the water and the trees around us.

I am running down the bank trying to keep up with him, but the current is too strong. Matus can't get out. Our gunners are still returning fire. I jump in the river trying to grab him, but he is yanked away from me. I am now being swept along in the powerful current. My arms are useless to move me in any direction but downstream. I have now lost sight of him.

"Matus! Matus," I shout. "I am here. My god, help us. Where are you?"

I am now frantic, looking. My eyes are darting about the rapids and churning water. He is gone. I grab on to a rock and pull myself on to the bank. We search the river far downstream, but there is no sign of him. Our mission has paid a big price. There will never be another Matus. He was the best we had. He always brought his squad home intact, but we couldn't bring him home. We return to our huts with the pain of our loss.

Chaya, his wife meets us. "Where is Matus? Julie, you are dripping wet. What has happened?"

We are silent. I avoid eye contact. I am overcome with loss and guilt. He was right there in arm's reach. How did I miss pulling him out? I can never forgive myself.

"Where is Matus," she screams? "Tell me, you bandits, Where is he?"

My eyes are full of tears as I look up, and whisper in a fractured voice," Chaya, he is gone."

Chaya falls on the grass in convulsions. Foam comes to her mouth. Her bulging eyes are wide open, and she shakes all over like she has a fever. Eighteen months ago she fell ill when the Nazis threw her two small children down the well in the Gorodok day of selection. Now her Matus is dead.

Two days later we find Matus downstream. His body is swollen and green. We bury him in our growing graveyard on the hill overlooking the forest.

Chapter 24

German POW's

June 1944

The Allies are pushing the Germans out of Italy with the fall of Rome. June 6, "D" day begins as 155,000 troops start landing on the beaches of Normandy. The US is winning the war in the Pacific. The US and Britain are pushing the Japanese out of Burma and India. June 9, Stalin launches an attack on Finland with the intent of defeating Finland in a land grab before pushing on to Berlin.

1 June 1944, a cool mid-morning on the edge of the Naliboki Forest

Expecting the worst, we block the roads leading into the forest. I have four White Russians to help me watch the main road to the village of Naliboki. Each has an old rifle with twenty rounds of ammunition. We are on top of a hill and behind a barricade of newly cut trees. There is the smell of pine and the music of busy birds singing, as the sun is coming up in a bright blue sky. I am looking down on a long straight dirt road and the budding and greening forest. Shattering the tranquility is the faraway sound of shooting and explosions. I stand watch while my troops eat breakfast.

Suddenly I notice a figure in a German uniform, a hundred and fifty meters away. I alert the boys. I'm hesitant to open fire. It's quiet with no small arms fire close by, and he doesn't look aggressive. I remain cautious and wait. He vanishes for a few minutes and reappears. I wave a white handkerchief. He sees me and stops. He then starts to approach. I wave again and he comes in with his hands on top of his head. My finger is on the trigger - ready to shoot. He has a hand gun, but no rifle. I order one of the boys to take his pistol and bullet belt and search him for any pictures and letters. I have him sit down and the boys offer him some of their breakfast. From his papers I see he is Corporal Fritz Webel, age forty.

"Hitler is finished," I say in German. "But you, Fritz, will live and be home in a few months. Where are your friends?"

Nervous and dejected he responds, "Two more are in the forest."

"Stand up and call them." I command.

"Lander! Peter!" he shouts several times.

Two men come out of the forest onto the road about a hundred meters away and walk in with hands on top of their heads. Each has a hand gun, but no rifle. The boys are glad to empty there pockets of papers, knives and money. From the papers I see they are Corporal Erich Lander, age 39, and Corporal Peter Ryzgs, age 26.

"You are welcome," I begin. "Hitler is kaput. You will soon be home. Rommel committed suicide after organizing a failed attempt to kill Hitler. Hitler has retreated to his bunker and left the rest of you to die for his cause. All of these territories are under our control. We have thousands of guerillas here, so you have no choice but to be our guest. You will be shot if you try to run, and there is nowhere to escape to. You will be treated fairly. We do observe international law for POW's, even if you Germans don't."

By noon the three are seated in our dugout for POW's. I am still at my post waiting for my replacement. Finally relief arrives. Our platoon leader, Vanya Lesnov, smiles, and embraces me.

"Where are the three hand guns?" I ask.

"I have the Magnum pistol," he says, showing me the gun. "The Commissar and his assistant have the Brownings.

"I captured them," I object. "I talked them into submission, so I should have a handgun."

Don't worry," says Vanya with a pat on the back. "I'll talk it over with the Commissar. I'm sure he will find something for you. I brought Jeremy as your replacement. Since you know German, I need your help interrogating the prisoners. Walk back to camp with me."

Vanya goes to the Commissar tent while I wait. He comes back with the Commissar's Russian revolver, and I accept it. I wanted the Russians to know that a Jew captured three Germans.

We go to the POW hut and Vanya starts the interrogation in Russian, as I translate into German for the prisoners. With pen and paper the Commissar's secretary is writing down the testimony as I translate the prisoners' German into Russian.

"Corporal Webel," begins the interrogation. "Tell us your history. Where are you from and what events brought you here today. If we find that you are not telling the truth, you will be shot. We have your letters to verify you testimony."

"I grew up in Dusseldorf. I met and befriended Erich in school. I was a truck driver for a bakery company. I am married and have two daughters. Erich and I were drafted into the infantry in the spring of 1942. We were given six months of training and sent to the Russian front in time for the battle of Stalingrad. In October of 1943, the rains came and turned the whole countryside into mud. Every step forced me to pull my leg out of the stinking mud that was sometimes knee deep. We were soaked to the skin and chilled to the bone. We retreated in a slow but orderly fashion - mowing down Russians and falling back again. We got reinforcements and attacked again and gained most of what we had lost. Then we were told to halt and dig in. After five days, we were ordered to retreat. The retreat was hell, because we had destroyed all the bridges and anything we could use for cover. After a few weeks the Russian artillery barrage began. They broke through and encircled us north of Smolensk. We fought our way out, losing half our troops. First Erich was wounded in the chest, and then I was shot in the upper right arm and in both legs. I fainted from the pain and came to in an auxiliary hospital with Erich in the same room. We were sent to a Berlin hospital and spent five months in bed. We were sent back to the front as truck drivers."

"The three of us served as truck drivers delivering food and munitions to the garrisons of Witebsk and Minsk. Four days ago, we were ambushed on the Zaslav-Minsk road. We lost ten trucks. Our guards were killed instantly. The three of us ran into the woods and escaped. We were trying to get to the garrison at Molodeczno and got lost."

"Corporal Erich Lander," queries Vanya. "Do you agree with Corporal Webel's testimony?"

"Yes," replies Corporal Lander. "Our history is the same for the Army. We have been friends since childhood. We asked to be allowed to serve together when we were drafted. I worked in a garage as a mechanic before my service. I have a wife and a boy, six and a girl, ten. They are lost without me. I am ready to go home and for the war to be over."

I check the letters and find that Webel and Lander are telling the truth, but I am suspicious of the Lithuanian. Peter was tall, handsome, and the son of a rich farmer. He speaks broken German and very little Russian. He was born in 1918 in the city of Showl.

"How long have you been in the Army," I ask. "Did you volunteer?"

"No," he answers. "I have been in for three years. The Germans drafted me when I was twenty-three."

"Into what unit?" I ask.

"I was first mobilized into the police, and then I went to the Army."

"Don't lie," I warn him. "All the police were volunteers. Ever been in the S.S.?"

"No," he answers while looking at the floor.

I show him his photo and ask, "What do you see in this picture?"

"I was a corporal in the Lithuanian police," he says still looking at the floor.

"This is a Lieutenant's uniform," I spit out as I clench my teeth in anger. I can see that he is trembling. I continue, "You said you were not a member of the Nazi party. What is this round button on your uniform?"

With a shiver he answers, "That's a sports medal. I was a good runner."

"No!" I spit out. "National Socialist German Workers Party is written on the badge. For once tell the truth. How long were you in the party?"

"I was forced to join the party only a year ago."

At the end of the interrogation with Peter, I take Fritz and Lander outside and ask them what they know of Peter. They say that Peter had boasted of killing Russian POW's and had participated in massacres of Russians and Jews. I report all this to Vanya.

An hour later a military court is called to try Peter. Three young guerillas serve as judges. Vanya reads the results of the interrogation. He puts down his papers and adds, "I appeal to you judges to punish this despicable representative of the Nazis. Today he must answer for his crimes. He has participated in mass killings and inhumane atrocities. In the name of law and justice and in the name of millions of the tortured and murdered, I ask you to find Peter Ryzgs guilt."

"May the defendant rise and answer the charges," the Chief Judge asks.

Peter stands handcuffed and shivering and says, "Please take into consideration that I was misled by my friends, who all joined the Nazis. Bishop Bryzgis appealed to us to help the German Army. I do not wish to minimize my guilt. I want to point out that the German Government is responsible for all the atrocities committed in Russia. You should consider that I surrendered to you without resistance. Please spare my life, so that I may atone for my guilt."

The verdict is guilty and the sentence is death by hanging. We march Peter from the military court to the nearest tree and hang him. Justice is done in one day.

It's dark when I get to Hannah's hut. She has just returned from the hospital hut. I tell her about the capture of the three Germans and the execution. She hugs me and says how proud she is of her husband. She has been having vivid dreams of her mother and father and her two sisters. She tries to stay busy caring for the injured, but nightmares are torturing her.

231

"Julie," she weeps. "I can't sleep.

I am looking into her tired, tearful eyes and the stress lines in her face. I put my arms around her and pull her to me and say, "The war is coming to an end. We will leave this unhappy land and go to Palestine and have five kids. Will anyone believe the story of our love - of how we met and survived so many chances to die and how our love lives through it all."

"I do love you, my Julie. Please hold me tight. Be with me always. We must make the most of the time we have. It could be the only time we have."

"I will love you forever and always be here for you," I whisper as I kiss her neck, her cheek, and her lips. I kiss her eye lids shut," and tell her, "I have a surprise for you."

"What," she says as she looks up from my shoulder with a curious smile."

"Look in the corner under your coat."

She breaks away and finds a wooden box. I sit up on the bed to enjoy her reaction, and say "I have brought you medical books in anatomy, pathology, and surgery, so you will be able to pass your exams to be a doctor."

"Darling, thank you so much," she says as she inspects each one of her treasures. "You must be reading my mind. I have been wishing for a medical book."

"Now for more important things," she says as she takes off her shirt and kicks off her pants exposing a perfect body and the pleasure of my life. She pulls my shirt over my head. With a hand to my chest, she pushes me back down on her bed and pulls at my pants until they are off. She then mounts me with her black silk hair falling about my face. I massage her tight shoulders into softness and work my hands down her back to her buttocks as I nurse her breast. She pulls me into her and I sink my lips into hers. Passion builds like bellowing clouds

232

that become a violent, flashing storm; igniting tears that fall on wide smiles. She gasps and moans, "Oh God, I love you. Be with me always."

15 June 1944, Naliboki Forest

Moscow orders us to intensify our activities. In reaction, the enemy starts a partial blockade of the forest and pounds us with heavy guns, which only succeed in making firewood. Our order is to cut all railway lines. At midnight the thousand partisans of our brigade move on the rails in ten different places. Every ten minutes a flare burst overhead. The Germans are out in force. My platoon is out in front and approaching the rails, when we hear heavy machine gun fire and bullets striking the trees around us. We all hug the ground. Two of us are hit. The moans and cries of the wounded are haunting me, as Vanya and I stand up behind trees with our automatic rifles and wait for our chance. The flashing light of the German heavy machine gun reveal three soldiers about eighty meters away. One of them is firing and another is feeding a bandolier of cartridges to the machine gun that is making a hundred degree arc in our direction. I wait until their gun is pointed at the other end of the arc, before I raise my gun, hold my breath and fire. Vanya does the same on his end. After three minutes the enemy gun is silent. We find them with their grenades still in their hands. The lieutenant has his belly blown out and the other two are face down. We take their boots and their weapons as our sappers blow up the tracks. More explosions can be heard in the distance. At dawn we are back in our dugouts with two wounded. Five of us are killed out of a thousand. It will be four or five days before the Germans can move anything on the rails.

24 June 1944, Naliboki forest near the Partisan base camp

I am collecting fire wood, when I discover a gypsy wagon with a red round top. A horse is grazing nearby. A brightly dressed woman with a black arm band is bent over tending her fire with a covered pot. She stands up to greet me with a straight back. Black intense eyes radiate from a strong determined face with deep smile lines.

"My son, I know you," she says as I approach. "You are Yehuda. My two boys, Sashka and Marka were with you in the guerillas. Do you remember them?"

"Yes, both were excellent horsemen and scouts who rode with Matus. They were ambushed on the road not far from Volozyn. They were the first to discover two enemy platoons waiting to ambush our company. Both were shot several times but were able to ride back and warn us before they died. They lie with Matus, in our grave yard."

"From my family of twenty, only my son Yashka and I live," she says as tears collect in her eye. She takes a breath and blinks to dispel them. "I am a gypsy, but every day I read your Holy Scriptures. It helps me see the future by looking at the past. I can see your future." she says as she pulls out a pack of brightly decorated cards from a skirt pocket and gives them a professional shuffle. "Take three cards."

I take a nine, ten and queen of clubs that I show with apprehension.

"Don't worry Julie," she smiles with the comfort of a mother. "You don't believe in the cards, so why worry. If you believe in something, then it will happen. Believe in this, it will save your life. The nine and ten show that you will see seventeen months of crosses, and the hardest part of your journey is still ahead. The queen of clubs shows you are bold and courageous enough to survive."

Chapter 25

Russian Tank Offensive from Minsk

To East Prussia

Russian Operation Bagration

22 June 1944- 29 August 1944

In April 1944, Russian leaders selected a plan to attack the German Group Center holding a bulge in Belarus and the Ukraine. Russian forces spread false intelligence that the offensive was to be made against German Army Group South in Ukraine, reinforcing something that the Germans expected. When the operation launched, the 1st and 3rd Ukrainian Armies were deployed to further support that ruse. The Germans fell for the deception and made their Army Group Center weaker; for instance, most armor in the German reserves was transferred south to Northern Ukraine. The German reaction to the Normandy invasion also weakened the available forces in the Russian front. On the morning of 22 June 1944, the Russian army with 1,700,000 Troops and 6,000 tanks rushed against 34 surprised German Divisions, nearly achieving a 10 to 1 numerical advantage in tanks and a 7 to 1 advantage in aircraft. The German lines quickly fell apart, and Minsk came under Russian control on 3 July 1944, capturing 50,000 prisoners of war. Ten days later, Russian troops had marched across Belarus and reached the Polish border. By the end of July 1944, the entire German Army Group Center ceased to exist, losing 300,000 men to death and 120,000 captured. 2,000 tanks were lost as well. On the Russian side 60,000 were killed and 3,000 tanks were lost. The Bagration deceptive tactics became a model for Soviet Army Cadets.

3 July 1944, Noon, In the Naliboki Forest, west of Minsk

"Fight for Mother Russia," the radio blares out. "Our tanks attack again and again with six or seven waves. Gradually we wear them down and reduce their numbers. The enemy can no longer hold on. Our Russian Blitzkrieg is beating the Nazis at their own game. Salute General Cherniakhovsky! His tank division has captured Minsk. His tanks will be in Berlin before the snow. Salute Stalin! Salute the High command! Kill the Nazis!"

Our huddle of Partisans circled around the radio break into a wild joyous dance. Screams echo through the camp, "Minsk is ours! Fuck the Germans! Freedom! We are free!" Guns fire into the air bringing people out of the dugouts. Vodka is gulped down, streams down our faces along with the tears of joy and goes right to my head. Laughter, screaming and dancing bring me to the point of exhaustion. For the first time in years, I feel only happiness in my heart. I hug and kiss Hanel as our tears flow together.

Two hours into our celebration, five T-34 Russian tanks roll into camp. The crews that climb out of the tanks are no more than nineteen years old. They are laughing, kissing and embracing us. We are amazed at the soldiers' morale. My spirits are lifted, but compared to them; I am a tired old man at thirty-one. They are young, invincible and have the Germans on the run. Their families have been murdered, so they have all the strength of anger and revenge. Our strength feeds on theirs.

When they show off their tanks, we see the T-34 is clearly superior to the German Tiger Tank. As they shoot off their anti-tank guns and small arms, we can hear the thunder and feel the vibrations of Russian heavy artillery pounding the German defenses. After three years of fighting, Russia has an unlimited supply of trained infantry, artillery and tanks. It is clear that collectively and individually we are stronger. None of us would surrender to the Germans under any circumstances. Their atrocities have scarred our souls. Revenge will be ours, and we will never have enough.

Later after eating and much Vodka, we see an American jeep drive up with a driver and two Russian officers and Ehrenburg, the famous Russian writer and war correspondent. The experienced partisans are called to headquarters.

Colonel Kryzanovski, who is one of the tank commanders speaks to us, "I am Commander of the Tatzinsky Tank Corps. We take our name from our victory at Tatzin near Stalingrad. I need your help in the fight for our homeland. We now have the latest generation of weapons; three hundred T-34 Tanks, unlimited artillery, American trucks, small arms, light artillery, anti-tank guns, rockets and heavy artillery. Our army is young and fresh, and we are a better army than the Germans, who are tired and beaten. We want you to join us in kicking the bastards back to Berlin, if any of them live that long. Are you ready? Whoever wants to join up, step forward?"

We all volunteer. The Colonel scrutinizes each of us. One by one he puts his hand on the shoulder of his selection and says, "Congratulations, welcome to the Tatzinsky Tank Corps."

Among those selected were Michael Lidsky, the Spingers, Abram and me. When he came to me, it was obvious that he knew of my capture and interrogation of the three Germans.

"So you are Yehuda," he says with a smile. "You must come with us. There is not a single person in our unit who speaks good German."

"Sir, I would be honored to serve with you," I say as I feel his heavy hand on my shoulder. There would be no way to refuse him, even if I wanted to. We are dismissed and told to report for duty at eight in the morning.

As I leave the tent I see some partisans have gathered around Ehrenburg who is smoking his pipe and listening to the accounts of how we survived in the swamp and blew up the rails. He asks if there was anyone who could write him and keep him informed of the battle as it progressed and answer questions he might have. I volunteer and we exchange addresses. I have never been so close to a famous person. I am impressed with his knowledge of the military and the ongoing battle. We shake hands and he gets in the jeep and drives off with the Colonel. As I walk away I am excited about corresponding with Ehrenburg, the greatest Russian writer of our time. He is also Stalin's propaganda minister and a Jew.

The tank corps is going to be more structured and disciplined than I am used to, but at least there won't be vodka drinking on duty, I hope. I never felt safe with the Russian Partisans who were drinking while we were trying to blow up a train.

I find Hanah in her hut. I lie down beside her on the straw bed. She reaches over and grabs my hand. I can feel the warmth of her love.

"Oh darling," she says as she rolls over on top of me and kisses me. "I am looking forward to being with you alone on our three weeks of furlough. There will be a parade and celebration in Minsk. We will be given medals and money for being partisans and risking our lives for so long. We have a free hotel where we can have a proper honeymoon. Aren't you the least bit excited? What's wrong?"

"I won't be going to Minsk," I say.

She rolls off of me and glares, "Why not?

"I am going the other way, to Berlin," I say. "I have been selected by Colonel Kryzanovski to join the tank corp. He doesn't have anybody who speaks German, but me."

"No need to talk to them - just kill them all."

"I would have joined anyway."

"Why? You have done enough," she says bitterly. "We deserve some time to rest and to be together. I am looking forward to getting out of the swamp, having some clean clothes and being a woman again. Most of all, I want to be with you. I have lost my family. I don't want to lose my husband. I want you close to me. I don't want you ever to be out of my sight. The war can be over for us. This damn army has put a wedge between us by keeping us apart for too long. We have done our duty. Please let's run away."

"Where would we run? Until the war is over, the Russian Army is the best place we could be. Jews are finished in this part of the world. Our homes and communities are gone. Still we aren't welcome in much of the gentile community. Our partisans have bullied and punished a lot of peasants, which didn't help relations that were already bad. Someday we will go to America where my cousins are. Until the war is over, you and I and every Jew must do his part to defeat the Germans. We have come a long way from being victims to fighters."

"I know," she says bowing her head in disappointment. "I didn't expect you to go so soon. I know you are not afraid, but I am afraid for you and us. I love you so very much. Please don't take unnecessary risks. Don't volunteer for anything. You must stay alive for me. I will do my part for the war in some field hospital. I wish we could be together for just two weeks. I am ready to have children and get on with our life."

I kiss her hands, her eyes and her salty tears. Exhausted, I fall asleep in her arms. I wake in the early morning hearing the artillery duel all around us sounding louder than the fieriest thunder storm. Hanah's face is beautiful and relaxed. I don't want to wake her. I just look, search her face, and memorize everything about her. Her silk hair spills across her breasts. Her active life has made a perfect body with a hard stomach and strong arms and legs. I want to remember her like this. God, please don't let anything happen to her. She is the most precious thing I will ever know. After a while she starts to wake up. I snuggle next to her and kiss her awake. I inhale the first breath of her morning. With passion she grabs and kisses me. I feel her love powerful and flowing through my chest, stomach and my whole being. We are all consumed and completely lost in each other. We make love like it may never happen again, and we must remember it always.

Exhausted, we are left wrapped in each other's arms. Her face is on my chest and her warm breasts are pushing against my stomach. Her long beautiful hair is draped around my neck.

"I hope you got me pregnant," she whispers. "It is that time of the month."

"It will be a child of passion," I smile. "How many do you want?"

"About a million."

"That will keep me busy."

"I had a terrible dream last night," she says as she hugs me for security. "I was surrounded by Nazis." she begins to laugh in half-hearted amusement. "I have similar dreams about twice a week. You would think I would get used to it and dismiss them before they happen. It is always like for the first time. I wake up shaking and frightened. I am glad I don't always wake you up. This time they came to my dugout with knives, damn long knives. They were as long as bayonet's. I am going to miss you when I wake from nightmares, and you are not here to hold me."

"I am going to miss you every night I am not sleeping with you and every morning that I wake up without you."

She kisses me and says, "I need to know your commander and your unit, so I can keep up with you. Of course I will write, but who knows if you will get the letter."

"I am in the Third Guard Brigade of the Third White Russian Front. My commander is Colonel Kryzanovski. He is Jewish, and so is his General, Cherniakhovsky, the Commander of the White Russian Front."

"There are a lot of Jewish Cherniachovskys in Vilnius, he must have family there."

"I must slip on my clothes and go. I have about twenty minutes to be there. I love you, my Hanele."

"I will dress and go with you."

As we climb out of the dugout, I see a tall blond man in his early twenties coming toward me with a big smile. It is Chonele Elterman of the Tchkalovs partisan brigade. I embrace him like a brother. I have known him since I was a school principal and he was the best soccer player in town. The last time I saw him was on the road. He was with his brigade and carrying a heavy machine gun. I had to shout to greet him as my platoon was headed in the opposite direction. His partisan command had also recommended him to join the Tatzinsky tank corps. We are soon joined by Michael Lidsky and the Springer brothers. We are all feeling a warm pride in our chest and a spring in our step that we have been chosen as the elite among a thousand partisans and have the honor of serving in a tank corps that is famous for its victories over the Germans at Stalingrad and the battles that drove the Nazis out of Russia to where they are now.

I feel a hand on my shoulder and turn to see Grishka's smiling face.

"I come to say goodbye," He says in his husky voice. "I wish you well and hope to see you in Palestine."

"Why aren't you coming with us?" Michael asks.

"They asked me," he chuckles. "I told them if you make me the General in charge, I will consider it. Even then, there are orders from General Stalin, the biggest asshole of them all. And if I saw Katkof, I would have to kill him. That wouldn't be good for either one of us. I've had too much of orders and the Russians. I quit. Anyway, the guerillas are being disbanded. For the moment I am in charge of me, so after the celebration in Minsk I will take two horses and ride toward Palestine. Fogel is coming with me, if he doesn't find a widow before we leave. We will be like Don Quixote and Sancho Panza. The truth is that I can't stay here. What Jew would want to be here? I have robbed every peasant within a hundred kilometers. Several would like to shoot me in the back. My family is dead and the Jewish community is gone. Now it is up to you. You must kill all the Germans, run away from the Russians, and please stay alive. You are my family. I love you."

We all hug good-bye to the best among us. I hope to see Grishka again. I know he will survive. But will I? With an upheaval of emotion, I take Hanah's hand, and we resume walking. I wish I had a way of telling her how deeply and completely I love her. We stop near where we must say good-bye, and I find a large tree for cover. We hold each other in a tight embrace. She is sobbing into my shoulder. It is futile to hold back the tears or my embarrassment in having them. We have never been apart for more than a couple of days since we married. We are the only family we have left. I take one last long kiss. She dries my eyes on her handkerchief and puts it in my hand with a lucky horse shoe. She watches me climb up on my tank and disappear inside. I assume my position as the machine gunner.

* * *

The writer Ehrenburg with the Tatsin tankmen at the front in 1942.

5 July 1944

We break through the German defenses about one hundred kilometers northeast of Minsk in the vicinity of Orsha and Borisov. We are advancing swiftly westward and not allowing the enemy to dig in. We have Infantry, four artillery battalions, rockets and three hundred T-34 Russian tanks. Our tanks are superior to the German tanks in speed and fire power. General Ochsner, the German commander has tanks, infantry, and artillery. After two days they retreat leaving small artillery units about every five kilometers to hold us back. In this fashion, the enemy is falling back, moving from position to position westward. Our tanks are moving around the Germans through the forest and marshland with our guerillas serving as guides, so our tanks and artillery don't get stuck. On my first day of fighting, our tanks are able to move swiftly and encircle 100,000 Germans.

Ehrenburg with General Chernyakhovsky at the front in 1942

6 July 1944

We are having a few hours rest while the tanks refuel and the supply lines catch up. I sit on the back of our tank with my tank-mate, Chonele Elterman, who was one of the first Jewish Partisans.

"How did you escape the Nazi net and join the partisans?" I ask. "I'm curious, because it took me six months?"

"Six months?" questions Chonele. "You were clever, lucky and resourceful to have lived through it with no means of support and being hunted like a rabbit. I made the transition from prisoner to soldier in about a week; that was the easier way. My parents, two sisters and I escaped the Selection by constructing a hiding place in the synagogue. Next we moved in with some Polish friends who hid us for several days until the policeman, Nikolay, saw something that gave us away. He came with his partner, Timur, for the bounty money while we were eating supper. I dived out a window before they could shoot, and they were too fat and slow to catch me. They executed my family the next day. I was furious for revenge. Nikolay was living alone, so it was easy to break into his house. With a knife from the kitchen, I waited for him to come home from work and grabbed his chin from behind while he was washing his hands and cut his throat. I shot Timur with Nikolay's gun as he was walking home and took his pistol. After killing two policeman, I had to go somewhere in a hurry. The two pistols were my ticket to the partisans. Like you, we were blowing up trains, and I also gave cover with the heavy machine gun and taught myself how to repair it."

"Some you couldn't break and others stayed broken," I reminisce. "Hirsh said you taught him how to fix them."

"We figured it out together. With heat, friction and the movement of rapid fire, things need maintenance after every use. I loved my gun, played it like a fiddle, and it gave me the power to make a difference. Once I saved our unit with my machine gun. We had just blown up a train and gone to a farm house to sleep. I couldn't sleep, so I got up and stood guard; I had gut feelings the Germans were pursuing us. Soon I heard dogs and saw lights; I opened fire and held them off while my unit escaped."

"You always gave a hundred percent to your soccer game and are the best I've ever seen. Now you are an amazing soldier. I'm sure you will be exceptional at operating our tank cannon. We will all be safer, in good repair and more effective with you around. It is an honor to be serving with you, my friend."

We jump in our tanks as the order is given to tighten the noose around the enemy. We fire artillery and rockets into the circle and charge ahead with our tanks. The Germans know they are in a cauldron and try desperately to break out, but it is too late. By five o'clock enemy corpses litter the road from Borisov to Minsk. The bodies are rotting and stinking in the summer sun.

Our General Cherniachovsky stops on the road to see the extermination camp at Mali Trostenets on the outskirts of Minsk. Jews from Vilnius, Minsk and nearby villages were exterminated here. Our General is Jewish and had cousins in Vilnius. The Germans blew up and burned the camp in an attempt to destroy evidence of genocide. In their haste to leave, the Nazis left thousands of bodies only charred. Thirty-four huge grave pits were discovered. Maybe two-hundred thousand were murdered here. It is the first death camp captured by the Allies. Many in the West do not believe our reports of the carnage.

With tears in his eyes, our general listens to the partisans as they tell of the atrocities, the annihilation of Jewish communities, and the killing of prisoners of war.

Talking to the foreign correspondents, Cherniachovsky shows the open graves and says, "Here are some of the millions killed by the Nazis. We will get the murderers. We are not pursuing the Germans from the east. That is too difficult. We shall surround them and take them from all sides. They are not yet completely crushed. Many divisions will resist stubbornly, but they are in our hands."

The atrocities at Mali Trostenets fuel our anger and determination to annihilate the enemy. At this moment, fifty thousand prisoners taken at Minsk are on their way to march through Red Square. After the parade, they will be shipped to Siberia. Few prisoners will be marching away from this battle. It will be a bloody road to Berlin. Revenge will be ours. The Germans know they are fighting for their lives, so it is not going to be easy.

The German Junkers are coming low, spraying our tank column with bullets. The firing of my machine gun, long burst of antiaircraft fire, the whistle of rockets, the clatter and groans of the tanks make a symphony of sweet music that muffles the screams of the dying.

The Germans have set up three defense lines stretching back five kilometers in order to protect a railway station that will allow them to retreat by rail. Without it they are at the mercy of our tanks. We dig in and wait for our artillery to get in place. After two days our Russian cannonade begins with hundreds of rockets flying overhead into the German positions. Big thundering shells explode and shake the ground. I am trembling and overwhelmed by the magnitude of the artillery barrage, so that I can't stand and must sit down. Now I know what power is driving the Germans out of the occupied territories. We are the soldiers and heroes who will soon bring freedom to the oppressed peoples of Europe.

The cannonade stops and we move on to the railway station to cut off the German retreat. The tank's exhaust is so sweet that I inhale it. I love everything about my state of the art tank and this whole mechanized army. I like having new first-class weapons with the Germans on the run. I gladly give up my old rifle for my place in the tank. Thank God I am in a tank rather than a scout on a motorcycle. Eight of the Partisans were assigned as motorcycle scouts. After a few days four of them are dead. I am sure some of them were killed because they were still drinking their vodka and didn't notice the snipers.

15 July 1944, Lithuania

Vilnius is captured. Brest and Litovsk have been taken in the south. German artillery stops us twenty kilometers east of Marijampole. Sounds of shells are flying overhead like express trains. Our artillery is answering. Shells are falling all around us on an already pockmarked hay field. We are ordered to leave our tanks and dig trenches. We dig deeper and deeper in the wet sticky soil with our clothing becoming heavy, soaked and skin like. I am too cold to enjoy the supper of beans, potatoes, barley soup and beef. The meat is marked "USA" in aluminum cans. Most of us won't eat. We know in case of a bullet to the abdomen, it easier to operate on an empty stomach. I am too nervous to sleep, talk or joke. Two more of our guerrillas are killed by the bombardment.

At first light, we are ordered to build an observation post to observe the attacking enemy. A wire is run for a phone to the General's command post in case his radio is knocked out by the heavy shelling that is shattering the forest around us. We are lucky to be in trenches. A hundred meters away, we hear screams. The lieutenant orders me to investigate. I crawl over and check. Four bodies are mangled with blood and body parts thrown about and two possible survivors. I radio for a medic. One man is conscious and bleeding from the head. I find Michael Lidzki gasping for air and groaning. It is the same Michael who jumped from the Gorodok truck with me and for years tried to get a British visa to go to Palestine. His eyes close and his face becomes pale but peaceful. I touch his hand and find no pulse. His body is warm and there is no blood or sign of injury. Maybe he is in a coma from a concussion. I give him artificial respiration until the medics arrive. The doctor pronounces him dead and finds a small shell fragment has pierced his heart. The soldier with the head wound seems okay. We bury the five in the dugout with Michael on top. I don't know if I can watch another friend die. You think you would get used to it, but it's like another stake in your heart and more pain to carry around. It's better to go to war with acquaintances - not with people you love.

16 July 1944

At five in the morning, from our observation post we are able to see the Germans move out of their trenches and move slowly in our direction. They are so far away; they look like small grasshoppers crawling out of their holes. The figures are bent with their heads drooped under the weight of their helmets like they are searching for something on the ground. Our infantry starts firing. Our artillery and tanks are quiet. More and more emerge from the trenches. The gray figures come on slowly. Now and then one of them plunges headlong into the undergrowth. They are now two hundred meters away. There are thousands, and too many for a machine gun to get rid of before they reach us. The rough terrain, underbrush and fog are not in our favor. I have the feeling we are about to be over-run. What are our guns waiting for? The Germans start their bombardment.

"Now is the time," I scream. And it comes from all sides.

The Germans are caught in a pocket. There is crossfire of rockets and artillery from all sides. The air is thick and murky with smoke. The enemy launches a heavy rocket attack and is still fighting back. Our tanks move in to stop the massive rocket attack. Thousands of grey soldiers are on the ground. Bodies, alive and dead, are torn to pieces by the treads of our tanks. I become indifferent to the screams of the live ones as my tank crunches over them. Our tanks smash through their lines. Our artillery targets the rear of the retreating enemy to prevent reinforcements. Now that the enemy is isolated, our infantry moves in to mop up the remnants. A thousand Germans raise their hands and shout, "Hitler kaput."

As evening approaches, what is left of the enemy is in full retreat. I am ravenous and devour my supper. I drink some vodka and spread my coat on the ground and sleep satisfied from a good day's work.

17 July 1944

At two in the morning we rise to chase the enemy. We move twelve miles west of Marijampole. Our reconnaissance reports the enemy is again entrenched. The terrain is marshy and the famous German tank division, Gross Deutschland, is prepared to meet us. We have lost twenty tanks and need rein-forcements. We know the Germans will defend East Prussia with all their resources. I feel it's the quiet before the storm as we build our defenses. We dig trenches - deep narrow and zigzagged. I know that only mother earth can save us from the

German artillery. We are divided into three gangs. Each gang works at a furious pace, knowing this is an emergency. Men resting roll cigarettes, measure the working crews' progress, and tell light jokes that didn't bring a laugh. Everyone loves our platoon leader, Viktor, who is a professional actor and singer from Leningrad.

"Boys," He says. "We are thirty kilometers from the Prussian border. We will make it. All is quiet, and the trenches are finished. Let's sing something you know. He starts in a strong baritone voice.

"Dark is the night
Bullets are whistling by
Rockets are flying high
In May, the enemy will be defeated.
My beautiful lady will meet me with my baby
Every Nazi will hang on a rope
Peace will come and we will see our girls"

We all sing along and forget our fear of the pending bombardment and for a moment are lighthearted. Our singing has attracted attention. I see some officers moving our way. Viktor shouts, "Attention." Among the officers is our Colonel Kryzanovski and Elie Ehrenburg, the famous novelist. His words on the radio are inspiring us to fight even harder to defeat the enemy. I can't believe I am seeing him again.

"Comrades," he says. "We broke the enemy's spine on four thousand miles of front line, from the Baltic to the River Donau in Romania. We are relentlessly chasing a retreating army. Some of your units under the command of your General Cherniachovsky have already crossed the German border. Radio Moscow announced one hour ago that General Stalin expresses his gratitude to your General for having the first Soviet tank brigade on German soil. That means you. Congratulations!

Long live Stalin! Long live General Cherniachovsky! Long live Colonel Kryzanovski!"

"We thank Comrade Ehrenburg for his inspiration," says our Colonel. "We are adopting him as an honorary tanker."

Ehrenburg shouts, "Kill the Fritzes!"

We answer with, "Hooray! Kill the Fritzes!"

We have a relaxed lunch and think we will be moving soon, but it doesn't happen. The German Junkers dive in at 2:00 PM and throw down a blanket of bullets. Several dozen of us are hit before we are able to dive for the cover of the trenches. Our antiaircraft guns are busy spraying the air. The German heavy bombardment begins, and doesn't stop. I am huddled face down in the dirt, trying to be smaller than my helmet. I expect to be hit. We are pinned down and dare not raise our heads. Ammunition trucks are blown up. Pockets of panic break out. I know the end is coming. I hear men screaming and crying as they are hit.

Our Colonel jumps on a motorcycle and checks on his platoons. He tells us, "Soon, the bombardment will stop. Our big guns and rocket launchers are in position.

Our artillery regiment with its "Stalin Organs" starts to shell the enemy with a barrage of rockets. The horizon is lit up with our artillery shells. I come out of the trench smiling and thanking God for each precious breath. Our heavy seventy-fives are moving their barrels back and forth, targeting a fifteen kilometer front. They are knocking out the German artillery and tanks. Our planes arrive by the hundreds. We have gained the initiative. The German artillery is silent. Now they are pinned down like we were, kissing the dirt and breathing smoke. Reconnaissance reports ammunition trucks blown up, and horses used to pull the artillery pieces are galloping wildly about.

The enemy is retreating. We enter East Prussia in pursuit as the sun breaks through the morning mist and rain, it promises to be a warm day. We find the country side to be rich in cattle, wheat and vegetable crops. There are big brick homes and stone barns filled with fresh crops. All the roads are paved and lined with large oaks. I have never seen this much wealth.

19 November 1944, Thirty miles inside East Prussia

On the outskirts of Tilsit, we stop our advance and the command sends out word that we would not harm the population. Because of my German, I am given the job of inviting young German women to our kitchens to eat good American beef, from cans of course. They say "Hitler kaput" and they are glad to spend the night with our young soldiers. I strike up a conversation with Erica, an attractive young blond. Her husband is in the German Army, and she hasn't seen him in six months. She has been left to take care of her farm and two small children.

"Why did you accept our invitation to dinner," I ask.

"Several reasons," she replies looking at the ground. "First I was hungry for some meat. The German Army has taken my pigs and sheep. I was also afraid of being raped and killed. Many wounded and dead have come down this road in recent weeks. There have been reports of massacres and rape. I thought if I gave myself willingly, my life and my children might be spared."

"You are safe enough with me," I say looking into her eyes. "I have a wife, Hanah, whom I love very much. I haven't seen or heard from her in several months. We have been moving so fast the mail can't keep up with us. I write letters, but get none back."

'You seem to be a kind, sympathetic person. Can we go somewhere and talk?"

"We could go to my tent," I say with a rush of excitement that contradicts what I said about her being safe. I am not sure that I am safe from my impulses. She is twenty-five and attractive in spite of facial worry lines and coarse muscular hands. She follows me to the tent and I pull back the flap for her. She sits on my bed of blankets and I sit down beside her. We are touching. She smells clean and fresh without perfume.

"Thank you," she sobs.

"I haven't done anything,' I say.

"Just being here with you makes me feel safe. I don't know if I will ever see my husband again. I don't know if my house and my farm will be spared. If there is an occupation, will I be able to keep them?"

"I don't know the answer to those questions," I say as I take her hand to comfort her. "I don't even know if I will live through tomorrow. I was almost killed yesterday. It has been like that for a long time. Somehow I know I will survive. I have been through the worst of it. I started out in a work camp and jumped out of the back of a truck that was taking me to be shot. I was caught and had to escape again. Finally I found my wife and the Partisans and a gun and was able to fight back. I have used up ten of my lives. I don't know if my luck will last. I have lost my entire family, every blood relation and my village to the Nazis. If I die getting my revenge, it will be worth it."

"I can understand your pain," she says squeezing my hand. "I have been a victim too. There are only old men in our town. I don't know if any of our men will come back from the war. If my husband is killed, I will die a widow. Please hold me. I need a man to hold me."

I hold her and we talk through the night and fall asleep in each other's arms. Just as dawn is breaking we make love.

"I must go see about my children," she says as she puts on her clothes. "I want to be there when they wake. I can be home in an hour of walking."

I walk Erica to the edge of the camp and we hug good-by. I walk back to my tent tired from the visit. I make my bed and straighten things up and get ready for the day. As I am putting things away, I notice the letter from Ehrenburg, the writer, is missing. Did she take or did I misplace it? Maybe she is working for German intelligence and trying to find out how we hide our tanks on the edge of the forest, so they couldn't be seen. There is nothing of military importance in the letter. Being a letter written by a famous writer, it is valuable.

After breakfast, I get my first letter from Hanah.

Dear Julie,

I am worried about you. Since you joined the tank division, I haven't received the smallest communication from you. We had a tremendous reception in Minsk. About six thousand guerrillas gathered. High-ranking generals talked to us, embraced and honored us with distinctive medals as "Honorable Guerillas for the Motherland". I received a medal for bravery.

You know I left medical school when the Nazis came. I decided to finish and get my diploma. I went back to Lvov University, and many of the professors recognized me. Even though the university was destroyed, I found data from my last semester in school. I had less than a semester to complete. The professors advised me to study hard and pass my final exams. I worked very hard for two months and got my doctor's degree. Believe me, it was difficult. In the forest, I never dreamed of finishing my studies. You see dear, I had to do this. I had to be busy and not think about our tragedy. Thinking about it could have killed me. The first weeks after the liberation, I was depressed. No one was left from our families, and you had volunteered to kill our enemies.

I hope and pray to see you again. I know that you are risking your life every day to take revenge for us. Good luck to you, dear Julie.

Your loving Hanah

P.S. I volunteered for the southern front under Marshal Vailevsky. My address is Post 321 - 1st field hospital. Dr. Hanah.

Our Medical Staff: Katherine, Boris and Me

I answer her immediately.

My Dearest Hanele

I am happy that you are okay. Your letter arrived today. It was a big joy to read, and I love your picture. We had parades here also. Nazi prisoners of war paraded before us. Their homes were on fire. Their cities and villages were in flames. You would have felt satisfaction in seeing their dead, their blackened walls, their smoldering timbers, and their cattle lying dead with their bodies swollen. Furniture, bottles and torn clothes were strewn among the ashes. We are having our revenge.

We had a great number of casualties. We received replacements twice with T-34 tanks and newly trained drivers. Do you remember there were fifteen guerrillas who volunteered for the tank corps? Today there are eight of us. Seven died in combat. Let us hope there's a better future for us. Michel Lidsky and Michael Springer fell in battle. Abraham Retzkin was seriously injured and taken to the hospital.

Often we catch collaborators like ex- policemen and Lithuanians in SS uniforms. Our justice is swift - a court martial and then a hanging. Do you remember the policeman, Smolski? He killed the only surviving Jews in Gorodok. Imagine, he volunteered in our army. I reported him, and the captain answered," Don't worry. I'll take care of it." A few days later he was killed by a sniper. Later in checking the body, we found some money in his shoes. So, as you see I am doing my best. Do you want me back in your arms? Pray for me and I will pray for you. My martyred mother once warned me, "If you survive when all your family is dead, your life will be miserable." I am afraid of losing a hand or a leg and later suffering the rest of my life. When the shells fall, my heart pounds, but little by little I have gotten used to it. I know I will come back to you. I am still keeping a diary. I am now describing the mood of our soldiers and the bravery and character of my Colonel Kryzanovski and the Commander in Chief of the 3rd Russian Army, Cherniachovsky. They are both Jews. The first is a native of Leningrad and the second of Vilnius. Now here is a bit of gossip. My colonel is in love with a young lady from Moscow, Dr. Anya. He is about fifty and she only finished medical school last year. He told me his family died of starvation in the Leningrad blockade of 1942-44. I admire his intelligence and our officers respect him and don't dare touch his girlfriend.

I love you. Soon we will march ahead. Please write again.

Yours,

Julie

How ironic to have sex with another woman and to get a letter from my wife two hours later. I'm trying not to feel guilty.

It's something that just happened. Maybe it needed to happen. I haven't spoken from the heart or been intimate with anyone in four months. I wanted to be close to a woman - to hold and hug someone. I needed a release of feelings that I can't express to a man. On the other hand, I am glad Hanah is not here to look into my eyes, she would know. I hate keeping anything from her. If she ever asks, I will tell her. What if she took a lover? She is attractive enough to have any man she wants. I am sure there are men who want her. Regardless of what she needs to do, I know she loves me. That is all I need to know. She is the love of my life.

21 November 1944

I wake this morning and check the date and realize November 22 is the second anniversary of our marriage. I haven't written a poem since the war started. I wonder if I still can. We are waiting for orders to move ahead, so I have time. Finally by noon I have it and put it the mail.

Hanele

I'm dreaming of your black silk curls
* tickling my face*
as I kiss your breast
* and your nakedness*
* with all its smiles and tears.*
I look through the peepholes in your eyes
* and turn back the laminations of years*
* until I reach the seed that germinated you,*
Speak of the things that hurt,
* let's kiss and hug and cry*

and lay down together
and dream the same dream
that we will always be together

I am thinking of you on our anniversary. I miss and love you so.
Love,
Julie

25 November 1944, the outskirts of Telsit, in the northeast of East Prussia

Our supply lines have caught up with us and we are given orders to move southwest towards Konigsberg. As we approach the River Pregel, we see railroad sidings, industrial back yards and chemical factories giving the cities a bizarre look. Our tanks become locked in a duel for a bridge over a fifty meter width of the river. We dig in. Artillery shells are exploding on both sides. We know the 250 tanks of Gross Deutschland are waiting on the other side of the river. Reconnaissance tells us the enemy has placed its defenses on a 15 kilometer line between many natural and artificial lakes. It is easy to defend because of the marshy terrain.

"It is clear," says our colonel. "We cannot maneuver our tanks and artillery on the marshy terrain. We must approach Konigsberg from the south. It is the same trap that the Germans set for our General Samsonov in 1914. He lost his entire army in the bog. We will retreat south and join our main force. We are already too deep in German territory. The Germans are at this moment trying to encircle us in a pocket as we have done to them so many times. Before we leave we must blow up the bridge to slow down their pursuit."

A sapper commando, Abram Michele and his corporal swing themselves under the bridge attempting to plant explosives. They work fast under heavy continuous fire. Abram is hit in the chest and the corporal has a bullet in the arm. Both wounded, they activate the charges and jump off the bridge into the river. They swim ashore and run 200 meters before the bridge blows, throwing them to the ground. They are brought back bleeding and unconscious. The corporal survives, but Abram dies from a bullet in his lung.

By the time we start moving south, the enemy has enveloped us. They engage our rear units, and we slow their advance. Our tanks break through their southern flank, and at the same time, we launch a counter offensive on our rear, eastern and western flanks - losing thirty tanks. We know what it is to be encircled and fear being annihilated. My colonel orders me to stay close to him.

"Maybe," he says smiling. "Maybe you will be our German interpreter."

I was with the command when we received a desperate radio message from General Burdainy, who was shouting, "Black Crow, Black Crow. We are encircled. Tell me where the exit is."

"This is the Fox at the railway junction," we answer. "Go on the road 65 South to the railway junction, 45 kilometers south of Goldap."

Our orders are to continue south in an orderly retreat. We are warned of a predawn German offensive. It is about 10:00 PM as we are passing through villages and cities. To make sure no one is shooting at us, everything is set afire including houses, barns, crops, towns and factories. A section of East Prussia 25 kilometers wide is burning.

"This is the German theory of terror," says my Colonel. "The Prussian General, Carl Von Clausewitz who fought against Napoleon, prescribed terror as a proper method of shortening the war. He believed civilians must feel the pressure of the war, so they would force their leaders to make peace. Now we are placing the Germans in an oppressive situation, so they will surrender."

After fifty kilometers, it is three in the morning, and we have escaped the trap. We are on a dirt road with a steep shoulder that falls into a ravine, so it is dangerous for our tanks to turn left. Viktor gives me a white flag and instructs me to direct the tanks to the right. The first sixty go by with no problem. I look up and see the sixty-first tank is not turning but coming right at me. There is no time to jump back. I drop to the ground and the tank's screeching treads crunch the ground with a deafening noise as they pass on either side of me and crash into the ravine. I am too shaken to speak. I recall how my tank treads chewed up the bodies of screaming Nazi soldiers. I especially remember one young boy who lost the lower half his body to my tank as he died. I still remember his screams and face. I never fully appreciated his pain until it was almost mine. It must be the worst way to die. I shiver at the thought. How many lives do I have left?

Chapter 26

The Battle for Konigsberg and East Prussia

3 January - 9 April 1945

The East Prussian Offensive was planned by the Soviets to prevent flank attacks from the North as they marched toward Berlin. During the initial planning, Stalin ordered his Generals to annihilate the German forces. The Soviets had a ten to one numerical advantage over the Germans. The Russians made slow progress due to a web of mine fields and fortifications. There were extremely heavy losses on both sides in the first twenty days. By the end of January, the Soviets reached Vistula Lagoon on the Baltic Sea, cutting off all supply routes to Konigsberg by land and sea. On February 10 as the Soviet encirclement tightened around Konigsberg, the Russians diverted half their troops to the Pomeranian Region of Poland and Germany on the Baltic Sea. This allowed the Germans to capture a corridor between the Port of Pillau and Konigsberg that they kept until the fall of Konigsberg on April 9.

It is reported that the Russian advance and capture of the city were characterized by arson, plunder and rape. Atrocities were expected as retribution. The many Nazi atrocities were fresh in the minds of the Russians. Russian radio propaganda encouraged troops with words such as, "Crush forever the Fascist beast. Break the pride of the German woman. Take her as your legitimate booty."

Konigsberg was protected by fifteen forts with walls twelve feet thick arranged in three concentric circles supported by pillboxes and foxholes. It had 130,000 defenders made up of 35,000 regulars and 95,000 young boys and old men. By the end of the battle eighty percent of the city had been destroyed. The Russians had 60,000 casualties. The Germans had 50,000 military casualties and 80,000 were taken prisoner. The Soviets sent 28,000 to forced labor camps. Konigsberg and most of East Prussia were ceded to Russia by the Allies in the Potsdam Agreement, because Stalin wanted an ice free port. The entire population of East Prussia was evacuated by the Germans, or killed or expelled by the Russians. The names of the towns and the population became Russian. Out of three million East Prussian civilians, 500,000 died. Many of the deaths could have been prevented, but Hitler refused to order an early evacuation. The same is true of military deaths; Hitler refused to allow his generals to retreat when they needed to.

6:00 AM, 10 January 1945, On the Lithuanian border about 10 kilometers inside East Prussia, near the railway at Ebenrode

In the coldest winter in anyone's memory, my hands and feet are freezing. I let my beard grow for warmth, and now it's making icicles. The biggest challenge is staying warm. Every day we march, exercise and run in place. We have been in this spot waiting for the thousands of lakes and marshlands to freeze over, and we have been freezing in the process. What once was a defensive barrier for Konigsberg is like a highway for our tanks and artillery to roll over. The rail lines that once served the Germans are now bringing supplies and troops to our front lines. Hundreds of tank cars full of diesel fuel are parked on the rails that will be used to run the tanks and trucks. Box cars full of ammunition, canned goods, sides of beef and pork, cigarettes, coffee, and vodka are here too.

This hurry up and wait operation has given me the time to work on my diary and write poetry again. The Army has supplied me with pencil and paper. Last night, I dreamt of the last time I saw my family at the Krasno Work Camp. I was haunted by dreams of the dead and dying. I wake, and cry as I write this poem.

Screams of the Dead

Again I see his terrified face
    and hear the screams of the blond boy
    not yet with a beard,
    with his legs being crushed
    by the treads of my tank.
Screams of this child's mutilation
    are multiplied by a thousand,
    as I see everyone I love
    naked and burning,
    screaming and then silent,
    as flesh burns to bone
    in the hell of a Nazi fire.
The list of the dead grows every day.
    Will there be anything left of us?
    And those that live
    will be living without their hearts,
    and ears that no longer want to hear
    the screams from the fire.

5:00 AM, 13 January 1945; A fog is hanging over the battle field on a bitter cold morning.

One million and six hundred thousand Russian troops, 3,300 tanks, 28,360 artillery pieces and 2,800 aircraft are now beginning the assault on East Prussia. I am jolted out my poetic dreams as I drop down into my tank and back into the reality of death and destruction.

We are trying to break through in several places on a ninety kilometer battle line to form bulges that will expand once we have penetrated the German defenses.

The big guns are pounding the German positions, while our aircraft wait for the fog to lift. It is three hours before dawn, the first wave of infantry is moving behind our tanks across farm fields and frozen marsh toward German fortified trenches. More foot-soldiers are following behind. When there is a break in the ranks, it is filled by a man from the rear. Once the first wave hits, the second, third, fourth and fifth waves of cannon fodder will be on their way. The fields have been lightly bombed to set off any land mines, but occasionally a soldier finds one and is blown up or loses a leg. Enemy lines left and right are defined by flashing gunfire as far as I can see. We don't want to give them a target, so we are not yet firing. With only helmeted heads above the enemy trench, we don't have much to shoot at. Our artillery is still keeping them low in the ditch and from having maximum fire power. At a hundred meters, I am given the order to open fire with my machine gun. The troops are running along with our tanks screaming battle cries and then with agony as they drop to the ground. They are doing their job. The first wave is there to catch the bullets, so the rest of us can overrun the ditch. The second, third, fourth and fifth waves are charging. Russian bodies are piling up, but they don't have enough bullets to stop all of us. Finally our machine guns spray their trenches like it's an infestation of rats. It is too dark to take prisoners, and we would rather see them dead.

We are almost to the second defense line as the first soft yellow light is reflecting in the gray spackled sky. The bastards are up and firing in spite of our artillery barge. I am pulling the trigger on my machine gun trying to keep their heads down in the ditch. At 100 meters before contact, we have lost most of the first wave. At fifty meters the second wave followed by the third, fourth and fifth waves are all charging at full gallop. Again we are in the ditch eradicating Nazis.

We stop, so the artillery and aircraft can weaken the third defense line and to be resupplied with foot soldiers and ammo. The reward of living to reach the ditch is looting the pockets of dead and live Germans. We are finding watches, fountain pens, better cigarettes, lighters, wallets and a quality of goods not found in Russia or Poland. I find the most delicious chocolates and a Swiss watch. I see it as a precursor of looting of the towns. It reminds me of finding some good boots when I was in the guerrillas, but these Germans have better stuff than the Lithuanians. We take some prisoners and send them back to our command post. Maybe they can tell us something.

We wait for three hours while our artillery and air craft pound them with everything we have. We want them to be to the point of waving a white flag before we get there. Again, our foot soldiers take a beating. We kill all the Germans in the ditch. My new watch is showing four-thirty. We have been at this for almost twelve hours and will do it again tomorrow. We have advanced 1.5 kilometers. This is no blitzkrieg but trench warfare.

19 January 1945

Staying warm is still a problem in a damp cold that is sinking into my bones. Except for my feet, it's warm enough in the tank out of the wind.

We are going through foot-soldiers like firewood on a cold day and still making only two kilometers a day on our drive to Konigsberg. We have an endless supply of teenager soldiers who grew up to avenge the death of their fathers and brothers and now are forced to die for Stalin. Their courage to charge the enemy's barrage of bullets comes from vodka and the threat of being shot by a Russian machine gunner, if they retreat. The age old tactic of frontal assault still works, if you have an overwhelming force and don't mind losing a lot of soldiers.

22 January 1945

The sky is clear enough that our artillery and planes are able to pound the German defenses. Most of our 2,800 planes are in the air. Our tank reserves are called into action. They are in such numbers the German anti-tank guns are not effective. We break through the German defenses at Guttistadt. Our advance gains momentum and we began to form our bulge. The towns and villages are burning. German bodies are again crunching under the treads of my tank. We are told to execute any Nazi civilian official.

West of Guttistadt, we discover Russian POW's were shot as the Germans evacuated.

24 January 1945

We have just overrun the ancient fortified town of Lotzen. It is noon and the sun has broken through the grey clouds to illuminate a horrid scene. Buildings are burning, the looters are looting, the drunks are drinking, and the rapist are raping. It is a madman's holiday. The Emperor Nero didn't do better. I am sitting on my tank with my crew in the town square waiting to be resupplied with diesel. I am taking it all in without wanting to be a part of it. At the sidewalk entrance of a small hotel is a young girl that has been fucked to death on a bloody mattress by god knows how many and not likely alive for all of it. The mattress looks like it was dragged to the sidewalk to be picked up with the trash.

A bloody, disheveled, fortyish woman in tears is yelling insistently, "Kill me. Please kill me." She falls to her knees on the street and continues the rant.

Tired of her noise, a young, drunk soldier takes his pistol and fires three times before she is quiet. He then goes about his business of playing with a music box, one of the new toys he has scattered about on the sidewalk.

All the women have been raped and their men killed. Everything that can be carried away has been taken by people who have never seen such wealth in huge houses with electric lights, fine clothes, paved roads, brick barns, motorized gadgets, and private luxury cars. We were riding in wagons down dirt roads and plowing fields with horses when the Germans invaded. Everyone is asking, "With all their wealth, why did they come to rob and kill us?"

It was for the oil, and the wheat fields.

February 1945

I received a letter from Hanah today.

My Dearest Julie
There is heavy fighting in the territory of Hungary, especially around Lake Balaton. We have many casualties. Sometimes it is difficult to step through the injured lying on the floor, begging for first aid. I am trying to do my best. We and the Germans are both paying with our blood for the insanity of Hitler and the fanatics who follow him.
I lost my friend, Katherine, who was one of our female doctors. She was an only child and my closest friend here. An artillery shell hit nearby throwing a chunk of dirt that smashed her skull.
I am sure I will see you soon, dear husband.
Love
Hanah

I respond immediately.

My Dearest Hanele
I am sorry about your Katherine. I wish I were there to hug you. I am losing friends too. Let's promise to stay alive for each other. The bloodiest battle of the war is going on here. It is reminiscent of WWI trench warfare. Bombs and mind fields are every meter of the way to Konigsberg. This is where the Russian Army was defeated by the Germans before the 1917 Bolshevik Revolution. Thanks to our tanks, we have the upper hand. We have chased the Germans from Stalingrad across Poland to their homeland. Now they have their backs to frigid seas of the Baltic, and they can retreat no more. The Nazis know we would rather kill than take prisoners, so they are fighting for their lives. Every day the ring tightens. We have cut their supply lines and they will soon be out of bullets and food. A million and a half Russians are marching behind tanks shoulder to shoulder. We are pushing them back 2 kilometers a day. At this rate we will reach Konigsberg in April.

Today we captured a Nazi mayor of a small village. I was asked to inter-rogate him and determine if he had committed war crimes. I found that he was a member of the SS. The Jury sentenced him to hang from the nearest tree.

With our love and the protective spirits of our martyred parents, I know we will get through this war and have a wonderful life together.

You are in my dreams every night.

Love,

Julie

18 February 1945

Today our General Cherniachovsky was killed when a shell hit his jeep in the town of Mehlsack, 35 kilometers south of Konigsberg. He was a Supreme Commander and a General of the Army and the youngest ever to hold those ranks. He was thirty-nine. He will be buried in Vilnius as the liberator of that city. We are heavy hearted. He was a brave and noble man.

1 April 1945

After a two month siege, we have broken through all the defense lines surrounding Konigsberg and are now at the gates of the city. It has taken the Russian Army 79 days and 60,000 casualties to go 160 kilometers. We have a secured a line from Lithuania to the Baltic, keeping Konigsberg from being sup-plied by land the sea. At this point they must be eating shoe leather. Again our request for a German surrender is denied. They would rather die fighting than surrender to another kind of death; they would miss the torture and humiliation.

Our artillery begins a five day bombardment of the city. I can see German tanks all around us with their crews dead and crushed. Some tanks are still smoking. Many artillery pieces are overturned. There are burned and flatten homes and fields. We have passed through a wasteland of destruction. Bodies of people, dogs, and cattle that last week were white and frozen stiff are thawing and stinking.

6 April 1945

After three hours of shelling and aerial bombardment, the assault on Konigsberg begins. A squad of infantry is assigned to each tank. Our squad assaults a designated target under the cover of my tank. Once the stronghold is captured, our tank and crew turn their attention to the next one. At last the enemy is coming out of their bunkers. A young boy in a baggy uniform opens the steel doors, takes a deep breath and cautiously steps outside. Our bullets are still whizzing by. He frantically waves his white flag. We hold our fire. Two bent old men come out behind him and stagger down the debris laden street toward our lines. It takes four days to get the last one out of his bunker.

Three-quarters of the city is destroyed. Its inhabitants have fled. The 20,000 who stayed are living in bomb damaged buildings. There are busted sewers and gas lines, dead soldiers, civilians, dead and injured dogs, cats, and horses, all stinking and littering streets paved with shattered glass, building parts and wrecks of assorted trucks. Multiple rapes and looting are going on as we take the city.

9 April 1945

Our Colonel Stefan Kryzanovski's tank was hit this morning; he died in the flames. He was a friend and a Jew from

Leningrad, who asked me to join the Communist Party and wanted me to become an officer. His girlfriend, Anya, is our company doctor. She and all our soldiers are stricken with grief. He was a friend who respected me and appreciated my education and language abilities. As my boss, he cared for my welfare as he did for all the soldiers in his command. I feel more vulnerable to the whims and anti-Semitism of the Russian Army now that he is gone.

At 6:00 PM, the Germans offer to surrender Konigsberg. At twelve midnight, it is accepted.

10 April 1945

The rape scenes of Lotzen and other towns are repeated as vodka takes over the victory celebration. The German women are trading sex for their lives. Some are gang raped and killed anyway. The looters are out shopping in the richest town they have ever seen. It is hard to find someone who is not drunk. Thank God for some functioning drunks who can feed us. Things are so far out of hand; I want no part of it. I have the urge to run to escape injury.

I find Sabitai and we take vodka and go to the waterfront in search of a quiet place. We are the only two guerilla volunteers of the fifteen that are still in action. Sabitai has been in charge of two platoons of infantry that specialized in taking out small pockets of resistance. Lucky for him, he wasn't in on the frontal assaults. We sit down on a pier with our legs hanging down toward the black sloshing water.

"I'm sorry to hear about your brother," I say.

"Henach's death devastated me. He was the last brother I had. I was so depressed I wanted to die. My four brothers were all killed fighting for Russia. Like you, I'm the only one left in my family. Henach shouldn't have died. He stepped on a mine and damaged a leg. They put it back together and said he would be okay. I came back a week later and he was dead from neglect. The infection went up his leg to his heart and killed him. I wanted to grab that damn doctor and strangle the bastard."

"Somehow we've got to carry on and make a new family," I say with hope. "The last thing my mother said was you got to stay alive and give me grandchildren."

"That's my plan. Lucky for you, you found Hanah."

I laugh, take a sip of vodka and say, "Don't worry, a woman will find you. You were always the best looking among us and the most intense. Your demeanor is saying, 'Don't argue with me, because I'm ready to kick your ass, if you disagree.' You've got that tough guy thing that women like."

"Well bring them on. I am ready for a woman. Maybe there will be one in Palestine. I know there is one somewhere. Why can't she be here tonight?"

"Henach dying and the death of your brothers, Jeremy and Michael, make me think of all the good men we have lost," I say reminiscing.

"There is Ele and Michel Lidsky who were both killed in Lithuania. Matus Simoncholntz, who was the best guerilla we had, died saving your sorry ass. You know the Russians thought he was Russian. They couldn't believe a guy that smart and fearless was a Jew. He never told them anything different. There were a lot of Jews that pretended to be Russian. They were just doing what they had to do to survive. Maybe we should have done the same."

We are sitting there looking out to sea, when a cute girl of six or seven, dressed in pants and a sweater, walks up, stares at us a minute and asks in German, "Do you want to rape my mother?"

THE BATTLE FOR KONIGSBERG AND EAST PRUSSIA

"What are you talking about?" I say as I stumble to understand.

"You look like a nice man," she says studying me. "My mother will be raped tonight. I want you to rape her."

A pleasant looking woman of thirty walks up and addresses the child, "Mimi, what are you doing?"

"I am trying to save your life, Mother," she says in a strong voice. "This man will rape you and not kill you."

Her tall thin frame is lost in an oversized army coat that must also serve as her bed. Her reddish hair is bundled on top her head. I can tell from her face that she is smart, determined and a survivor.

"I am Julie," I say standing up. "I see you need some help staying alive tonight."

"Yes, I'm Maria. We have been hiding in the bombed out buildings. A soldier tried to rape me earlier. When he handed me his vodka bottle I hit him in the head with it and was able to get away. We saw a woman gang raped and killed tonight; that's what Mimi is talking about."

"I'm married and have a job that starts early in the morning. My friend, Sabitai, is not married and free tonight. He doesn't understand German. Do you know Russian?"

"Yes," she nods. "Enough."

"Then I will arrange for you to stay with him." I turn and address Sabitai. "Did you know that all things come to those who are not looking?"

"No," he responds. "Who said that?"

"I did."

He laughs and says, "Then it must be true."

"Didn't I tell you that women find you attractive? Didn't you say that you are ready for a woman? I know it's been six months since I last found you one. Well here she is. Her name is Maria. She likes you and finds you attractive. She wants to spend the night with you. Can you help her out?"

"Sure," he says as he stands and pulls his thick brown hair back out his face with both hands. "So she likes me better than you."

"Yes, you were always the pretty boy."

11 April 1945

The POW's are housed in a German Army camp outside the city. Supervised squads of Germans are being used to clean up the city and restore services.

We take over the hospital after the Germans are evacuated to the prison camp. There aren't so many patients to move. Many of them died when a horde of looters attacked the hospital and demanded watches. They turned patients out of gurneys and beds upside down. Only the strong survived. A sixteen year old soldier pointing a machine gun threatened a room full of patients. He was red faced and crying that he was going to kill everybody, if he didn't get a watch. He was like a kid with no present on Christmas. Within a few minutes the nurses found two watches.

Our company plans a memorial service for our Colonel tonight. Anya is organizing it. Some ashes have been collected from his tank.

Because of my education and fluency in German, I am drafted into Smersh, the Russian military police, and made a counterintelligence officer. I am given a private room in the barracks next to the old police station that has now become Smersh headquarters. After supper on Anya's instructions, we meet in a park overlooking the river. It is sunset and the orange and red sky is reflecting in the dark water. There are about thirty of us. The rest are carousing in the city and becoming part of the drunken victory celebration. Anya is the most beautiful widow I have ever seen. Her slim feminine figure is muted by the Army uniform. Her electric blue eyes have softened with grief. She reads something while blotting tears. Several of us speak and Anya throws his ashes in the water.

I express my condolences to Anya.

She kisses me on the cheek and says, "I am so glad you are here. I need your help. We will talk. Wait for me."

The last person leaves and Anya motions for me to sit on a bench overlooking the river.

"They have moved me into the Hospital compound as one of the staff doctors. I have an apartment there. I want you to join me there tonight. Before you say anything, let me explain. Stefan's death has been devastating for me. I have had two sleepless, crying, screaming nights. I can't be alone again tonight. I need someone with me or I'll go crazy," she says as she sobs into her handkerchief.

I put my arm around her to comfort her and say, "Yes, I am here for you."

She turns and buries her sobbing face in my shoulder. We just sit and hold each other and watch the orange sunset disappear in the water. Hand in hand we walk through twilight streets echoing with celebration shouts, screams, and laughter that disjoints us and is out of place with our grief. We try to shut it out, but it is too loud to ignore.

We come upon a street dance fueled by vodka, a screaming accordion, foot stomping and hand-clapping. Cossack dancers are leaping over a fire with its flames licking their boots and pulling at me to escape into the dance. I take her hand and reluctantly she gives into the contagious frivolity, fun, and rhythms that grab us and send us flying hand in hand, leaping across the fire. We skip on the cobblestones until we are forced to stop and catch our breaths. She smiles, the first of the night, looks into my soul and grabs my arm and pulls me toward her apartment.

We kiss and start taking off our clothes the moment we step into through the door. With her bright eyes and blond hair falling about her shoulders, she is even more beautiful than I expected. There is something about a death when it is close, that makes us want to make love and embrace life. All the love we ever had is flowing between us. All the passion that I have suppressed for months is rushing out.

She collapses in my arms, kisses my neck as her tears fall on my chest. I hug her and kiss her forehead.

"I'm sorry," she says as she tries to dry her eyes.

"Please cry," I say as I kiss her ear. "Crying does help. I wish I could cry more than I do. So much grief is buried in both of us."

"I need you to be with me for a while." she says as her voice cracks. "If I am not with someone, I will be with everyone. Do you understand?"

"Yes and yes, I will be with you as long as you need me."

She kisses me on the lips and her face falls on my chest as she says, "It's been a wonderful night. Please come back tomorrow after work."

12 April 1945

We wake with just enough time to get to our jobs. I slip on my clothes and have a long kiss goodbye.

"Tomorrow," she says with a smile of love. "I will be here by eight."

"I'll be back at eight-O-five," I beam as I throw a kiss from the open door.

It is my first day on the job. I am now a Lieutenant. I climb into attics, check basements and other hiding places looking for Germans. By interrogation and looking at their papers, I decide if they are Nazis or honest citizens. I look through their eyes into their souls and determine their character. Now the shoes of justice are on my feet. I decided who lives or dies. In my eradication of Nazis, I wonder if I will become like the SS bullies that eliminated Jews in the selection. I am now having my own selection with two assistants who wait outside to catch anyone running from the building. They are present during the interrogation to write down the testimony. It goes much like the interrogation of the Germans I captured in the Naliboki Forest.

We finish at four o'clock. I go back to my room and wash myself from a bucket. I am thinking how beautiful this place once was. What would it be like to enjoy the city with Anya, before it was bombed? The thought inspires a poem that I think she will like.

Supper is still out of cans and the cook is proud of his dish. We sometimes ate better in the guerillas when food was fresh from the field. As I walk through the streets, I see some progress is being made to clean things up. I climb the stairs of her partially bombed-out building and find Anya has heard my footsteps and is standing in the door looking amazingly sparkling and fresh. I can see she has decided not to be a grieving widow.

We kiss and she shuts the door behind me.

"I wrote a poem for us," I say with a burst of excitement. "How fun it would be to go out on the town in Konigsberg when there was a town to enjoy, and to be embraced by music that our passions can ride on. Ravel and Dvorak make me want to leap and twirl in the air. And I love a gypsy violin. In the right hands the violin grips my soul. I must have gypsy blood."

"Okay, Gypsy Julie," she says. "Then let's hear the music of your poem."

A NIGHT ON THE TOWN

I want to sit in a cafe with a strong cigarette and coffee
  and hold your hand across the table
  and see your smile grow radiant
  as we talk of your dreams, and
between kisses, we feed on passions of Dvorak's
  Slavonic Dances and Ravel's Bolero
  in an ancient concert hall,
  with carved gargoyles flying with our spirits
that take us to a café
  where a gypsy violin screams
  under a bobbing chin
  igniting a room of flashing eyes
compelling us to leap and dance on the table with clicking heels,
  shouts and claps expanding
  until we're wild enough to be thrown out,
and then I sink down with you
  in a soft feather bed
  and wake up to your smile.

"I love it," she says with a kiss of appreciation. "I wish to be in a town that wasn't bombed out, and that we had the soft feather bed. You can wake up to my smile."

Our next kiss ends in bed. Love making is even more wonderful the second time. I roll over and she snuggles into my right side with my arm pulling her to me. I look up at the spider-cracks in the ceiling and feel completely relaxed, content, and then realize I am in love with two women. I have guilt but no regrets. Somehow I must have an honest relationship with both women, but Hanah is too far away, communication is impossible. And will we both live through the war? I can't mention it in a letter – it would drive her mad.

Anya gets up and slips on a house coat and brushes her hair. She pulls out a bottle of red wine, some white cheese and bread from her bag and places them on the table next to two glasses.

"Stefan's assistant gave me this today," she says as she lifts the bottle. "Quite a prize in this devastated city. Can you open it?"

"Sure," I say as I slip on my coat to avoid the chill of the room. I cut out the cork with my pocket knife and pour the wine. We lift and strike our glasses and both say, "To life."

"That's a Jewish toast, "I say. "Are you Jewish?

"Of course," she smiles.

"Is that why you were attracted to me?"

"Yes," she giggles with a little wine spilling from a corner of her mouth. "I am not attracted to all Jewish men. Only one at the moment. Is that why you were attracted to me?"

"I thought you were beautiful and bright and Stefan, a very lucky man. I was attracted to you, but I didn't think about you being Jewish."

"Tell me about your wife," she asks as she puts down her glass and stares into my eyes searching for the truth.

"Hanah is a doctor like you, working in a field hospital," I say while feeling a little uncomfortable. "Like you, she is up to her neck in blood in a hospital in Hungary. She went to medical school in Lvov. Her passion is music and the piano. She has a full head of black tangled hair and sparkling eyes. We fell in love and married ourselves in a barn where she was hiding. We were together in the guerillas for two years, before I joined the tank corps."

"You haven't seen her in nine months. Do you still love her?" she asks looking into my soul.

"Yes, I love her."

"Do you love me?"

"Yes I do. I love you very much."

"Maybe you shouldn't," she says, looking into her empty glass. "I am not like you country Jews. I'm a wild city girl. I'm whimsical, jealous, and can be a bitch. I might throw you back and catch another."

"I must take that chance," I say as I pour more wine. "Never have I been able to control were my heart goes. It is yours as long as you take care of it. I've been close to death every day for four years and almost killed a dozen times. I've learned to embrace now and live for today without a care for tomorrow which may never come for us. Each minute with you is precious. I love this moment, because this is the only time there is. Carpe Diem, seize the day. With death all around us, behind us and our own deaths in front of us, it is fantastic to be holding on to life with you on the edge of the abyss. Do you love me?"

"Yes I do love you," she says as she gets up with her breast falling out of her house coat into my face.

She sits down in my lap, and I nurse her nipples as she caresses my face. I take her in my arms and carry her to bed.

"I am becoming completely addicted to you," I say as I place a pillow under her head and kiss her lips. "I can never give you up."

15 April 1945

I have been at my new job three days and have processed about a hundred people. I am now looking at the remains of a five story apartment building. The smell of urine hits me at the front door. The stairs are still functional, so I don't need a ladder. There is evidence throughout of camping vagrants. Furniture has been used for firewood. Bare mattresses have been soiled by dirty bodies. Sheets have been ripped and used for ass wipes. The place is so torn up, bombed out and stinking, the owner wouldn't know whether to tear it down or fix it. I tie a handkerchief over my mouth to mask the stench, as I search. I open a third floor closet and find cute, little Mimi crouched in front of a frightened Maria with a vertical finger over her mouth that is saying don't tell anybody; like it's a game of hide and seek.

"Please," Maria whispers. "Just walk away and don't tell anyone we are here."

"After a hesitation I say, "I can't. It is my job to evacuate these buildings and find Nazis."

"Don't blame it on your job. I am sure that's what all the Nazis are telling you. It was their job to exterminate Jews. Now it is your job to exterminate Germans. You are no better than the Gestapo."

I take a deep breath and try to stay professional as I say, "You and your daughter will be assigned to a deportation camp and transported to Germany."

"I suspect that your deportation camp is just a depository for whores to service your soldiers. How do I know we won't be shipped to Siberia," she says as they both burst into tears. "Hitler's war has killed our men and destroyed our country. We are victims, just as you are. After being abused by Nazis, now you Russians are stealing and raping us."

I hear the heavy footsteps of my help trudging up the stairs. I can tell by their faces that their plea for compassion is over.

"Take them and put them in the truck," I tell my sergeant.

Maria's jaw drops in disbelief and then clinches in anger as she shouts "Go tell your friend, Sabitai, about this; he protected and cared for us. I am sure you don't have the guts to confront him."

She looks at me to speak, but I'm silent.

"Sabitai will never forgive you," she spits as she is pulled away.

"You are not a nice man," screams Mimi as she kicks my ankle. "I was wrong about you."

I am still depressed about my day when I reach Anya's apartment.

She greats me with a kiss and I collapse in a kitchen chair and place my elbows on the table with my hands rubbing the tension out my face.

What is wrong," she asks as she massages my neck.

"I feel like I sent two innocents to be executed. I didn't know how to help them. There was a woman and her little girl that we took kicking and screaming to the deportation camp. I met them on the street on my first night in Konigsberg, and saved them from being raped and killed during the victory celebration."

"How did you do that?"

"I had Sabitai take her home. He took them for a few days, but he had to go back to his unit that is being shipped south."

"You must give it up. You can't save everyone. You can't save anybody but yourself. Don't carry this around – you'll go nuts. Why do you think I have a drink when I get home? I try to leave the bloody mess at the hospital. When you come through that door leave the worries of the day behind. Bring happy Julie here. I don't like the sad, worried one."

"Yes, you are right. Give me the joy juice."

23 April 1945

The central city has been searched; we are now working in the outlying areas. Today we begin by searching a large brick home on the river. I immediately notice some soldiers have been partying down stairs and have left vodka bottles, cigarette butts and shot holes in the walls and ceiling. The three story house has one of its wings missing and part of its roof. I search the rooms and closets and find nothing. I climb the narrow stairs to the attic. I turn my flashlight around the room and find a pair of eyes in the dark.

"Come out," I command in German. "I can see you. I am the police. I am here to help you."

She is tall and thin with straight black hair and blue eyes that are dripping with tears. "Thank God someone is here," she sobs. "Last night I was attacked by three men. Because they were drunk, I was able to escape before being raped. I've been hiding here all night while they searched, fired their pistols and screamed for me."

"I'm sorry," I say as she grabs my arm. "You could have been killed. You are also lucky to live through the shelling. Whose place is this?"

"This was my father's house. We were safe in the basement during the shelling. My mother and father died of starvation after our food was robbed in January. They didn't tell me they weren't eating so that I could. After they died, I was saved by a neighbor who shared some flour and beans. Where can I go to be safe?

"I'm not sure," I say. "How old are you?"

"Twenty-two," she says.

"What is your work experience?"

"I've worked as a nurse and kept books for my father's wholesale business."

"Do you know any Russian?"

"Yes, I once studied ballet in Leningrad."

I'm thinking she is too pretty. If I leave her here, she will be killed by rapists. She will be in danger, if I place her with the deportees; the guards will take advantage of her, if the inmates don't.

"Are you interested in working in a Russian hospital?" I ask.

"If that will keep me alive, yes."

"I can't take you with me now. I will be back the minute I get off duty. Go back to your hiding place. Oh, what is your name?"

"Rebecca."

"I'm Julie. Come out when I call your name. It would be good if you wear a scarf and a long coat to hide your face and figure in case we see your attackers. I am sure they will be looking for you.

It is five o'clock before I can get back to the house on the river. I was able to get some food from the cook that he put in one of his tin cans. I go back to the attic and call Rebecca. She comes out and I give her the food and a spoon. She devours it before we get to the front door.

We walk arm in arm until we reach the park on the river where we had the memorial service for Stefan. We find a park bench and sit and wait for sunset.

"Why are you helping me," she asks in a timid voice.

"I'm not sure why I am sticking my neck out for you," I say as I search for an answer in the water. "My family and most of the Jews in my village were murdered by the Nazis. For three years I have been seeking and finding my revenge. Everything I loved was destroyed. A way of life and the people that lived it are dead. They did similar things in Russia. That is why we devastated this place - for revenge. The Nazis killed twenty-five million Russians and millions of Jews and Gypsies. Now Stalin is making East Prussia a Russian state. There won't be a single German alive here. You are an innocent and too beautiful to be slaughtered. I can see the same agony and fear in your suffering that I saw in the work camps and in myself. You have lost your family as I lost mine. And you have nowhere to go. I feel your hurt as if it were my own."

"Maybe it's because I am Jewish," she says. "My mother was Jewish."

"Then we must save you somehow," I say as we embrace. "How did your parents meet?"

"They met at the University in Berlin. My mother wasn't a practicing Jew, so she wasn't thought to be Jewish when my father brought her home to Konigsberg. Her family was killed in the selection."

"My girlfriend is a doctor. Maybe she can find you work. The Russians are like the Germans, if you can be useful they will keep you."

I take her back to my room in the police barracks. There are men taking women to their rooms, so it doesn't cause notice.

"Lock the door behind me and don't open it until I call your name," I instruct. "I'm going to talk to Anya."

I find Anya in bed waiting for me.

"I've been waiting forever," she says. "I had to drink the wine by myself. Don't explain or say anything, just fuck me."

I've never seen her so lose and uninhibited. It must be the wine. I try my best to keep up with her as she takes over the love making and gets on top.

"Yes! Yes!" she screams as she falls down on me exhausted. "That's what I needed. I love you."

"I love you," I say. "I need to talk to you."

"Okay, talk," she says as she dismounts with a huff and puts on her house coat. "Come on what is it?"

"I found a Jewish girl in an attic today, and I don't know what to do with her. She was almost raped by three soldiers. If I take her to be deported, she will be raped. She is a nurse and has experience in caring for the wounded. I thought you might be able to use her at the hospital. She speaks Russian."

"Why do you think she will be raped, if you place her to be deported?"

"She is young and absolutely gorgeous."

"So you are in love with her. Is she your new girlfriend?"

"No, just someone who will be dead tomorrow without help.

"Where is she?"

"In my room."

"How long has she been there?"

"Two hours."

"Bring her here, and we will talk about it. Go on, get out of here. You have ruined my escape from bloody reality."

I get to my room door and knock and call Rebecca. There is no answer. I try the door and find it unlocked. Pudgy Harold, the guy next door, is looking gross in his underwear. Rebecca is lying naked in my bed with her arms crossing her breast and her beautiful face twisted in fright.

"I thought you wouldn't mind if I entertained her while you were gone," an apologetic Harold says as he grabs his shirt, pants and shoes and is out the door.

I lock the door behind him and turn to Rebecca with, "I'm sorry. Please forgive me. Did he hurt you?"

"No," she says," as she pulls up the sheets to her neck. "He frightened me. He showed me his knife and said he would cut my throat, if I didn't take off my clothes. Do you want to make love to me? You can if you want. I just don't know why I'm here," she says as she sobs.

I sit down on the bed and hold her hand and say, "I am so sorry. I didn't know I would be gone so long. Put on your clothes and I will take you to a safe place to sleep."

Back at Anya's, the girls are sitting at the round dining table getting acquainted while I am lying relaxed on the bed being ignored and lost in my thoughts.

"Anya," I say reaching for her attention. "Don't you think it strange that our general and colonel were both killed in the last days of the last battle of the war? And killed when they were no longer needed?"

"Do you think they were killed by Russians?"

"It is possible that they were murdered," I say as I sit up on the side of the bed. "Because they were Jews and in position of power."

"Stefan was only a colonel."

"But he was next in line to be a general and would have been promoted with our general's death. They were both completely blown away with nothing left of them. No body to examine or bullet to extract. I think they were both hit by a shell from one of our big guns. A forward observer could direct a shell or mortar fire with accuracy enough to hit a Jeep or a tank. We don't know what direction the shells came from. The German artillery didn't have spotters directing their fire. They were just firing in our direction. With over a million Russian soldiers as targets, how did they get lucky enough to get our top brass?"

"We had about 60,000 killed," Anya says. "So one in twenty Russians was killed."

"Yes, but most of those were foot soldiers who were blown away in mine fields or slaughtered in making frontal assaults. No one was killed above the rank of Major except our colonel and general. There is no better time to murder someone than in the heat of a battle."

"But why kill them?"

"I think they were victims of anti-Semitism and the cleansing of Jews from the upper ranks. Whoever did the dirty work will advance in rank. Stalin himself could have ordered it. For the murderer, I would look for a colonel in the artillery that is soon to be a general."

"That's crazy. Ivan was his best and most famous general."

"Yes, that is why he was killed. Our General had become a national hero. Stalin doesn't like to share the lime-light. He would rather give us a marble statue. A live hero can be a threat to his power. I think the General was the main target. They saw Stefan as a Jew about to be a general, so why not kill him too."

"How did Stefan and Ivan rise in the ranks, if they were Jewish?"

"They both had Russian names and were not thought to be Jewish. It was only later that they were discovered to be Jewish. And anti-Semitism has been growing with the help of the Germans. First they conquered us with their propaganda, before they brought in the tanks."

"So Mr. Detective," she asks. "What can be done about it? What are you going to do with your theory?"

"Not a damn thing. It is just one more reason to get the hell out of Russia."

"And time to go home, my dear Julie," she says with a kiss as she sits down beside me. Rebecca will stay here tonight and go to work with me in the morning."

Not wanting to give her up for the night, I grab Anya and we roll over in the bed and hug and kiss again. She pushes me away, and reluctantly I get up to leave. Rebecca gives me a spontaneous hug of appreciation that ends with tears in our eyes. She squeezes my hands as we pull apart, and her eyes thank me again and I feel her love.

24 April 1945

It's dark when I arrive at Anya's door and knock and say, "It's Julie."

"Go away," she commands without opening the door. "I'll call for you when I want to see you."

I walk away depressed by her rejection and wondering what happened? She must have another man. I'm jealous of whoever it is. I knew she was fickle, but didn't think I would be gone so soon. Then she did say she would call me. I don't like the idea of sharing her. Who is it? I'd like to know. I stop, and think about going back to her door to find out, then think better of it and continue to the street. What if I were caught looking through the keyhole? And to see something that would only bring hurt. I'll find out soon enough. I did say I was content to have her for the moment. She did warn me that she was impulsive. I do have a wife out there somewhere. I'll go back to the bombed-out library, and see if I can find another book. If I want to get drunk tonight, I can find plenty of company. The streets are growing with more night life and noise. Several bars are rising from the ruins.

28 April, 1945

I am writing letters to Hanah, and still I am tormented by the absence of Anya. I am tempted to knock on her door but don't. At work, we are still searching buildings for Germans and finding half the people are Nazis. They all express regrets like that might have some effect on the way I judge them. The best they can hope for is ten years in Siberia. Somebody else will decide that.

30 April 1945

I wake an hour before sunrise at the time Anya and I would be making love. I can't quit thinking of her. I light a candle and write a poem. I put it under her door on the way to work.

BEFORE DAWN

I wake gasping for breath
with my hands trembling and cold.
I look for you,
but you are only a pillow.
Loneliness seeps in,
and I close my eyes and find you again,
and I hold and kiss you and wait for your love.

I think of you loving someone else,
and me being married,
and still our love is real,
as it throbs and breathes
and sparkles in your eyes.
I love you forever.
Our love is ours alone.
It is the most precious thing I have.
Don't let anyone touch it.

1 May 1945

After breakfast, we get the message that Hitler is dead. Russia has declared victory over Germany. There is celebrating and much vodka drinking in the streets and in our barracks. I am dressed for work, but there is no work today. Who could work or want to. The devil is dead. Has any human caused as much death and suffering? My eyes welt up in tears of relief that it is over. There is shouting and guns going off. I can hear a chorus of men singing badly in the street and a cannon boom on the waterfront.

I am hit with a feeling of isolation and loneliness in the middle of a wild celebration. I have no friend in the barracks or in the street that I can hug, drink and dance with. Last week my tank was put on a rail car along with my crew. So many responsible for the victory are dead, including my colonel and general and most of the guerillas who joined the tank corps. I am feeling no joy in this victory, just relief that it is over. There is a part of me that would celebrate with vodka, but none has been offered. Maybe with enough vodka I could forget the flood of pain.

"Jew boy," says pudgy, hairy chested Harold as he staggers through the door in his underwear and offers up a half empty bottle. "Have a drink." He raises the bottle higher, loses his balance and tries to steady himself.

He reminds me of Stumpy when he was feeding me cheese. My impulse is to grab his bottle and break it on his stupid head. I should have beaten him when he tried to rape Rebecca. Offering a drink is his way of apologizing. He got off to a bad start with "Jew boy." He is standing like a statue offering the clear glass army issue vodka. Just to get rid of him, I take a sip and give it back to him. With cloudy eye contact, he nods his head, and I nod back. He takes a swig, turns and walks out thinking everything is okay between us. You never know what is hiding behind a veneer of politeness. He was kind enough to tell me that the reason I don't have roommates is because I'm a Jew. I was there, because they were desperate for German speakers. Maybe if my family had adopted a Russian name like my General and Colonel did, maybe I could have avoided discrimination. The other half of assimilation would be to give up the synagogue, and I have done that. I spend the day working on my Diary.

It is about five o'clock when I hear a knock. I put down my pencil and open the door to find Rebecca, whom I haven't seen in a week.

"I've come to escort you to Anya's," she says with a smile.

I grab my jacket for protection against a cold misting rain. I lock the door and ask, "How are you doing? You look much better."

"Yes," she says. "I am eating again. My hair is no longer falling out. Look, I'm even putting on weight and my cheeks are red. I am working in the hospital as a nurse and liking it. As you might have expected I am living with Anya. Neither one of us knew we loved women too. It was just a happy accident."

"Not so happy for me," I say with a forced pout. "I have been catching up on my reading."

"I do feel guilty about that," she says as she looks into my eyes and squeezes my arm. "You did save me - I'm grateful and you are my hero. Because Anya often talks of you, and the way you were sympathetic and listened and shared your life with me, I feel that I know and like you very much. We are both missing you, so tonight we have fixed a few things to eat and there's wine and vodka of course. We are celebrating and you are the only guest."

Anya has decorated the apartment with candles and several shades of brightly colored paper.

She is dressed only in her house coat that falls open as she puts her arms around my neck and plants a long passionate kiss on my lips and whispers, "Thanks for the beautiful poem. I love you too."

"Welcome to the party," Anya says with exuberance as she spreads her arms in a grand gesture. 'No army here, so first you must take off those ugly clothes and put on this house coat. Then we will sit at the table and enjoy good conversation over some wine and hors d'oeuvres'.

I open the wine with a real cork screw and pour. I raise my glass and toast, "To the freedom to have a new life."

"And where are you going to have your new life," asks Anya.

"Texas," I say. "I have cousins in America."

"In America, I like New York and California," Anya says. "We are going to Paris. We want you to come as our husband."

"That is such a wild idea," I say. "I'm speechless."

"No need to talk, just get in bed, and we will do the rest."

Surrounded and caressing soft feminine curves bathed in the flickering yellows of candle light, I tingle with shivers of goose-bumps as I embrace the growing affections of two gorgeous, loving women. Anya is full breasted and curvaceous with eyes electric with desire. Rebecca is thin and light with the straight back bearing of a dancer. Her black hair frames her loving blue-eyed smile and falls on pointed breast. We massage each other and relax into the warmth, discovery and excitement of new love. They kiss me and then each other as we fall into a kissing, embracing triangle that ends with them giggling and whispering. I look for what is coming next as I search their mischievous faces. With laughing eyes glued to mine, they attack with strokes, caresses - showering my face and body with kisses as I lie on my back in helpless bliss and embrace the intertwining of our spirits, tumbling over ourselves with desire to give, to please, to relish and possess each other for the brief moment that we become one. Then we relax into a tranquility that flows into our dreams.

We sleep snuggled in Anya's bed. I wake with the girls reaching across me to embrace. Here we are in a place with a hundred men for every woman, and I'm in bed with two fantastic girls. That's my happy accident. I love them and wouldn't want to be without them, but I do love and miss my Hanah. This is the conflict that I am sure to ignore until it resolves itself. I treasure all the love that has come my way and hold it tight. I never want love to die, ever again.

Anya is right; there is a difference between city and country Jews. I would never have thought to have two women in bed or even two women in my life at once. But the death of everything I know has taught me to escape the past by living in the moment and embracing the feast of life as it is served.

8 May 1945

It is official; WWII is over in Europe with the Germans signing an unconditional surrender with Russia in Berlin. I am wondering how soon I will be discharged from the Army, and when will I be allowed to leave and go to America? When will I ever see Hanah again?

There is more celebrating in the streets. Again I am remembering my family and my dead comrades. I don't know why the celebration is triggering depression. Maybe it's because people I love are not here to celebrate.

I'm having another adventure with Anya and Rebecca. Anya's place is still decorated from the last party.

"No more Army!" shouts Anya. "We are now free spirits."

"If only our spirits could fly and take our bodies with them," I say as I open the wine.

"I am working on that," she says with a sly smile. "Don't ask, I will say no more."

I bypass the wine and go for the vodka. After a few drinks I give up my remorse for the dead. I feel more comfortable with the girls and become a solid part of the laughter in the room. Rebecca has become more aggressive and sure of herself. The physical closeness that we all leaped into is evolving into a solid emotional bond. Our triangle is growing stronger.

19 May 1945, 7:00 PM

It is Saturday, and Sunday is my day off. Anya opens her door with a smile and hands me my house coat. I have been sleeping with them every night. We have become a family with Anya in charge. She is the glue that binds us together. As usual, I wake up in the morning with the two of them snuggled together, and I have the other half of the bed. Anya fixes a breakfast omelet with eggs and cheese she has brought from the hospital. I can see her offering her contagious smile to the cook in exchange for groceries. As always Anya gets what she wants. Beauty and brains in one body are a powerful force.

After breakfast Rebecca takes us to some of her favorite spots that include the public gardens which we find neglected. We pick a hill in a park where the river begins to flow through marsh lands and have a picnic lunch. Pushed by a stiff wind from the west, puffs of white clouds fly overhead with a threat of rain on the horizon. Gulls screech as they flap to catch the wind's up draft and then circle effortlessly as they fish. One by one they make fearless dives that end with white splashes in the dark blue water. I would love to throw up a kite into this wind and watch it catch a cloud and sail out of sight. Spring is happening in our blood and our spirits are blooming with the flowers. The girls pick and crush wild flowers and run their fragrant hands through their hair. Giggling, they attack me with their fragrance, and we end with a three-way hug. We are bathing in a spring of peace and normality as nature renews itself in contrast to the manmade mess around us.

Rebecca is crushed by the destruction. What was once an ideal, privileged life is gone forever. I can't keep my eyes off her. She moves with the grace of a dancer with her shiny black hair being tossed about her shoulders. Today in the bright light of spring she is a jaguar with piercing blue eyes. Tonight she could be a cuddly kitten purring in my lap. She is one of those gorgeous creatures that attract the gaze of anyone with eyes. Her parents must have spoiled and sheltered her, for she is naïve and vulnerable and easily manipulated. Rebecca hasn't realized the power of her presence. She knows she needs a protector and for the moment it is Anya, and I am also becoming her shield.

On the docks, we buy a fish fresh from the boat. Anya cooks it Greek style with a can of tomatoes that I found on one my searches.

After supper, Anya says, "I got a letter from my father this week. He is a professor at the Moscow Medical School where I studied. He likes my plan to move to Paris. He says there will be occupation troops in all the countries that Russia pushed Germany out of. They won't be discharging anybody from the service for more than a year. At home there is a shortage of doctors, teachers, engineers and most professions. They are not going to let a doctor out of the country. Now would be the time to leave before Stalin is able to gain control of the borders and in the confusion of so many people moving about. The port is now open and with boats going in and out. A bribe could get us on one of those ships. Julie, please come with us."

"I can't," I say looking at the floor. "I can't leave Hanah behind. You are right. Now is the perfect time to go. I've done my duty. I've had my revenge. I'm ready to leave."

"Then come with us," she insist as she caresses the back of my neck.

"I wish I could," I say. "This place is going to be hell without you. You two are the only friends I have here."

"And lovers," she says retreating with her sly smile. "Think it over; you can change your mind. You told me how your father came home to marry your mother and wasn't able to get back to America. You could lose your chance to leave Russia, if you wait on Hanah."

3 June 1945, Sunday

I wake trembling with tears. Finally there is faint pink light on Anya's white plaster walls that repels the dead, hidden in the dark. I have talked to my mother and my brothers most of the night. Is there any way to fill the emptiness? My mother was the most vivid and loving as she embraced me.

"I am so proud that you have come this far alive." she beamed as I felt her fingers in my hair and her nails on my scalp. I was taken back to our last embrace. Everyone I love is still living in my dreams.

I snuggled into Anya's backside and smell the fragrance of flowers in her hair, as I put my arm around her and she closes her hand around mine and pulls it to her breast. After a moment, she turns into me and we embrace and my love melts into hers. She knows that I need her. Rebecca moves to my back and slips her thin arm in a hug around my chest. I am sandwiched in a cocoon of love that is the comfort I need.

"Do you love us?" Anya asked.

"Yes." I whisper as my voice breaks with emotion. "I never want to be without you."

"Then why won't you come with us?"

I collect myself and say, 'It is not a matter of loving Hanah more than you. I can't abandon her. She needs my help in leaving Russia."

"And you need my help in escaping. Take advantage of me. I know how to get things done, more than you do. You need me. We are your new family."

5 June 1945, Tuesday, 7:00 PM

I'm in my room reading, when I hear a knock and Anya's voice. I open the door and she falls into my arms. It's passionate, intense and spontaneous. We don't even speak. We are taking off each other's clothes like the first time we made love.

When it is over, I know that this is the last time. I might never see her again. The thought of losing her bringing tears to my eyes. "I love you," I say.'

"I love you," she says. I have missed you. My affair with Rebecca is like my wine and an escape from the blood, the dying and ruined men that I see every day. I realize I'm not complete without you. It's your maturity, strength and intellect that I need. I want an equal not a dependent. I have found a boat to Copenhagen. From there you can come to Paris with us, or any place you please. I love you enough to want the best for you. You won't find happiness in Stalin's Russia. Don't let Russia or Hanah be your prison. Don't let Hanah or anything else keep you from your freedom."

I am remembering the last thing my mother told me, "You will have a chance to escape, and it will last only a second, and you must take it without thinking of me, or anything but saving yourself. I refuse to be the ball and chain that keeps you here." Hanah would be telling me the same, if she were here. I am torn and don't have an answer, but listen for myself to speak for whatever comes out. And would my answer change in five minutes? Whatever I choose, I'll want what I give up. Why must we give up one love for another? I don't want to choose and loose Anya or Hanah. I look into Anya's loving eyes and think of living with her and Rebecca, the fun and adventure of Paris and the world beyond the fence and the beautiful children we could have.

"I do love you," I say with tears and a broken voice. "But I can't leave Hanah."

"You are being a damn fool," she says as she dresses to leave. "You aren't the first person to be a sacrificial idiot for love. I just wish you would be a fool for me and yourself. You are choosing to be a slave of the state, maybe for the rest of your life, rather than freedom. I wish you loved yourself enough to give Julie what he needs. If you change your mind in the next hour, come to my place. I will never forget you, and I will never stop loving you."

"I will never stop loving you," I say as I get up and kiss her good-by with a long silent hug that she finally breaks away from.

Anya's tearful, loving smile stays in my head as I shut the door. She lost Stefan, and now she is losing me. I am feeling loss and guilt. With my eyes clouded with tears, I lie back down and look at the ceiling. I take a deep breath to let go of the tension and think about what has happened. I now have the choice of continuing with one of two happy accidents. By chance I found Hanah, the love of my life. I know we will be content, supportive and loving each other no matter what life's adventure brings. If I left tonight with Anya, my heart would still be in Russia with Hanah. Choosing Hanah doesn't soothe the devastation of losing Anya and a chance to go to Paris and America. I am a fool no matter what I choose. But somehow I am still alive and have the miracle of life that is not without joy and pain.

Epilogue

After the War in Gorky

In 1932 the City of Nizhny Novgorod was renamed for the writer Maxim Gorky, who was born there. Gorky is an industrial port on the banks of the Volga River which connects it to Moscow. It has extensive iron works and a truck factory built by Henry Ford. As railroad hub and river port, it has always been an important trade center. The old city dates back a thousand years with forts, castles and many historic buildings.

I am discharged from the Army in December of 1945 and given a position as a math teacher in Gorky. I like walking the cobblestone streets and river bridges of the old city and being in a place untouched by bombs. I entertain myself in the city library and work on my diary until Hanah joins me as my wife in June. She is exhausted from the sufferings of the war that still bring recurring nightmares. There is a food shortage. People are going to work hungry. No one can understand why we are so poor when we won the war. We are living in one small room with a hot plate for a kitchen. Hanah becomes depressed from the claustrophobia of our quarters and the pervasive poverty.

After a year of waiting, we get a small two bedroom apartment that begins filling up with babies. Finally we are having the grandchildren my mother wanted. The children are the blessing that brings joy back into our lives. I love watching their personalities grow. The teacher in me likes planting seeds of thought. Right away I am teaching English and some Hebrew and the love of books. After so much death, Hanah enjoys bringing new life into the world as a pediatrician in the city hospital. In spite of our difficult life, I never regret staying in Russia for her. She is still the love of my life. Most guerillas have gone to Israel. We stayed in the army too long. Now Stalin has shut the door and no visas are being given, and he's not likely to let a doctor or a teacher leave. Like everywhere else in Europe, Russia is slowly recuperating from the war with the loss of population, consumer goods and agricultural production.

I am able to buy a radio on the black-market that allows us to listen to "Radio Free Europe". We realize that so much of our news is propaganda. We put in applications to emigrate but nothing comes of them.

Finally Stalin dies and some restrictions are lifted. In 1959, Khrushchev makes an agreement with Poland to let former Polish citizens return to Poland. Hirsh Berman and I decided to make the move with our families. Hirsh was our arms manufacturer in the guerillas. He rebuilt and repaired many old rifles. Hirsh grew up strong from working as a blacksmith with his father since he was eleven. He can repair most anything. The peasants liked and trusted him. After the war he married Matus's widow, Chaya, and settled in Gorodok. They have two girls. With family and friends gone, they found too many heart breaking memories in Gorodok and decide to leave when the chance is given.

After meeting with a dozen KGB officials and having our savings taken, we are allowed to leave Russia. We meet Hirsh and his family in Minsk and take the train to Wroclaw, Poland. We meet other repatriates, who tell us the Poles are still hateful and indifferent to our tragedy.

A fifty year old woman at the housing office tells us with a hostile glare, "If you were here in 1943, you would not be alive."

"What a nice homeland we have returned to," says Chaya holding the hands of her eight and nine year old girls.

Hanah and I are holding our three children who only speak Russian, and the Polish sounds terrible to them. I say, "Look into their eyes and you will know if they collaborated with Hitler and are thieves and murderers of innocent people. You can see the hate in her face. This woman behind the counter is one of them. It was my job in the army to discover people like her. If we were in East Prussia during the war, I could have her executed."

I turn to the women and say in Polish, "I was in the Russian Army, the military police, and a guerilla fighter before that. If you were found wearing your Nazi button when the Russians came through, you would have been shot. If the guerillas had known you were a collaborator, you would have been killed. You had two chances to die. You would be dead, not me, if I were here in 1943."

I start teaching math in the high school. The teachers are nice enough, but the bookkeeper figures my monthly salary and puts part of it in his pocket. When I show him his mistake, he laughs at me and barks, "Why did you come here?"

I don't say anything. It's clear we must leave. Hirsh is more aggressive. He has money from selling his house in Gorodok. All I have is a Russian piano. Hirsh and his family leave for Israel. A month later we get a letter. They are living in the biblical town of Ashkelon and are not happy. The country was ravaged by two wars. Food is expensive and there are strange uneducated Moroccan Jews. The children are afraid of them and keep saying, "Let's go back."

"Where can we go back?" Hirsh asks. "You can go to the USA," he tells me. "You can prove your father was an American citizen living in Waco, Texas."

With my cousins' help, we go to Texas. Hanah is forty-one and I am forty-seven starting over again in a new culture with a new language. I become a guard, and Hanah studies English with the children. It takes her four years to be licensed as a doctor. I get my teacher's certificate, and start teaching math. Hanah begins working in the emergency room and later has her own practice.

From the papers we learn about the violent American society. We are afraid to leave our house, because of the robbers, killers and rapist roaming the city. We don't understand the lenience of the judicial system or why the criminals are so quickly released back to the street.

Hirsh writes and tells me things have improved. He bought a house. The girls are married and living happily with jobs and homes. He says we need to come see him.

We fly to Ashkelon in 1973, just after the Yom Kippur War. Hanah is fifty-four and I am sixty finally getting to the Promised Land.

"I am proud of my sons-in-law," Hirsh beams. "They take good care of my daughters. They both risked their lives to defend our country and came home alive. The government, I am not so happy with. There is corruption, kickbacks on contracts and missing funds. The ultra-orthodox religious parties represent fifteen percent of the population, and try to push the country to the right with strict adherence to religious law and with prayers and religious education in the schools. They are looking for converts among our children and have found some. They have large families and multiply like rabbits. I have no use for them or their strict, stifling religion that they want to impose on everyone else. They want all of us to live by their rules. They refuse to take up arms and do nothing to protect Israel. Yet they want to tell us how to run it. I say if you haven't been a soldier, you don't vote. Religion and fanatics have no place in government."

Every day we walk to the beach. It is relaxing to watch the sun sparkling on the water and the rolling waves bursting into foam as they crash on the beach. During these walks, Hirsh likes to talk of the problems in Israel.

"During the war," he begins. "I was checking the buses. Often I am seeing young religious Jews of military age. I run after them shouting, 'Traitors! Hitler should have killed you first with your beards and pais. Why don't you fight for your country? You hypocrites! I'll beat out your brains with my hammer. For two thousand years, you have us wait patiently for the Messiah. Instead the Germans come and destroyed six million of us. The boys run like crazy. I won't hesitate to use my hammer on these bastards. I care about this country. It hurts when I see someone littering the street or our children's minds with bullshit."

"The guerillas who fought with the Russians want to send their medals back," says Hirsh as he throws a stone into the waves.

"I'll put mine in with them," I say. "The Russian Academy of Science has called the Holy Scriptures a bloody, racist, Zionist philosophy. They have taken up the Nazi banner. They are prosecuting Jews and sending them to prison as Zionists."

"Bastards," shouts Hirsh as he kicks up the sand. "They are cheating the Russian people out of a decent life. Jews are again outcast. I'll make sure every Jew who got a medal from the Russians sends it back, but not before we make it worldwide news with a truck full of medals."

I laugh at myself and say, "When I was in the tank corps pushing the Germans out of Poland, I thought we were liberators. We were giving the people of Eastern Europe freedom. Now it is obvious we replaced one tyrant with another. The Germans enslaved, robbed and murder us, but the Russians were clever and used us to our full potential as soldiers and in the professions we knew for the war effort, and then cast us aside."

"So what regrets are you living with," ask Hirsh?

"I regret that I didn't have a home to go to when the war was over, and that we didn't get out of Russia sooner. If I had never captured and interrogated those POW's in the Naliboki Forest, the Russians wouldn't have known about my German. They wouldn't have found me essential to the tank corps. But I might have joined anyway. I was so consumed with getting revenge for the murder of everything and everybody we knew. If we had left for the US in forty-five, we would have had more time to build a career and have a retirement. Hitler and then Stalin robbed us of twenty good years. Sometimes I think we should have come here."

"No," he says with a wave of his hand. "The first years were difficult. And even more difficult before I came. From its beginning, this has been a country at war. We are always living with the tension of a bomb blowing up somewhere on the street. A war could come anytime. But we are fighting for our land, not someone else's."

"And you have a large Jewish community," I say. "You are living in a Jewish village. I miss that."

"Then please, take a few orthodox rabbis home. Don't wish for something you don't want. We have not learned to be Jews without rabbis."

I laugh and say, "I like our rabbi, but I'm not religious. I enjoy the community, so I go to the synagogue. There is one more regret. I would have liked to have been involved in tracking down the Nazi war criminals. I can never have enough revenge for what they did to us.

* * *

Today we are visiting old friends in Haifa. My cousin, Itzchok, who lives here, is showing us around. He served in the guerillas and army like the rest of us. In thirty years Haifa has become a modern city. At night with thousands of lights, the city looks like a giant castle built in the middle ages on the slopes of Mount Carmel.

There are seventeen guerillas and their families from Gorodok who gather in the home of Abraham Retzkin overlooking Haifa and the sea. Among them are Abromitze, Itzke Rogovin, Sabitai Springer, Grishka Tsaffon, Lavit, Shapiro, Hirsh Berman, Itze Mever, David and Jeffa Lidsky, and Abram Itze. We start with a toast: L'Chayim (to life). With a few drinks the mood improves, and we start telling war stories. Rogovin tells how he ambushed the policeman who threw the Gorodok children in the fire during the massacre. That was the beginning of many revenge stories. We give up that conversation and talk of our new lives and our children. Somehow we survived and are happily married and have children and grandchildren. In many ways our lives have been similar. We lost our parents, our brothers and sisters. We lived in disguise among the peasants until we joined the guerillas. In the guerillas, we had revenge and helped destroy the Nazis and their fatherland.

I ask Grishka if he rode his horse to Palestine.

He laughs and says, "No, we took a train and a boat. I couldn't put my pregnant wife and three kids on a horse. It was Fogel's idea to find a widow at the guerilla celebration in Minsk. I found one before he did. Besides a wife, I brought Sonia Esser's daughter with me, who is now Doctor Rose Lubinsky with a husband and three girls. My adopted kids, Tacia and Betty, are grown with children and live in Tel Aviv. I have six grandchildren and two sons who are soldiers. So my family is prosperous and growing.

"I am happy you are doing well," I say with a hug to the shoulders. "I must see Rose before I leave. Please, tell me about Fogel."

He had his grandson's Bar Mitzvah today and couldn't leave it. He found a wonderful woman that has given him four sons and is the anchor and the rudder he needed. Fogel works with me in my dry-goods business. We are still peddlers. Fogel and I fought in every war, even the last one. I am now a Major and many bullets have come my way. I got one in the leg. You see how ugly it is? By a miracle I am still breathing. How are we still alive when we had so many chances to die?"

"I don't know," I say shaking my head. "I know my mother's spirit was there trying to protect me."

"The dead will always be with us," he laments as he returns my hug. "We miss you, my friend, and Hanah, who is as lovely as ever. Please, come share a meal with me tomorrow at noon. We will make it last until night. You are family."

A toast," shouts Grishka. "Mican lo nazya," (We will not retreat from here).

A group of survivors from Gorodok, where men, women, and children were massacred by the Germans in 1942

At far right, standing, is Sabtai Springer, surrounded by his family.

*Grishka Tsaffon with his grandchildren
in Petach Tikvah*

Yehuda in 1947   *Maria(Hanah)1945*

Yehuda Julian Adelman: January 5, 1913 - June 28, 1983

Maria (Hanah) Milner Adelman: April 23, 1919 – May 16, 2012

Adelman Family in Dallas, 1960
Maria Milner (Hanah), Joseph, Aleksandr, Roma and Julian Yehuda

Rose Lubinsky and her family. As a 2-year-old child she was saved from the massacre in Gorodok and Krasno. She is now living in Israel as a medical doctor in a hospital.

Yehuda's Medals for Storming & Capture of Konigsberg

& for Victory over Germany in the Great Patriotic War

The Kennedy Connection

Dear Billy

I would suggest you find "Dear Mrs. Kennedy: The World Shares Its Grief Letters, November 1963 ." My mother and father were great admirers of the Kennedy family. After JFK was assassinated in Dallas, FBI asked my mother to provide Russian interpreting while they interviewed Lee Harvey Oswald's widow, Marina, which she did for many hours. Later, my parents composed and sent a touching letter to Jacqueline Kennedy that somehow found its way to be published in the above referenced book.

With best regards,
Alex Adelman

Dear Jacqueline Kennedy

We come from the distant Russian City of Gorki on the River Volga. Three years ago, we left our Russian homeland, our beautiful Russian language, many friends, my MD career, and my husband's teaching job, because we could not stand any more of Khrushchev's propaganda about American animosity toward the Russian people.

During WWII my husband and I did our best in our Soviet units to resist the villainous German nationalism. I finished my medical school training and was immediately mobilized to help our young soldiers. Under heavy artillery shelling, we did our job and sometimes with our bare hands. When we were exhausted, you Americans came with moral help, food, medicine, and even bullets and artillery shells. Twice America fought with Russia against Germany. Now the biggest crime is that we fight against each other.

I hope that the free America can resolve this conflict between our countries. Your husband and our President began this job. I was sure that he would be reelected and would finish it.

Dear Jacqueline – this sad day for all of us came too soon. I could not help but cry for all of Friday. I felt like somebody hit me over the head and took a part of my soul and my hope. Many bad thoughts tortured me and my family. Why are people allowed to carry guns? Why is it permitted to sell guns to ex-convicts? Where else in the civilized world will you find such freedom to kill? Every day in Dallas we read about killings. Add to that the stealing, robbers, and racial violence and you are giving Khrushchev the best propaganda.

Mrs. Kennedy! There are many possibilities to finish this infamy. Don't leave politics. You must go on with the ideas of your late husband. Only in carrying on with his work you will find healing and keep away from dreary thoughts. Please begin now, and you will gain the crown of your late husband.

Yours sincerely, Dr. Mary Adelman, Julian Adelman and family

How the book happened

Why turn a memoir into a novel? For the same reason a movie is made out of a book - to bring it to life. So the reader can better live and experience the event. I was visualizing action and hearing the characters talk as I was writing. It was a movie happening in my head. I hope readers have the same experience. There are some holes in the story that I had to fill. What I have written is better than 90 percent true to Yehuda's memoir and what I was able to find out from his family.

In, "Heroes Without Medals," Yehuda's story is lost and scattered about in descriptions of Holocaust atrocities, the trials of Nazis, and 2,000 years of discrimination. The book reads like most memoirs - about as exciting as the encyclopedia. Those were the reasons Alex asked me to tell his father's story of survival and revenge.

I met with Alex Adelman in December of 1995 and agreed to write his father's story. I started writing in January, and with Peggy Barlow's editing help, I had something to show Alex when I saw him a year later. I kept working on the book, but came to a stopping point when Yehuda joined the Tank Corps. I had lost all my guerilla characters and I couldn't make the tank battles interesting enough for anybody to want to read it. I didn't know where to end the book, but I didn't want to end it at the Tank Corps. Over the years there were a lot of distractions from writing including my construction and oriental carpet businesses. In June of 2012, I started working on it. Once I got going, I thought the momentum would carry me through to the end of the book. I gave the first three chapters to my neighbor, Martha Weinstein, who did editing, liked it and wanted to see more. I kept giving her chapters, and we begin talking about it. Martha and my wife, Quincie, helped me get from one chapter to the next and through the tank battles to the end of the book.

Martha introduced me to Bonnie Gadless, whose father emigrated from Belarus before WWII. Her description of her father and the family dynamics was helpful. She edited the book and gave me suggestions.

Jeanne Tessier did an edit and made me realize that I still had a lot of work to do. My wife Quincie has given me editing help and suggestions from the beginning to the end. Betty

Guttmann, Lee Congdon, Helena Hotmarova, Huldah Huldah Simpson and Yvonne Richardson have edited and help me think about the book. As you can see, it has been a group effort. I was encouraged by everybody's positive reaction.

In Search of Art

After getting a degree in theater from the University of Florida, I studied clinical psychology and creative writing at Florida State University. After college, I created a one man show from my two volume poetry book, "Loafer's Bench" and "The Man that Lives Inside of Me." I performed my poetry and danced at bluegrass festivals, night clubs, colleges, and on TV and radio. WFSU TV made six short movies of me acting out my poetry that were aired on Public TV and Turner Broadcasting. To support my art, I have worked as an actor, airlines agent at JFK, computer programmer, building designer, and general contractor. I am now writing full time and living in Tallahassee, Florida with my wife, Quincie Hamby, and our son Henry.

I have been writing poetry since childhood. Writing fiction and creative non-fiction is a logical progression from my narrative poetry, where I become the character and tell his or her story from the character's point of view. Yehuda's Revenge" was one of four books aging in my computer. Maybe age helps with novels as it does with wine. Look to see two more books to be published in 2015.

Bill Gwynn

29725645R00184

Made in the USA
Charleston, SC
21 May 2014